I0009217

ARTIFICIAL INTELLIGENCE
FOR URBAN PLANNING

This book aims to introduce planners to AI, outlining essential concepts, terminologies, and methodologies. AI now promises to reshape urban planning, but as with many technological innovations, AI also introduces ethical, practical, and organizational challenges. Understanding both AI's current capabilities and its limitations is essential for planners, even as we acknowledge the rapid and unpredictable nature of its evolution. Chapters address some of these complexities, not by providing definitive answers, but by introducing urban planners to core AI topics. The book shows how planners can effectively use AI in their daily practices, engage constructively with technical specialists, and critically assess the appropriateness of these technologies in different planning contexts. This book will be of interest to both urban planning professionals and researchers.

Thomas W. Sanchez, PhD, AICP, is a Professor in the Department of Landscape Architecture and Urban Planning at Texas A&M University. He earned his PhD in City Planning from Georgia Tech and a Master of City and Regional Planning from Cal Poly, San Luis Obispo. His research and teaching focus on cities, planning methods, transportation, and technology. His most recent books include *Networks in the Knowledge Economy* (with Denise Bedford) and *Planning Knowledge and Research*. Sanchez serves as the American Planning Association (APA) Education Committee Chair and as a member of APA's Artificial Intelligence (AI) Foresight Community.

ARTIFICIAL INTELLIGENCE FOR URBAN PLANNING

Thomas W. Sanchez

Routledge
Taylor & Francis Group

NEW YORK AND LONDON

Designed cover image: linn meyers, untitled, 2024

First published 2026
by Routledge
605 Third Avenue, New York, NY 10158

and by Routledge
4 Park Square, Milton Park, Abingdon, Oxon, OX14 4RN

Routledge is an imprint of the Taylor & Francis Group, an informa business

ISBN: 9781032760476 (hbk)
ISBN: 9781032760469 (pbk)
ISBN: 9781003476818 (ebk)

DOI: 10.4324/9781003476818

Typeset in Joanna
by Apex CoVantage, LLC

CONTENTS

FIGURES

Illustrations by the author, with the assistance and feedback of Buzan Bishwas and Wasantha Kumari.

PREFACE

Writing about AI in the early stages of its adoption into urban planning presents unique challenges—technologies and applications evolve rapidly, and what we understand today may significantly shift tomorrow. Nevertheless, this book aims to introduce planners to AI, outlining essential concepts, terminologies, and methodologies.

My fascination with the intersection of computer technology and urban planning began 40 years ago, during my graduate studies at Cal Poly San Luis Obispo. My master's thesis, conducted under the guidance of my advisor, Steve French, was a survey examining computer usage among California city and county planning agencies. At that time, approximately 60 percent of these agencies had computers in their organizations, another 20 percent expected to have them soon, and the other 20 percent did not see a real need for computers. This early exploration, driven by Steve's guidance, sparked my long-standing interest in computers, data analysis, and applications to urban planning.

AI now promises to reshape urban planning, potentially exceeding even the impacts of computerization. Its capacity to analyze vast data sets, predict complex trends, and generate innovative solutions positions it as a profound force, not just for analytical methods, but also for creativity, problem-solving, and decision-making processes in planning.

As with many technological innovations, however, AI also introduces ethical, practical, and organizational challenges. Understanding both AI's current capabilities and its limitations is essential for planners, even as we acknowledge the rapid and unpredictable nature of its evolution.

This book addresses some of these complexities, not by providing definitive answers but by introducing urban planners to core AI topics—such as machine learning, neural networks, natural language processing, computer vision, and generative AI. By building this foundational understanding, planners can begin to integrate AI tools more effectively into their daily practices, engage constructively with technical specialists, and critically assess the appropriateness of these technologies in different planning contexts.

Ultimately, this work is intended as a starting point. It encourages planners to continue exploring and educating themselves in AI, preparing for a future where AI applications will become increasingly common, sophisticated, and indispensable in shaping our urban environments. In reflecting on the adoption of AI for urban planning, the words of Carl Sagan seem quite appropriate: "We've arranged a civilization in which most crucial elements profoundly depend on science and technology." This underscores planners' need to understand the powerful technologies we increasingly rely upon, ensuring they are used thoughtfully, ethically, and effectively.

ACKNOWLEDGEMENTS

I want to acknowledge the American Planning Association (APA) for supporting the initial work, "Planning Advisory Service Report 604: Planning with Artificial Intelligence", which was the starting point for this book—in particular, Petra Hurtado, Sagar Shah, Joseph DeAngelis, and Ann Dillemuth at APA. A special thanks goes to Ann Dillemuth for providing fantastic editing and insights for this book. I would also like to acknowledge the generous intellectual support from Marc Brenman, Tan Yigitcanlar, Xinyu Fu, Soheil Sabri, Claire Daniel, Norman Wright, Theo Lim, and Julio Carrillo on topics related to AI and beyond.

I would also like to acknowledge the role AI has played in the creation of this book. Just as AI promises to become a valuable tool in urban planning practice, it has served as an essential tool during the writing process. In particular, Microsoft Word's spelling and grammar checkers, Grammarly, Quillbot, and ChatGPT 4o provided assistance, helping to refine clarity, readability, and coherence. While AI certainly helped shape this book, the responsibility for the content and ideas remains entirely my own.

1

INTRODUCTION

Artificial intelligence (AI) is touching more and more aspects of our daily lives, leading to significant technical, social, and economic changes. This innovation also impacts urban development and the methods used by urban planners. Therefore, planners should consider how to deploy AI to maximize its benefits and reduce its drawbacks, particularly in the face of current uncertainties. Having explicit knowledge of what AI is and how it operates, and understanding the most important practical and ethical aspects surrounding its use, is essential to implementing AI in ways that best serve planning practice.

Claims about AI, both positive and negative, are often exaggerated, and the term "AI" is frequently misused or loosely linked to actual AI methodologies. Even among experts, there is an ongoing debate about AI's scope, definitions, and priorities. To develop better policies, accurately assess opportunities and risks, and critically evaluate claims, we must clarify what AI truly encompasses, the components that make

DOI: 10.4324/9781003476818-1

up an AI system, and the many ways performance, accuracy, fairness, accountability, and security intersect. Additionally, we need to consider the complexities of balancing these factors when designing high-quality urban environments.

This book provides a foundation on AI concepts, terminology, and methods and examples of how AI can assist or augment urban planning. The intent is to provide enough background so that planners can begin to recognize how AI methods fit into planning processes. While planners may not be able to build AI solutions, they should understand the general framework and language in order to communicate with the application developers or data scientists who can. A certain level of literacy will also be needed to facilitate transparency and openness with stakeholders who may be impacted by using these tools in urban planning.

Why AI, and Why Now?

In 2022, the American Planning Association (APA) and the Lincoln Institute of Land Policy collaborated to identify approximately 100 trends pertinent to urban planning for the first time (Hurtado et al., 2022). The resulting 2022 Trend Report for Planners identified several trends related to AI and urban planning:

- **Digital transformation of cities**. Today, digital technologies touch nearly every aspect of life, including how individuals live, work, learn, shop, and move around the city, how businesses engage with their customers, and how we communicate.
- **AI in everyday life**. Because AI is already transforming the local landscape, planners must comprehend how to apply AI fairly and effectively.
- **Urban infrastructure and AI**. AI systems are increasingly used in urban technology and infrastructure in the public and private sectors. This includes automating systems and their maintenance and optimizing these processes.
- **AI-based planning tools and upskilling needs**. Aside from the expected effects on cities and communities and the planners who work in them, AI is also likely to change the planning profession.

- **AI ethics**. Concerns about human rights, civil liberties, privacy, and social equity are significant when AI systems are used in communities or when AI is used as a planning tool.

In the following years, 2023, 2024, and 2025, the Trend Report for Planners updated and expanded on the potential role of AI in urban planning. One factor with significant implications is the accelerating rate of development and availability of open-source, consumer-grade AI. These tools are no longer limited to researchers but can be applied more broadly without extensive technical training.

Adopting new AI-based planning tools will require planners to learn new data management skills, understand infrastructure innovations using AI (Hurtado, Hitchings, & Rouse, 2021), and understand ethical concerns about AI (Sanchez, Brenman, & Ye, 2024). This will require upskilling or learning new skills through professional development and planning education (Hurtado et al., 2022).

While a significant proportion of the American public is concerned about the use of AI and computer applications to enhance human intelligence, they also express optimism about its potential benefits. A 2021 survey by the Pew Research Center suggests that these perceptions are frequently based on worries about autonomy, unintended consequences, and the degree of change these developments might entail for people and society (Pew Research Center, 2022). Survey respondents expressed the most significant concern for "loss of human jobs," "surveillance, hacking, and digital privacy," and "lack of human connection, qualities," while seeing "makes life, society better," "saves time, more efficient," and "inevitable progress, is the future" as potential positive outcomes (Pew Research Center, 2022, p. 21). The survey also showed that most people associate AI with video surveillance and self-driving cars and less with other capabilities such as analysis and decision support.

In the same year as the Pew survey, a survey of APA members asked about planners' knowledge of AI, perceived levels of appropriateness for planning, and the likelihood of adopting AI tools. The survey results suggest that planners have relatively low familiarity and experience with AI applications. At the same time, they have a generally favorable outlook on AI adoption within the planning profession (Sanchez et al., 2022). Respondents indicated that they expect AI to play an essential role in future planning, though only 7 percent of respondents planned to adopt AI tools in the near future. However, if general trends are any indication, opportunities for AI usage in urban planning will grow as technology advances. Just as computerization made its way into planning operations, so will AI.

What is AI?

AI is described in many ways. Still, at its core, it involves using computers to mimic or improve human intelligence processes, such as reasoning, pattern recognition, and learning over time. AI systems can analyze vast amounts of data, detect complex relationships, and adapt based on new information, making them powerful tools for solving problems across various domains. However, for many urban planners, AI is still a futuristic concept.

Urban planning relies heavily on data-driven decision-making, including land-use planning, transportation modeling, environmental impact assessments, and economic forecasting. Many of these processes involve repetitive, time-consuming tasks such as collecting and processing demographic data, running traffic simulations, or assessing zoning compliance. AI has the potential to remove or streamline these labor-intensive aspects, allowing planners to focus on higher-level decision-making and strategic thinking.

Beyond automation, AI also introduces new ways of understanding and interpreting urban complexity. Through machine learning (ML) and predictive modeling, AI can reveal patterns that may not be easily discerned through traditional methods. It can simulate future development scenarios, evaluate the potential outcomes of different policy choices, and even generate design alternatives for urban spaces. These capabilities position AI as more than just a tool for efficiency; it becomes a means of expanding the analytical and creative capacities of planners.

However, using AI in planning also raises important questions about bias, transparency, and the role of human judgment. While AI can enhance planning processes, it is not a replacement for the values, ethics, and contextual knowledge that planners bring to their work. Understanding how AI functions, where it excels, and where it falls short is essential for ensuring that these technologies serve the public good rather than reinforce existing inequities.

This book explores AI as a transformative tool for urban planning, outlining its capabilities and limitations and how it can be integrated into planning practice. By examining how AI can improve analytical efficiency and strategic decision-making, planners can better understand its role in shaping the future of cities and regions.

The term artificial intelligence includes many different technologies and methods. In the 1950s, AI pioneer John McCarthy defined it as "making a machine behave in ways that would be called intelligent if a human were so behaving" (McCarthy et al., 2006, p. 11). More than 60 years later, AI researchers Stuart Russell and Peter Norvig defined AI as "the study of agents that receive percepts from the environment and perform actions" (Russell & Norvig, 2020, p. viii). Though AI may be defined differently based on uses and objectives, its key elements, as in both of these definitions, include *intelligence* and *behavior*, or action based on that intelligence.

While AI refers to an extensive range of analytical methods, the primary elements involve inputs, analysis, and outputs (Figure 1.1). An AI process typically takes inputs of a large quantity of data, performs an analysis, and produces outputs, which can take various forms depending on the types of inputs and context of questions being addressed. What makes AI "intelligent" is its ability to use results from the analysis and outputs to improve the overall process—to learn. Planners might note that this process is not unlike the basic process of planning practice:

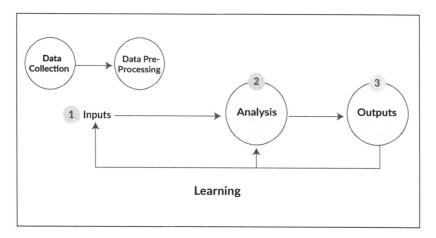

Figure 1.1 The basic analytical process for AI.

gathering information about an issue or a challenge, analyzing it to answer important questions, and producing plans or policies that address that challenge or problem.

Many years of AI research by computer scientists focused on understanding the complexities of human thought processes and logic. The objective was not only to understand how humans think, but also to develop the means to improve upon it in a way that could be applied to nearly anything that involves intelligence and decision-making (Batty, 2022). AI is now associated with a wide range of consumer goods and services we use daily, from product design to marketing to customer feedback. AI also impacts government operations and policymaking. Governments worldwide are using AI technology to inform their responses to some of the most pressing problems of our time, such as the COVID-19 pandemic, climate change, and the implementation of new data laws and governance structures. In the United States, agencies at different levels of government are now using AI-related tools to address the many challenges they face. One such example is state governments' growing use of chatbots to respond to information requests about such things as unemployment cases and COVID-19.

A BRIEF HISTORY OF AI

By some accounts, modern computing began in the 1940s when Princeton mathematician John von Neumann envisioned a computer-like process that could store programs (i.e., digital computer instructions). The computer program could be executed using stored memory, more closely achieving the functionality of a human brain. This aligned with the work of Alan Turing's World War II codebreaking device that successfully decrypted German military messages (featured in the movie *Imitation Game*). The device, known as "Bombe," far surpassed human manual processes for testing combinations and problem-solving but was an analog machine rather than a digital computer (Dyson, 2012).

An essential early AI milestone was a 1956 conference sponsored by the Defense Advanced Research Projects Agency (DARPA) at Dartmouth University. Participants included AI researchers Marvin

Minsky, Oliver Selfridge, Allen Newell, Herbert Simon, and John McCarthy. As noted above, "artificial intelligence" is commonly attributed to McCarthy, while Newell and Simon have been credited with one of the first AI programs, the Logic Theorist.

The Dartmouth University conference generated significant enthusiasm about the potential for a "thinking machine" with the capacity to "learn," and significant financial support began to flow from the government and businesses for this research (Buchanan, 2005). Substantial gains in AI during the next 20-year period included the General Problem Solver (GPS) algorithm, developed in the late 1950s, which was fundamental to more advanced cognitive structures and the AI programming language LISP. LISP is one of the oldest high-level programming languages, initially developed by John McCarthy for AI research.

Despite decades of well-funded international research, scientists could not build their envisioned "intelligent machines," and there was a relative lull in scientific advancement. Researchers struggled due to a lack of funding in an "AI winter" from the mid-1970s until the 1990s (see Figure 1.2). However, by the end of the 1990s, American corporations had gained renewed interest in AI, partly due to considerable advancements in computer hardware. This also included significant investments by countries such as Japan to create "fifth-generation computing" that enhanced computing speeds and AI. Over the last 20 years, corporations like IBM, Amazon, Google, and Baidu have successfully applied AI techniques in specialized fields to significant commercial advantage. Many digital services we use daily—the internet, personal computing, communications, navigation, and others—contain AI. As a result, these technologies are increasingly influencing many aspects of our lives.

The emergence of large language models (LLMs) such as ChatGPT, Claude, and LLaMA in the past few years has marked a pivotal moment in the widespread adoption of AI beyond the scientific community, signifying a shift toward more accessible and practical applications of advanced technologies. Unlike traditional AI methods, such as neural networks, which excel at recognizing patterns and making predictions, and natural language processing (NLP), which enables machines to understand and generate human language, LLMs integrate these capabilities to create interactive, conversational agents.

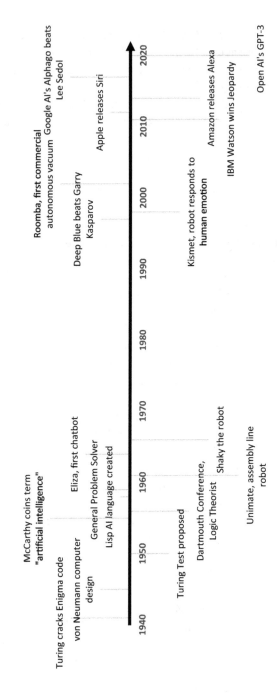

Figure 1.2 Timeline of significant events in the development of AI.

This integration allows a broader audience to harness AI for everyday tasks, from customer service to creative writing, demonstrating the transformative potential of AI in diverse fields and promoting a deeper public understanding of these technologies.

AI's Potential for Urban Planning

Research into AI for urban planning began in the 1960s, influenced by the development of computer technologies with a broad range of scientific and industrial applications (Brail, 1987). However, the lack of large-scale datasets and computing capabilities significantly limited the development and implementation of planning applications for transportation and land-use forecasting systems. Over time, academic and industrial research using advanced quantitative and spatial analysis commonly associated with AI has increased steadily; however, the planning profession has adopted few of these approaches. Much of the current planning-related discussion about AI concerns innovative city technologies that capture and analyze data for optimization processes, such as traffic management and energy consumption. Less attention is being paid to using AI in urban planning and associated decision-making activities, including scenario planning and generative designs, but this will very likely change with time.

Planning future cities will require appropriate expertise and proper planning methods. There is general agreement that urbanization will continue to increase as a function of economic opportunity. In contrast, equity, environmental pressures, and infrastructure needs will continue to be significant challenges. In addition, technology, connectedness, and digitalization will continue to increase in importance rapidly (Woetzel, Rajadhyaksha, & Frem, 2018; National League of Cities, 2022). AI is expected to play an essential role in future development activities and in planning and managing cities for sustainability, resilience, and equity in both the short and long term. Planners should be prepared for the changes that will lead to how future cities are planned, designed, and managed.

Like most other fields, the planning profession has dramatically benefited from adopting new or updated technologies to augment planning practices. Just as urban planning gradually adopted computer technologies during the 1980s and GIS during the 1990s, the profession is now on an inevitable progression toward adopting AI. Unlike in earlier decades, today data is widely available, computer technology is pervasive, and AI has already been adopted in many facets of daily life.

However, not all aspects of planning are suitable or appropriate for advanced analytical methods and other capabilities of AI. AI will not take a planner's job anytime soon (if ever) because of the complexity of planning and the processes involved with planning. Still, it can be a valuable tool, especially for repetitive and time-consuming tasks. As with other innovative tools and technologies, planners should assess the procedures they use against the capabilities of AI to identify opportunities for improvement and determine the steps required to make those changes.

AI offers various applications and techniques for urban planning, providing planners with advanced tools to analyze, visualize, and solve complex urban challenges. Understanding fundamental AI methods becomes critical for effective and innovative planning as cities grow in complexity. This book introduces five fundamental AI techniques (Figure 1.4), highlighting their distinct capabilities and transformative potential for urban planning.

- **Machine learning (ML)**: Machine learning algorithms can identify patterns and relationships within data, supporting applications such as land-use classification, predicting housing market trends, and optimizing resource allocation.
- **Neural networks (NN)**: These models mimic the structure of the human brain to recognize patterns and make decisions. In urban planning, neural networks can analyze complex datasets to identify trends and forecast future developments.
- **Natural language processing (NLP)**: NLP enables AI systems to understand and process human language. This capability is invaluable for extracting insights from large volumes of textual data, such as planning documents, public feedback, and regulatory texts.

- **Computer vision (CV)**: Computer vision techniques allow AI systems to interpret visual data like satellite imagery and traffic camera footage. This capability is helpful for many planning-related applications, such as monitoring urban green spaces, analyzing traffic flow, and assessing infrastructure conditions.
- **Generative AI (GenAI):** GenAI models generate new data that closely resembles the input data on which they were trained. This is one of AI's most innovative and transformative applications, augmenting content creation, design, scenario generation, visualization, and communication.

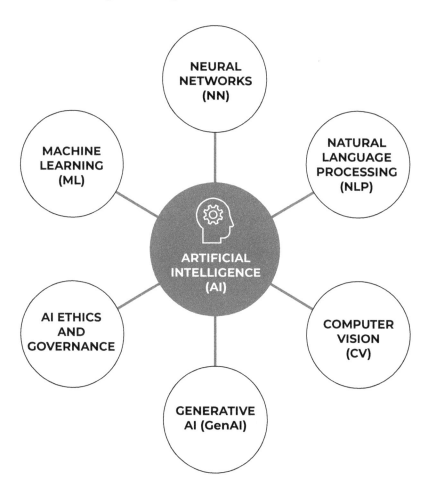

Figure 1.3 Areas of AI discussed in this book.

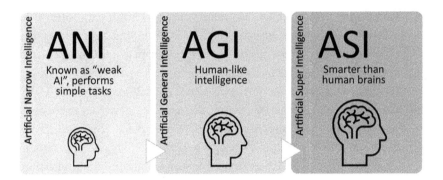

Figure 1.4 Levels of AI.

All of these areas are being tested on planning-related questions. Most of the current applications of AI can be considered "weak AI," which mechanizes limited human thought and behavior patterns. Still, the growing pervasiveness of AI technologies and the unforeseeable potential consequences of "strong AI" or even "super AI" concern many.

Only a small amount of AI is used in everyday planning practice despite a substantial and growing body of scholarship on the subject. Much of this research performs specific planning analyses, but these methods are yet to be used to prepare or evaluate plans or policies. Closing this gap has its challenges and will start with planning practitioners, researchers, and educators becoming aware of the opportunities and potential benefits of adopting new approaches. This book seeks to make those connections.

Levels of AI

Understanding the levels of AI is essential for contextualizing its current capabilities and future potential in urban planning. AI is not a monolithic technology but a broad and evolving field encompassing different degrees of sophistication, computational demands, and strategic objectives. These levels help us gauge the "stage" of progress we are experiencing at any given time and provide a framework for assessing how AI can be applied to planning challenges.

When discussing specific AI methods, whether machine learning models for land-use prediction, natural language processing for analyzing public comments, or generative AI for urban design, it is helpful to understand the evolution of AI approaches and applications. Different AI techniques vary widely in complexity, adaptability, and decision-making capacity. Without appreciating these differences, it is easy to overestimate or underestimate what AI can realistically achieve in a given planning context.

To navigate these distinctions, scholars and practitioners often refer to three general levels of AI: artificial narrow intelligence (ANI), artificial general intelligence (AGI), and artificial superintelligence (ASI). Bostrom (2014) articulated this framework, which is widely used in AI discourse.

ANI, which performs simple tasks, represents most of today's AI technology. Also known as "weak AI," ANI simulates basic human logic and behavior as defined by a limited set of rules and circumstances; it does not reproduce human "intelligence" in the larger sense. Examples include internet search tools, facial recognition, and text-to-speech conversion—systems that can be taught to carry out particular tasks. Online commerce and entertainment services such as Netflix, Spotify, and Amazon use ANI to classify user preferences, resulting in recommendations. In the past ten years, machine learning and deep learning advances have enabled significant advancements in ANI.

ANI typically only has a small amount of memory and is considered "reactive." Reactive AI mimics human thinking and handles various stimuli without accessing prior knowledge or deep reasoning; it usually lacks memory and data storage capabilities. A computer playing chess, a game with well-defined rules, is one example of ANI. More sophisticated AI can collect and store data, allowing computers to access previous facts to guide future decisions. ANI can be seen as a building block for larger systems that can be integrated with other AI tools and processes.

AGI, or "strong AI," is focused on performing a full range of tasks. It represents the proposition that machines can be trained to learn human behaviors, think like humans, and use the fundamental aspects of human consciousness. To perform with near-human levels of intelligence and carry out every task that a human being is capable of, AGI will need to master critical capabilities related to sensory perception, motor skills, natural language skills, human-like creativity, and comprehension of human social and emotional characteristics. This will produce powerful AI with extensive knowledge and cognitive computing skills that can handle data efficiently and at incredible speeds, giving it advantages over human cognitive skills.

Compared to ANI, AGI is expected to understand the context of a task, which leads to self-evaluation, learning, error correction, and improved performance on an unsupervised basis. A Level 5 autonomous vehicle (AV) without human intervention is one example of an AGI application. Being able to handle any or all scenarios that arise while driving illustrates the complexity expected from an AGI system.

Going beyond AGI, the concept of ASI has been described as "an intellect that is much smarter than the best human brains in practically every field, including scientific creativity, general wisdom, and social skills" (Bostrom, 1998, p. 1). ASI represents how robots (or other intelligent agents) will develop sufficient self-awareness and self-vigilance to outperform human intelligence and behavioral abilities.

Machines that possess "superintelligence" will have neural capacities exceeding that of the human brain, making them capable of conceiving abstractions and interpretations beyond that of humans. As conceptualized, ASI will replicate human behavioral intelligence, using better memory and processes superior to human intelligence to solve problems and digest information, events, and stimuli more quickly. Not only will ASI be able to comprehend human expressions, but it is also expected to communicate its own emotions, beliefs, and desires. Superintelligent robots will have decision-making and problem-solving abilities that are significantly more reliable and superior to humans.

As noted above, today's AI technologies fall to the narrow end of the AI spectrum. Scientists and engineers are still working to develop computers with cognitive abilities comparable to humans, though they have made some significant advancements, such as IBM's Watson supercomputer. Many scientists and professionals contend that AGI will not be viable for at least several decades, with predictions ranging from 2030 to 2060 before the arrival of such a system (Goertzel, 2014). Some experts predict that, given recent developments, ASI may exist by the end of the 21st century (Kelly, 2017).

Although having such powerful technologies at our disposal may sound enticing, the idea is fraught with unintended and unknown consequences. We can only speculate as to what effect this may have on the lives of human beings. Dystopian views of an ASI future—as depicted by science fiction in which robots dominate humans—assume that there is an innate evil within these systems and that the superintelligent agents will turn against the people who created them. English theoretical physicist Stephen Hawking has cautioned, "The development of full artificial intelligence could spell the end of the human race" (Cellan-Jones, 2014). Experts in the field have expressed a significant amount of concern, alerting us to possible dangers and encouraging us to be thoughtful about the potential repercussions of this new technology to maximize its benefits and avoid harm.

About This Book

The following chapters provide a structured and in-depth exploration of AI and its applications for urban planning, covering both technical and practical aspects. This book is designed to help planners understand AI's terminology, methodologies, and challenges, enabling them to make informed decisions about integrating AI into their work. However, this knowledge is not just critical for professional practice; it is also increasingly essential for personal awareness. AI is embedded in nearly every aspect of our daily lives, shaping how we interact with technology, access information, and navigate the world. Understanding its principles and implications is no longer optional; it is necessary for participating in modern society.

Chapter 2 introduces **machine learning (ML)**, a cornerstone of AI that enables computers to learn patterns and make predictions based on data. This chapter explains how ML methods are designed, applied, and interpreted, introducing supervised and unsupervised learning concepts. It provides concrete examples of how ML can be used in urban planning, from forecasting housing demand to optimizing public transportation systems. In addition to planning applications, readers will gain a broader appreciation of how ML powers everyday tools such as recommendation systems, fraud detection, and virtual assistants—technologies that shape decisions well beyond professional settings.

Chapter 3 introduces **neural networks (NN)**, a subset of ML designed to mimic how human brains process information. This chapter provides detailed explanations and practical examples of how neural networks can be used in urban planning, such as identifying spatial patterns in land use, modeling complex traffic flows, and detecting environmental risks. Understanding NNs is crucial for their applications in planning and for grasping their broader role in AI advancements, including facial recognition, speech-to-text processing, and medical diagnostics.

Chapter 4 explores **natural language processing (NLP)**, which allows AI to analyze, interpret, and generate human language. This chapter discusses how NLP can be applied in urban planning by analyzing public comments on development proposals, processing policy documents, and summarizing large volumes of regulatory text. AI's ability to interpret human language has transformed communication technologies from chatbots to automatic translation tools, making NLP one of the most influential areas of AI for both professional and everyday use.

Chapter 5 focuses on **computer vision (CV)**, the field of AI that enables machines to process and interpret images and video. This chapter provides examples of how CV can be used in urban planning, such as assessing land-use changes from satellite imagery, monitoring pedestrian movement, and detecting infrastructure deterioration. Beyond planning, computer vision powers many of the technologies we encounter daily, from facial recognition to autonomous vehicles, and understanding its mechanisms helps us engage critically with the expanding role of AI in visual data interpretation.

Chapter 6 discusses **generative AI (GenAI)**, the final central AI technique examined in this book. GenAI can create new content, including images, text, and urban design proposals. This chapter discusses how these methods can be applied to urban planning, illustrating how AI-generated design alternatives, scenario simulations, and automated report generation can enhance planners' creative and analytical capabilities. GenAI is also becoming deeply embedded in personal and professional life, from AI-powered image editing to automated writing assistance, making it essential for planners to understand its possibilities and limitations.

Chapter 7 shifts the focus to **concerns and challenges** surrounding AI. While AI presents remarkable opportunities, it raises serious ethical and practical concerns. This chapter discusses bias, errors, and misapplications that can lead to poor or harmful planning decisions. It also examines broader societal concerns, including privacy risks, data confidentiality, and the potential for AI to reinforce historical inequities. These discussions are crucial for planners and anyone interacting with AI-driven technologies in daily life, as the ethical deployment of AI is a shared responsibility.

Finally, Chapter 8 summarizes the book's key insights and offers guidance for future AI implementation in urban planning. It discusses how planners can strategically integrate AI today, anticipating its continued evolution. The chapter also considers AI's long-term trajectory, forecasting how its expanding scale will shape planning practice and the broader societal and technological landscape.

As AI becomes increasingly woven into the fabric of professional work and personal life, it is vital for planners—and everyone—to have at least a modest understanding of its capabilities, limitations, and ethical implications. This book serves as a guide for engaging thoughtfully with AI, providing readers with the background to make informed choices in their professional and personal interactions with these powerful technologies.

References and Resources

Andrews, Clint, Cooke, Keith, Gomez, Alexsandra, Hurtado, Petra, Sanchez, Thomas W., Shah, Sagar, & Wright, Norman. (2022). AI in Planning Opportunities and Challenges and How to Prepare Conclusions and Recommendations from APA's "AI in Planning" Foresight Community. American Planning Association, Chicago, IL.

Antunes, Miguel Eiras, Barroca, Jean Gil, & Guerreiro de Oliveira, Daniela. (2021). Urban Future with a Purpose: 12 trends shaping the future of cities by 2030. Deloitte. Accessed October 11, 2022. https://www2.deloitte.com/global/en/pages/public-sector/articles/urban-future-with-a-purpose.html

Barcelona City Council. (2021). Government measures for a municipal algorithms and data strategy for an ethical promotion of artificial intelligence. Accessed November 1, 2022. https://ajuntament.barcelona.cat/digital/sites/default/files/mesura_de_govern_intel_ligencia_artificial_eng.pdf

Batty, M. (2022). The emergence and evolution of urban AI. *AI & Society*, 1–4.

Bostrom, N. (1998). How long before superintelligence? *International Journal of Futures Studies*, 2.

Bostrom, N. (2014). *Superintelligence: Paths, dangers, strategies.* Oxford University Press.

Brail, R. K. (1987). *Microcomputers in Urban Planning and Management.* Rutgers University Center for Urban Studies, New Brunswick, NJ.

Buchanan, B. G. (2005). A (very) brief history of artificial intelligence. *AI Magazine,* 26(4), 53–60.

Cellan-Jones, R. (2014). Stephen Hawking warns artificial intelligence could end mankind. *BBC News,* 2(10), 2014.

City of Los Angeles. (2020). SmartLA 2028: Technology for a better Los Angeles. Accessed October 15, 2022. https://ita.lacity.org/smartla2028

County of Santa Clara, Technology Services and Solutions. (2021). FY22–24 Strategic Plan. https://it.sccgov.org/home

Dimock, W. C. (2022). What AI Can Do for Climate Change, and What Climate Change Can Do for AI. *Scientific American,* April 5, 2022. https://www.scientificamerican.com/article/what-ai-can-do-for-climate-change-and-what-climate-change-can-do-for-ai/

European Commission. (2018). 2018 reform of EU data protection rules. Accessed October 29, 2022. https://ec.europa.eu/commission/sites/beta-political/files/data-protection-factsheet-changes_en.pdf

Goertzel, B. (2014). Artificial general intelligence: concept, state of the art, and future prospects. *Journal of Artificial General Intelligence,* 5(1), 1.

Gomez, Alexsandra & DeAngelis, Joseph (2022). *Digitalization and Implications for Planning.* American Planning Association, Chicago, IL.

Hurtado, Petra, Hitchings, Benjamin G., & Rouse, David C. (2021). *Smart Cities Integrating Technology, Community, and Nature.* American Planning Association, Chicago, IL.

Hurtado, Petra, Shah, Sagar, DeAngelis, Joseph, & Gomez, Alexsandra. (2022). *2022 APA Foresight Trend Report for Planners.* American Planning Association, Chicago, IL.

Kelly, K. (2017). *The Inevitable: Understanding the 12 Technological Forces That Will Shape our Future.* Penguin.

McCarthy, J., Minsky, M. L., Rochester, N., & Shannon, C. E. (2006). A Proposal for the Dartmouth Summer Research Project on Artificial Intelligence, August 31, 1955. *AI Magazine,* 27(4), 12–12.

National Association of State Chief Information Officers. (2020). Chat with Us: How States are Using Chatbots to Respond to the Demands of COVID−19. Accessed November 2, 2022. https://www.nascio.org/resource-center/resources/chat-with-us-how-states-are-using-chatbots-to-respond-to-the-demands-of-covid-19/

National League of Cities (2022). Future of Cities. Accessed October 5, 2022. https://www.nlc.org/initiative/future-of-cities/

Organization for Economic Co-operation and Development (OECD). (2020) Using artificial intelligence to help combat COVID-19, April 23, 2020. https://www.oecd.org/coronavirus/policy-responses/using-artificial-intelligence-to-help-combat-covid-19-ae4c5c21/

Parikh, N. & Hohman, A. (2021). NYC Artificial Intelligence Strategy. City of New York, Mayor's Office of the Chief Technology Officer. https://nparikh.org/assets/pdf/nyc/nyc_ai_strategy.pdf

Pew Research Center (2022). AI and Human Enhancement: Americans' Openness Is Tempered by a Range of Concerns, March 17, 2022. https://www.pewresearch. org/internet/2022/03/17/ai-and-human-enhancement-americans-openness-is-tempered-by-a-range-of-concerns/

Rahnama, H. & Pentland, A. (2022). The New Rules of Data Privacy. *Harvard Business Review*, February 5, 2022. https://hbr.org/2022/02/the-new-rules-of-data-privacy

Russell, S. J., & Norvig, P. (2020). *Artificial intelligence: A modern approach* (4th ed.). Pearson.

Sanchez, T. W., Brenman, M., & Ye, X. (2025). The ethical concerns of artificial intelligence in urban planning. *Journal of the American Planning Association*, 91(2), 294–307.

Sanchez, T. W., Shumway, H., Gordner, T., & Lim, T. (2022). The prospects of artificial intelligence in urban planning. *International Journal of Urban Sciences*, 1–16.

U.N. Habitat. (2022). World Cities Report 2022: Envisaging the Future of Cities. United Nations Human Settlements Programme, Nairobi, Kenya. Accessed October 2, 2022. https://unhabitat.org/world-cities-report-2022-envisaging-the-future-of-cities

Woetzel, Jonathan, Rajadhyaksha, Vineet, & Frem, Joe. (2018). Thriving amid turbulence: Imagining the cities of the future. McKinsey & Co. Accessed October 2, 2022. https://www.mckinsey.com/industries/public-and-social-sector/our-insights/thriving-amid-turbulence-imagining-the-cities-of-the-future

World Economic Forum. (2022). Blueprint for Equity and Inclusion in Artificial Intelligence, Whitepaper. Accessed September 22, 2022. https://www.weforum. org/whitepapers/a-blueprint-for-equity-and-inclusion-in-artificial-intelligence/

2

MACHINE LEARNING FOR URBAN PLANNERS

As cities worldwide face social, economic, and environmental challenges, the need for innovative solutions has never been greater. Urban planning, a discipline as ancient as the cities it seeks to shape, has always adapted to its era's technological and methodological advancements. Today marks another era of significant transformation. Machine learning (ML) can analyze large amounts of complex urban data and predict trends and patterns to inform decision-making. ML suits the field since urban planning involves understanding intricate spatial, social, and economic dynamics. Its ability to detect patterns, optimize resource allocation, and model complex systems aligns closely with the analytical needs of planners, enabling more data-driven, responsive, and forward-looking urban policies.

The integration of ML into urban planning requires an interdisciplinary approach. This involves a mix of expertise from several domains, with the rich analytical, human-centric tradition of urban planning alongside

DOI: 10.4324/9781003476818-2

the innovative potential and analytical strengths of ML. The objective of this chapter is twofold: to introduce planners to the processes underlying ML and to highlight their practical implications for urban planning. By delineating the scope of ML's applications in urban development, from infrastructure planning to environmental sustainability, the intent is to demonstrate how planners can use these technologies to enhance the livability and resilience of urban environments.

In addition, an exploration of ML in urban planning would be incomplete without addressing the challenges and ethical considerations inherent in deploying these technologies. This chapter addresses these critical issues, recognizing that the promise of ML comes with significant responsibilities. From data privacy and security to the risks of algorithmic bias, there are potential ethical dilemmas that planners must navigate so that the benefits of ML are realized equitably across urban populations (Sanchez, Brenman, & Ye, 2024). This discussion serves as a reminder that ethical principles should guide technological advancement to benefit society.

Historical Background and Development

ML has its origins in the broader field of artificial intelligence (AI), which emerged in the mid-20th century as researchers sought to create machines capable of learning and problem-solving. The central concept of ML—machines learning from data rather than being explicitly programmed—was first explored in the 1950s (Russell & Norvig, 2016). One of the earliest pioneers was Alan Turing, who proposed the concept of a learning machine in his 1950 paper "Computing machinery and intelligence". In 1959, Arthur Samuel, a researcher at IBM, coined the term "machine learning" and developed one of the first programs that could improve its performance at playing checkers through experience. Around the same time, Frank Rosenblatt introduced the perceptron, an early type of artificial neural network that demonstrated how computers could learn to recognize patterns.

The field saw significant progress in the 1980s and 1990s with advancements in algorithms and computational power. Geoffrey Hinton played a crucial role in reviving neural networks through backpropagation, a technique that allowed networks to adjust their weights efficiently and improve learning. Other key figures, such as Yann LeCun, contributed to the development of convolutional neural networks (CNNs), which became essential in computer vision tasks. Meanwhile, Vladimir Vapnik and Alexey Chervonenkis introduced the support vector machine (SVM), a powerful approach for classification problems. During this period, ML transitioned from symbolic AI approaches, which relied on hand-crafted rules, to data-driven statistical learning.

The 21st century marked an explosion in ML research and applications, driven by the availability of large datasets, increased computing power, and improved algorithms. In 2006, Hinton and his colleagues demonstrated deep learning methods that significantly improved performance in pattern recognition tasks. This breakthrough laid the foundation for modern AI applications, including deep neural networks that power speech recognition, image processing, and natural language processing. More recently, researchers such as Yoshua Bengio and Ian Goodfellow have contributed to generative models, including the development of generative adversarial networks (GANs), which enable machines to generate realistic images, text, and even music.

Introduction to Machine Learning

ML enables computers to learn from and make decisions based on data, automating the analysis of vast amounts of information to identify patterns and insights. For urban planners, understanding these fundamentals is critical for effectively applying ML technologies to address urban challenges. This section lays the foundation by defining ML and how it differs from traditional computational approaches.

Machine Learning (ML): A subset of AI that focuses on building systems capable of learning from data rather than following explicitly programmed instructions.

To deepen our understanding of ML within urban planning, it's essential to cover some aspects that distinguish ML from traditional

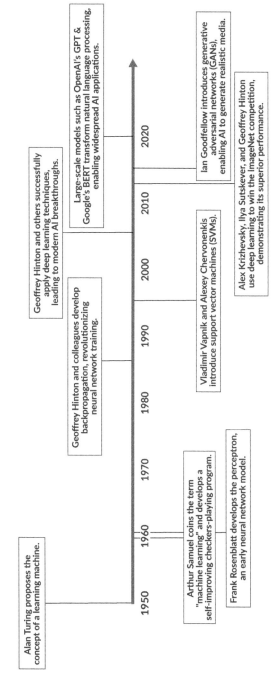

Figure 2.1 Timeline of important milestones in machine learning.

computational approaches. Unlike conventional algorithms that execute pre-defined rules, ML algorithms improve their performance as they are exposed to more data. This ability to adapt and learn from patterns in data without being explicitly programmed for specific tasks sets ML apart and underpins its potential across various fields, including urban planning.

Figure 2.2 illustrates the fundamental difference between traditional programming and the ML approach. In conventional programming, a programmer provides data and a predefined set of rules or instructions (the program), which the computer executes to generate results. In contrast, ML reverses this process by taking data and the desired results as inputs and using computation to infer the underlying rules or patterns, effectively learning from the data rather than relying on manually written instructions. This distinction is crucial for urban planning, where many challenges involve complex, interrelated systems that are difficult to model with explicit rules. By using ML, planners can analyze vast amounts of urban data, recognize patterns, and generate predictive models that support better decision-making.

In the urban context, this distinction provides many opportunities for planners to analyze complex urban data in novel ways. For instance, traditional computational methods might require a planner to manually (i.e., visually) analyze traffic patterns and predict congestion points. This task becomes complicated as the scale of data increases. ML, on the other hand, can process and learn from vast datasets—ranging from traffic sensor data to social media posts—to identify not only existing

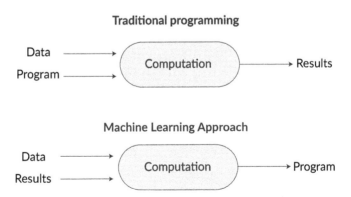

Figure 2.2 Traditional programming compared to the machine learning approach.

congestion points but also predict future traffic trends. This shift from manual analysis to automated, data-driven decision-making enables urban planners to address the complexity of urban environments more effectively, allowing for more nuanced and informed planning decisions that can adapt to change over time.

Fundamentals of Machine Learning

Essential ML concepts and terminology include algorithms, models, and training data. Understanding these concepts is crucial for grasping how ML can be applied in urban planning. At its core, ML is a method of using data to detect patterns, generate insights, and make predictions or recommendations without relying on explicitly programmed rules. Unlike traditional statistical approaches that often require predefined relationships between variables, ML allows systems to learn from data, refining their understanding and improving accuracy over time. This adaptability makes ML particularly valuable for urban planners, who must analyze complex and dynamic systems where relationships between variables—such as population growth, transportation demand, and environmental impact—are not always straightforward. By breaking down ML concepts with urban planning analogies, we can better illustrate their role in planning applications.

Algorithms form the backbone of ML, serving as the instructions that process data and identify patterns. In urban planning, algorithms can be compared to transportation models or land-use models that define how spaces should be organized and utilized. Just as zoning regulations help guide development by setting parameters for land use, height restrictions, and density, ML algorithms establish the rules for how data is analyzed and processed to extract meaningful insights. Different ML algorithms serve different purposes—supervised learning algorithms rely on labeled data to make predictions, unsupervised learning algorithms identify hidden structures in data without predefined labels, and reinforcement learning algorithms optimize decisions through trial and error. Selecting the correct algorithm is akin to choosing the appropriate planning framework for a project—a transit-oriented development model, a smart growth strategy, or an environmental impact assessment tool.

Models in ML represent the distilled knowledge and patterns learned from the data. This model can then make predictions or decisions in new, similar scenarios. For urban planners, understanding and utilizing ML models is like having a dynamic blueprint that adapts and improves with additional data, providing insights into future urban trends, population needs, or environmental impacts. For example, an ML model trained on historical traffic data could predict congestion patterns in growing metropolitan areas, much like a transportation model forecasts the impact of new infrastructure projects.

Training data is the cornerstone of building reliable algorithms and models. It is comparable to the surveys, studies, and historical data that urban planners collect before drafting a new urban development plan. This data provides the foundation for subsequent analyses, ensuring that real-world conditions and community needs inform the final plan. In ML, training data is used to "teach" the algorithm about the world it's analyzing, allowing it to learn the relationships between different variables and how they influence the outcome. The quality, quantity, and diversity of training data are critical factors in determining the accuracy and generalizability of an ML model. For planners, incorporating ML into their work means using vast amounts of urban data—such as census records, mobility patterns, real estate trends, and environmental factors—to train algorithms, enabling more nuanced, data-driven decisions that reflect the complexities of urban environments.

One of the key advantages of using more data in urban planning is its ability to reduce uncertainty, leading to more accurate and informed decision-making. Traditional planning models often rely on limited data, resulting in gaps in understanding and suboptimal outcomes. In contrast, ML models trained on larger datasets—such as real-time traffic flows, historical land-use records, or social media trends—can identify subtle patterns that smaller datasets might miss, improving predictions for congestion, zoning, and infrastructure development. More data enhances model generalization, allowing ML systems to better predict and adapt to new scenarios, such as rapid population growth or environmental changes. Additionally, diverse datasets help mitigate bias in urban analysis by ensuring that all communities, including underserved areas, are adequately represented, leading to more equitable planning decisions. Furthermore, processing large volumes of real-time urban data enables planners to respond dynamically to challenges like traffic congestion, air pollution, or energy consumption.

ML can be categorized into three main types: supervised, unsupervised, and reinforcement. Each approach offers unique capabilities to address different urban planning challenges. Understanding these categories is essential for planners seeking to integrate ML into their work, as each type is suited to specific kinds of data and decision-making processes. Supervised learning, for instance, is beneficial when historical data is available to train models for predicting future trends, such as forecasting housing prices or estimating traffic congestion. On the other hand, unsupervised learning can uncover hidden patterns and relationships within data, making it valuable for clustering neighborhoods based on socioeconomic characteristics or detecting emerging land-use trends. Meanwhile, reinforcement learning is well suited for optimization problems that involve dynamic decision-making, such as improving public transportation routes or managing energy distribution in smart cities. By recognizing the strengths of each ML category, urban planners can select the appropriate approach to analyze complex urban systems, optimize resource allocation, and develop data-driven strategies.

Supervised learning is an ML approach that uses a labeled dataset to learn patterns and relationships from input variables (features) to the output variable (target). The primary goal is to build a model that accurately predicts the output variable based on new input data. This process involves several steps. First, data collection is performed, which includes both the input variables and the corresponding output variable. Next, data preprocessing is done to clean and transform the data, handling missing values, normalizing features, and encoding categorical variables if necessary. Then, model selection occurs, where an appropriate supervised learning algorithm, such as regression, decision tree, or support vector machine, is chosen. Following this, the training phase uses the labeled dataset to train the model by minimizing the error between the predicted and actual output values and adjusting the model's parameters to fit the data best. Validation follows, evaluating the model's performance using a validation set to ensure it generalizes well to new data and avoids overfitting. Finally, testing assesses the model on a separate test set to determine its predictive accuracy and performance. Supervised learning involves the computer being "taught" by labeled data.

Unsupervised learning is an ML algorithm that works with data without labeled responses. Unsupervised learning aims to identify patterns, structures, or relationships within the data without prior knowledge of the outcomes or category. This type of learning is beneficial for exploratory data analysis and finding hidden structures in the data.

In unsupervised learning, the process begins with data collection that includes only the input variables (features) without any corresponding output labels. Next, data preprocessing is performed to clean and transform the data, handling missing values, normalizing features, and reducing dimensionality if necessary. The next step is algorithm selection, where an appropriate unsupervised learning algorithm, such as clustering (e.g., k-means, hierarchical clustering) or dimensionality reduction (e.g., principal components analysis (PCA)), is chosen. Following this, model training involves using the selected algorithm to analyze the data and identify inherent patterns or groupings. Clustering involves grouping similar data points, while dimensionality reduction consists of mapping data to a lower-dimensional space. The evaluation step assesses the quality and validity of the identified patterns or structures using appropriate evaluation metrics, such as the silhouette score for clustering. Finally, the results are interpreted to gain insights into the underlying data structure and inform further analysis or decision-making. In unsupervised learning, the computer "teaches itself."

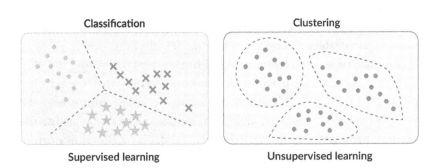

Figure 2.3 Supervised and unsupervised learning.

Reinforcement learning is an ML algorithm that trains agents to make decisions by interacting with an environment. The goal of reinforcement learning is to maximize the cumulative reward that an agent receives over time by taking actions that yield the highest rewards. Unlike supervised and unsupervised learning, reinforcement learning is based on learning from the consequences of actions rather than from labeled data.

The reinforcement learning process involves several key steps. It begins with defining the agent's environment, including the states, actions, and rewards. The agent starts in an initial state and takes actions to transition between states according to a policy, which is a strategy for choosing actions based on the current state. The agent receives feedback in the form of rewards or penalties after each action, which helps it learn which actions are more beneficial. The agent aims to learn an optimal policy that maximizes the cumulative reward over time. This learning process is typically iterative and involves exploring the environment to discover new states and actions and exploiting known information to maximize rewards. Various algorithms can be used to update the agent's policy based on the received rewards.

Each type of ML—supervised, unsupervised, and reinforcement learning—provides distinct analytical capabilities relevant to urban planning. Understanding these approaches is important because they determine how data is processed and which analytical methods are appropriate. Supervised learning helps predict future trends based on historical data, unsupervised learning helps identify patterns and groupings within complex datasets, and reinforcement learning supports

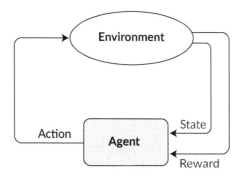

Figure 2.4 Reinforcement learning process.

decision-making in dynamic environments. Integrating these methods allows urban planners to improve forecasting, optimize resource distribution, and enhance public services.

The Machine Learning Process

This section outlines the step-by-step process of an ML application, from data collection to model deployment, using urban planning projects as examples. It highlights the iterative nature of ML projects and the importance of data quality and model evaluation. The ML process mirrors the phased approach urban planners are familiar with in their projects. For example, a city may want to optimize public transportation routes based on shifting demand patterns. Urban planners could collect real-time transit ridership data, traffic flow information, and demographic trends, then use an ML model to predict areas where transit demand will increase, allowing for proactive adjustments to routes and schedules to improve service efficiency. The following describes the steps in the process and the tools at each stage of the ML workflow.

1. Data Collection

The workflow begins with data collection, the first step akin to conducting surveys and gathering information for an urban development project. ML projects start by compiling relevant datasets, including anything from satellite imagery to social media posts, depending on the problem. For example, ML applications in urban planning could use data such as:

- **Satellite imagery**: To monitor urban sprawl or changes in green spaces over time, which can feed into ML models predicting future land-use changes or identifying illegal construction.
- **Social media posts**: To analyze public sentiment around new urban projects or understand how residents use certain city areas.
- **Real-time traffic data**: Collected from traffic sensors and used to build predictive models for traffic congestion to inform infrastructure investments.

2. *Data Preprocessing*

Just as urban planners may clean survey data or remove outliers from quantitative datasets, the data collected for ML must be cleaned and preprocessed. This involves handling missing values, normalizing data (ensuring consistency across data types), and encoding categorical variables. For example, raw data from sensors may contain missing values or inconsistent readings for predicting traffic congestion in a city. Data preprocessing might involve imputing missing values, normalizing traffic volumes, and encoding categorical data such as time of day (morning, evening) into numerical forms.

Additionally, if a dataset contains many variables, dimensionality reduction techniques such as PCA can simplify the data while preserving its most important patterns. These methods reduce the number of variables by identifying key features that capture the most relevant information, making analysis more efficient without significantly losing accuracy.

3. *Model Selection*

The model chosen depends on the complexity and type of data. For example, decision trees or random forests might be used to predict pedestrian safety risks at intersections based on traffic volume, road design features, historical accident data, and nearby land uses. For predicting housing price trends based on historical data, linear regression may be used if the relationships between variables (like location, building age, and proximity to amenities) are relatively simple.

4. *Training the Model*

Training involves feeding the data into the ML model to learn patterns and relationships. During training, the model adjusts its parameters to minimize error so that the resulting algorithm or model best fits the training data. For example, an ML model that forecasts traffic patterns could be trained using data collected from traffic sensors over several years, with variables like road conditions, weather, and time of day. The model would "learn" the relationship between these factors and resulting traffic congestion levels.

5. Model Evaluation

After training, ML models must be evaluated so that they perform reliably. Key evaluation metrics include **accuracy**, which measures the overall correctness of the model's predictions; **precision**, which indicates how many predicted positive outcomes are correct; and **recall**, which reflects how well the model identifies all relevant positive cases. These metrics help determine the model's effectiveness, robustness, and ability to generalize totheew data, often assessed through techniques like cross-validation.

The model mustn't overfit the training data, which means it should perform well on new, unseen data, much like an urban plan should be adaptable to future conditions. For example, a model predicting which neighborhoods are at risk for gentrification might be evaluated using historical property value trends, rental price increases, and demographic shifts. Planners can assess the model's accuracy by comparing its predictions with observed patterns of displacement, business turnover, and changes in housing affordability over time.

6. Model Deployment

Once the model is trained and evaluated, it can be deployed to make real-time predictions or inform decision-making. For example, an innovative city initiative could deploy a traffic prediction model in real-time to adjust traffic light timings dynamically based on predicted congestion patterns. This real-time deployment improves traffic flow and reduces commute times for residents. Or, an ML model predicting land-use changes might be integrated into a city's analysis process. Urban planners can use the model to simulate different development scenarios. This allows them to visualize how different zoning decisions could impact housing density, commercial areas, or green spaces over the next ten years.

7. Monitoring and Maintenance

Just as urban plans require ongoing evaluation and adjustments, ML models need regular monitoring to be sure their predictions remain accurate as new data becomes available.

For example, a model to predict traffic congestion must be periodically retrained with new traffic patterns, especially as cities evolve and new infrastructure is developed. This process ensures that the model remains relevant and valuable for long-term urban planning efforts.

Machine Learning Tools and Technologies

The tools and technologies that power ML include software libraries and platforms. Integrating ML with Geographic Information Systems (GIS) for spatial data analysis is particularly relevant for urban planners. This section aims to familiarize planners with the technological landscape of ML and how it can be harnessed for urban analysis and planning.

There is a rich ecosystem of software libraries and platforms designed to make ML accessible. Just as skilled urban planners and designers utilize various tools—from CAD software for design to statistical packages for demographic analysis—ML practitioners rely on a suite of technologies tailored for different aspects of ML work. Key among these are software libraries such as TensorFlow and PyTorch, which provide comprehensive environments for building and training complex ML models.

Platforms and programming languages are used to develop a wide range of ML algorithms, from regression to clustering. This is similar to urban planners using GIS software to integrate and analyze spatial data, providing insights into land-use patterns, infrastructure networks, and environmental impacts. The integration of ML with GIS marks an essential advancement for urban planners. By combining the spatial analysis capabilities of GIS with the predictive power and pattern recognition of ML, planners can discover more insights into urban phenomena, from predicting traffic congestion to identifying areas at risk of environmental degradation.

Programming Languages

When implementing AI for urban planning, Python and R are two of the most commonly used programming languages, each providing distinct strengths and capabilities. Both languages are highly relevant to the field as they provide powerful tools for data analysis, ML, and visualization, all essential for modern urban planning. Understanding the costs and benefits of each language helps select the right tool for different urban planning applications.

Python Programming for AI in Urban Planning

Python is widely known for its versatility and popularity across various fields, including AI and ML. This language provides a broad range of capabilities, from fundamental data analysis to complex simulations and predictive modeling. Python's ecosystem includes numerous libraries facilitating AI and ML applications, such as TensorFlow, sci-kit-learn, and PyTorch. These libraries make it easy to build models for predicting traffic congestion, analyzing land-use patterns, or even simulating urban growth.

In addition to its strengths in ML, Python is also highly effective in geospatial analysis. Libraries like Geopandas, Shapely, and Fiona (for example) enable planners to work with spatial data, mapping everything from population density to transportation networks. Integrating Python with GIS platforms such as QGIS and ArcGIS enhances its utility for urban planners who need to process and analyze geographic data.

One of Python's key advantages is its adaptability. It is helpful for AI applications and can handle various other data collection, cleaning, and visualization tasks. This flexibility allows urban planners to integrate AI models into broader workflows, such as optimizing real-time traffic signal timings based on predictive algorithms. However, Python does come with a learning curve, mainly when working with advanced ML algorithms, which can require considerable computational resources, potentially leading to additional hardware or cloud services costs.

R Programming for AI in Urban Planning

R, in contrast, is a language tailored for statistical analysis and data visualization, making it particularly strong in areas where detailed data analysis is required. Urban planning projects that involve large amounts of census data, housing market analyses, or socio-economic studies can benefit from R's extensive statistical libraries. Tools like ggplot2 and leaflet make R popular for data visualization and for creating detailed graphs, maps, and heatmaps that convey essential insights into urban development trends or public sentiment around new projects.

R also supports spatial analysis through packages such as sp, sf, and raster, which can be used to analyze the geographic distribution of green spaces or study urban crime patterns. This makes R a powerful tool for those who need to perform advanced spatial statistics. Despite its statistical analysis and visualization strengths, R is less suited to large-scale ML projects than Python. While R has ML libraries such as Caret and Random Forest, it is generally more limited in building and deploying complex AI models.

R's strength lies in its ability to handle detailed quantitative analysis, making it ideal for planners working on econometric models, traffic flow predictions, or environmental impact studies. However, for tasks that require integrating AI models into broader systems or real-time applications, such as traffic management systems or smart city platforms, Python is usually a better choice.

Comparing Python and R in AI for Urban Planning

Python and R have their places in AI-driven urban planning but cater to different needs. Python is often preferred for complex AI projects involving ML, automation, and real-time decision-making. It excels in deep learning and can easily integrate with other tools, making it suitable for applications like traffic prediction systems, urban simulations, and smart infrastructure management. Python's versatility allows urban planners to streamline workflows across multiple domains, from data preprocessing to model deployment.

R, as previously mentioned, is more specialized in statistical analysis and data visualization. R's statistical capabilities make it a valuable tool for urban planning studies that require a detailed analysis of housing markets, population growth, or transportation patterns. R is handy when planners need to produce high-quality visualizations or perform complex econometric analyses. Its role in urban planning focuses on extracting insights from structured data, making it a preferred tool for research and policy evaluation.

Python and R are open-source and free to use, a significant advantage for municipal governments or planning agencies with limited budgets. However, the hidden implementation costs come from training and infrastructure. For urban planners unfamiliar with programming, both languages require time and investment to learn, and many planning organizations may need to hire data scientists or consultants to leverage these tools entirely. Additionally, the computational demands of AI and ML models—especially those run on large datasets—may necessitate investments in cloud computing services or more powerful hardware.

Tools like ChatGPT significantly impact how programmers approach coding in Python and R, enhancing productivity and reducing the learning curve. For Python, ChatGPT can assist in generating scripts for tasks such as data preprocessing, ML model development, or Application Programming Interface (API) integration for setting up traffic prediction systems or automating real-time data analysis workflows. It can provide explanations of complex concepts like neural networks, provide debugging advice, or generate boilerplate code for tasks like setting up applications for smart infrastructure management. For R, ChatGPT is effective for crafting efficient statistical models, creating intricate data visualizations, and automating repetitive tasks, such as cleaning survey data or running regression analyses. It can guide planners through econometric modeling, suggesting optimal packages and libraries for analyzing transportation or housing data, and even help refine ggplot2 visualizations to communicate findings better.

Choosing between Python and R ultimately depends on the specific requirements of the project. Python is ideal for projects that require large-scale AI integration, real-time processing, or deep learning applications, while R shines in projects centered around statistical analysis and data visualization. As urban planners increasingly incorporate AI into their decision-making processes, understanding the capabilities of both languages is essential to maximizing the potential of these technologies.

Applications of Machine Learning in Urban Planning

ML's ability to predict and simulate makes it a powerful tool for planning urban infrastructure and development projects. This section highlights how ML models can optimize designs, forecast demand, and enhance management, providing planners with insights to make data-driven decisions.

ML stands apart from traditional computational methods primarily because it can process and learn from data iteratively. While conventional programming relies on explicit instructions defined by developers to perform tasks, ML utilizes algorithms that can analyze data, learn from it, and make predictions or decisions without being explicitly programmed for each step. The algorithm's exposure to large datasets facilitates this iterative learning process, from which it identifies patterns and adapts its responses. Such capabilities are particularly advantageous in urban planning, where dynamic and complex datasets—ranging from traffic flows and utility usage to social demographic shifts—can provide insights into urban conditions. By harnessing ML, urban planners can transition from static models and assumptions to dynamic, data-informed decision-making frameworks, enabling more responsive and efficient urban management and development strategies.

An example of how ML models change over time can be seen in traffic flow prediction for smart cities. In a traditional model, urban planners might rely on historical traffic data and fixed rules to predict congestion patterns at certain times of the day. These rules may be static, such as anticipating heavier traffic during rush hour and lighter traffic at night, without considering real-time variables like accidents, weather conditions, or sudden population surges.

In contrast, an ML model designed for traffic flow prediction continually learns and adapts as new data is fed. Initially, the model might be trained on historical traffic data. Still, as it is exposed to real-time data—such as daily traffic patterns, weather updates, event schedules, or road closures—the model iteratively refines its predictions. For example, suppose the city hosts an unexpected significant event or experiences a major road blockage due to an accident. In that case, the ML model will recognize how traffic deviates from the norm. Over time, it adapts to account for these deviations, improving its accuracy in predicting traffic patterns in similar future scenarios.

As the ML model processes more data and learns from its previous predictions, it evolves from simple assumptions to a sophisticated system capable of accounting for various dynamic factors. The iterative nature of ML allows it to adjust predictions based on current conditions and identify patterns that a static, rule-based system might miss. This dynamic learning process enables real-time traffic management solutions, such as dynamically adjusting traffic light timings or recommending alternative routes to alleviate congestion, leading to a more responsive and efficient transportation system.

ML models can address complex urban challenges by enabling data-driven decision-making across multiple domains. Cities generate vast amounts of data from transportation networks, environmental monitoring systems, public services, and emergency response operations. ML can process and analyze this data to uncover patterns, optimize resource allocation, and improve efficiency by predicting infrastructure maintenance needs and optimizing land-use planning to enhance environmental sustainability and improve public safety. The following sections explore key applications of ML in urban infrastructure and development, environmental planning and sustainability, and public safety and emergency response, highlighting how these technologies are shaping the future of urban planning.

Urban Infrastructure and Development

In urban infrastructure and development, the application of ML provides significant potential. ML can predict future infrastructure needs, optimize sustainable building designs, forecast project delays and cost overruns, simulate urban growth and zoning optimization, and predict traffic and infrastructure stress points. Integrating ML into planning and development processes will better equip urban planners to address the multifaceted challenges of modern urban environments.

Predicting future infrastructure needs. ML algorithms can analyze historical data on urban growth, resource consumption, and population dynamics to forecast future infrastructure needs (e.g., roads, schools, hospitals) with increasing accuracy. By integrating data sources such as census records, migration patterns, economic trends, and land-use changes, ML models can identify hidden patterns and predict where demand for infrastructure will increase. This predictive capability allows for a more effective allocation of resources, ensuring that urban infrastructure can evolve with demographic and technological changes.

For example, an ML model could analyze past population trends alongside factors like housing development, employment shifts, and transit accessibility to predict changes in population density across different districts over the next decade. Figure 2.5 presents a chart of predicted population change, highlighting scenarios with significant development or decline. Planners can use these forecasts to prioritize investments in public transportation, utilities, and social services, ensuring that infrastructure expansion aligns with projected demographic shifts.

Optimizing building designs for sustainability. ML can optimize building designs by simulating configurations to identify those that maximize energy efficiency, occupant comfort, and sustainability. By analyzing vast datasets on building performance, climate conditions, and material properties, ML models can predict how different design choices will impact energy consumption. These models can incorporate variables such as insulation materials, HVAC efficiency, window-to-wall ratio, and building orientation to recommend configurations that minimize energy waste while maintaining thermal comfort.

For example, an ML model can evaluate historical energy consumption patterns and environmental factors to predict how a proposed building

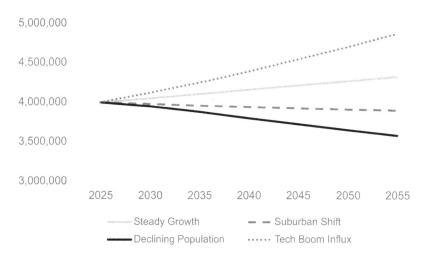

Figure 2.5 Chart of population scenarios.

will perform under various conditions. By simulating thousands of design variations, the model can identify optimal layouts that reduce heating and cooling demands while improving indoor air quality. Figure 2.6 presents a before-and-after comparison chart showing energy consumption (in kilowatt-hours) for a building before and after ML-driven optimizations. This visualization highlights the tangible impact of AI-driven design adjustments, demonstrating how predictive modeling can lead to significant energy savings. More examples of this will be discussed in the generative AI (GenAI) chapter.

Predicting traffic and infrastructure stress points. As described above, ML models can analyze real-time traffic data and historical congestion patterns to predict future stress points in the city's infrastructure. By integrating data from sensors, GPS tracking, traffic cameras, and public transportation usage, ML can identify recurring congestion areas and forecast how infrastructure will perform under varying conditions, such as rush hour, weather events, or population growth. These predictive insights allow urban planners to take a proactive approach by recommending interventions before bottlenecks become critical issues.

For example, ML models can analyze patterns in vehicle flow, pedestrian movements, and accident reports to determine where roads,

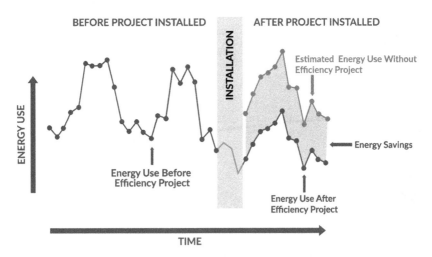

Figure 2.6 Before-and-after comparison chart showing energy consumption (in kilowatt-hours).

intersections, or transit networks are most vulnerable to overload. The model can assess factors such as road width, signal timing, traffic density, and public transit accessibility to highlight areas that may require upgrades, such as lane expansions, signal optimizations, or new transit corridors. Figure 2.7 presents a network map of city roads with color-coded traffic stress points, illustrating where congestion and infrastructure strain are most likely to occur. By using this data-driven approach, planners can prioritize infrastructure improvements, deploy adaptive traffic control systems, and develop long-term strategies for mitigating congestion, ultimately enhancing urban mobility and safety.

Figure 2.7 A network map of city with predicted traffic stress points.

These examples demonstrate how ML can support urban infrastructure and planning through data-driven insights. Graphics such as heat maps, 3D simulations, and scenario comparisons provide helpful visualizations that make these scenarios more straightforward to interpret and apply in real-world planning contexts.

Environmental Planning and Sustainability

ML can aid in environmental planning and the promotion of sustainable urban development. By analyzing ecological data, ML can help planners assess the impact of development projects and monitor pollution levels, contributing to healthier and more sustainable cities.

Assessing Development Impacts. Integrating ML into environmental planning and sustainability efforts marks a significant advancement in how cities approach urban development with an eye toward ecological health. ML's ability to process and analyze extensive environmental datasets—ranging from satellite imagery and remote sensing data to sensor networks measuring air and water quality—enables predictive modeling of the ecological impact of urban development projects. By using real-time and historical environmental data, ML models can identify trends, assess risks, and simulate various development scenarios to guide sustainable decision-making.

ML applications in environmental impact assessment rely on diverse data sources. Satellite and aerial imagery are used for land-use classification, deforestation tracking, and urban heat island detection through convolutional neural networks (CNNs). Sensor networks, including Internet of Things (IoT)-enabled devices, collect data on air pollution, water quality, and noise levels, which ML models analyze to detect anomalies and predict future conditions. Climate and weather models incorporating historical climate data, combined with ML-based predictive analytics, help forecast potential shifts in temperature, precipitation, and flood risk due to urban expansion. Additionally, geospatial and GIS data allow ML algorithms to analyze spatial patterns of development and their impact on ecosystems, such as habitat fragmentation and wetland loss, often using clustering techniques like K-means or DBSCAN.

Various analytical methods support ML-driven impact assessments. Regression models such as Random Forest and XGBoost estimate pollution levels or temperature variations based on urban density and land-use changes. Neural networks process satellite imagery to detect changes in vegetation cover, water bodies, and built environments over time, predicting how development affects biodiversity. Time-series forecasting methods, including Long Short-Term Memory (LSTM) networks, model long-term environmental changes due to construction, such as increased stormwater runoff and soil erosion. Agent-based modeling further enhances impact assessment by simulating the influence of human activities and policy interventions on environmental systems, helping planners explore potential mitigation strategies.

Figure 2.8 presents a citywide map illustrating the development impacts on different areas, highlighting regions where ML models

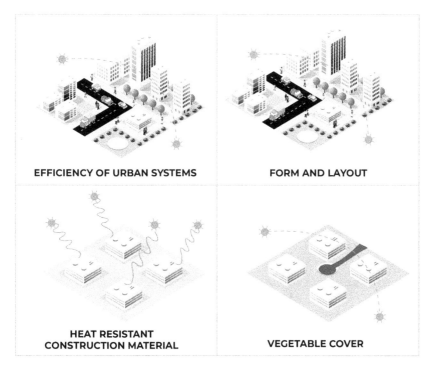

Figure 2.8 Assessing development impacts.

predict significant ecological changes due to urban expansion. The map visualizes areas at risk of increased air pollution, heat island effects, or water contamination, providing planners with a spatially explicit tool for assessing environmental vulnerabilities. By applying ML techniques to development impact assessments, planners can gain a more nuanced understanding of how construction, infrastructure expansion, and urban activities influence the natural environment. These predictive insights allow for informed decision-making that minimizes ecological disruption, optimizes resource use, and ensures that urban projects align with long-term sustainability goals.

Monitoring Pollution Levels

ML algorithms can play a crucial role in monitoring pollution levels across urban areas by analyzing vast amounts of environmental data to identify pollution sources and predict fluctuations. These models integrate data from multiple sources, including real-time sensor networks, satellite imagery, weather data, and traffic patterns, for a comprehensive assessment of pollution dynamics. By processing this diverse data, ML enables city planners and environmental agencies to detect pollution hotspots, anticipate changes in air and water quality, and implement targeted interventions to mitigate environmental harm.

ML methods used in pollution monitoring range from supervised learning models that classify pollution levels based on historical data to unsupervised clustering techniques that identify emerging pollution trends. Regression models such as Random Forest and XGBoost analyze relationships between pollutant concentrations and contributing factors like vehicular emissions, industrial output, and meteorological conditions. CNNs process satellite imagery to detect areas of high particulate matter concentrations or water contamination. Recurrent Neural Networks (RNNs) and LSTM networks model time-series data to forecast pollution spikes based on seasonal variations, traffic congestion, or changing wind patterns. Additionally, reinforcement learning approaches help optimize pollution control strategies by simulating different regulatory scenarios and evaluating their effectiveness.

Figure 2.9 presents a citywide prediction of pollution levels and sources, illustrating areas where ML models have identified significant emissions from transportation corridors, industrial zones, and densely populated districts. The visualization highlights anticipated pollution fluctuations based on traffic congestion, factory operations, and weather conditions, such as wind direction and temperature inversions. By using these predictive insights, policymakers can design proactive interventions such as adjusting traffic flows, enforcing stricter emission regulations, or strategically planting urban greenery to absorb pollutants. Ultimately, ML-driven pollution monitoring enables more effective regulatory measures and targeted interventions, contributing to improved air and water quality and healthier urban environments.

Figure 2.9 Predicting pollution levels and sources.

Challenges of Machine Learning

This section addresses the critical data privacy and security issues associated with ML. The collection and analysis of urban data raise significant privacy concerns, the importance of ethical data handling practices, and the challenges of securing sensitive information.

Data Privacy and Security

The collection and use of large amounts of data in urban planning, while valuable for informing decision-making and city management, necessitates a rigorous examination of data privacy and security issues. Urban data can contain sensitive information about individuals and communities, from location data derived from GPS and mobile devices to personal details collected through public engagement initiatives. If mishandled or accessed by unauthorized parties, such data could lead to significant privacy breaches, undermining public trust and potentially harming the individuals involved. Therefore, ethical and responsible data handling becomes critical, requiring urban planners and data analysts to adhere to strict privacy regulations and ethical standards. This includes implementing effective data anonymization techniques, ensuring that personal identifiers are removed and that the data cannot be used to re-identify individuals. Furthermore, the transparent communication of data collection and usage policies with the public will be increasingly important, allowing individuals to understand how their data is used and the potential risks.

Beyond privacy concerns, securing the large amounts of data collected for planning activities from cyber threats poses a potential challenge. As cities become increasingly digitized, the potential for cyberattacks that could access or corrupt sensitive urban planning data also rises. Such breaches risk exposing personal information and could disrupt urban infrastructure and services, leading to broader public safety concerns. Implementing comprehensive cybersecurity measures should become a standard procedure to mitigate these risks. This involves securing data storage and transmission and continuously monitoring and updating security protocols to address emerging threats.

Moreover, there is a need for collaboration between government agencies, technology providers, and cybersecurity experts to develop and enforce industry-wide standards for data security in urban planning. Addressing these challenges is critical for realizing the benefits of data-driven urban planning while safeguarding the privacy and security of individuals and ensuring the ethical stewardship of the data that cities will use in the planning process.

Bias and Fairness

The potential for bias in ML models poses significant ethical considerations for urban planning. Transparency and fairness in ML applications are paramount for equitable urban development outcomes. This also involves methods to clean and correct data used by ML models and techniques to detect biased outcomes (Sanchez, Brenman, & Ye, 2024).

Bias in ML models can stem from various sources, notably from the data on which these models are trained. Urban datasets may reflect existing inequalities or historical biases, such as disparities in housing, employment, and public services across different neighborhoods. When ML models are trained on such data without appropriate checks and balances, they are likely to perpetuate or exacerbate these inequalities in their predictions and recommendations. This can lead to urban development strategies that inadvertently favor certain groups or areas over others, undermining efforts toward inclusive and equitable urban growth.

Addressing these challenges requires a concerted effort toward transparency and fairness in developing and applying ML models in urban planning. Transparency involves making the datasets, model algorithms, and decision-making processes accessible and understandable to stakeholders, including the public, to scrutinize and question their fairness and implications. This level of openness is crucial for identifying potential biases and building trust in ML applications. Furthermore, actively incorporating fairness as a core consideration in ML model development is essential. This includes employing techniques to identify and mitigate bias in training data, designing models sensitive to fairness criteria, and continuously monitoring and adjusting models in deployment so that they produce equitable outcomes.

Moreover, engaging with diverse communities in the urban planning process can provide valuable insights into the needs and concerns of different groups, helping to guide the development of more fair and representative ML models. By prioritizing transparency and fairness, urban planners and data scientists can harness the power of ML to drive urban development strategies that are not only effective and efficient but also just and equitable, ensuring that the benefits of urban innovation are shared broadly across all segments of society.

Sustainability and Accessibility

Another important application area is the environmental implications of deploying ML technologies and the importance of making these tools accessible to urban planners across different contexts.

Integrating ML technologies into urban planning opens new avenues for efficiency and innovation and brings to the forefront the imperative of sustainability and the democratization of technology. The environmental impact of running complex ML models, which require significant computational resources, is a growing concern within the context of sustainable urban development. These operations can consume vast amounts of electricity, contributing to the carbon footprint of data centers and technology infrastructure. As such, there is an increasing need to adopt more sustainable ML practices, such as optimizing algorithms for energy efficiency, utilizing green computing resources, and considering the lifecycle environmental costs of technology deployment in urban planning projects. These strategies aim to uphold the benefits of ML without compromising ecological sustainability, aligning with broader goals of creating eco-friendly urban spaces.

Furthermore, the accessibility of ML technologies poses another critical challenge. The technical complexity and resource requirements of ML can create barriers to entry for urban planners, especially those in under-resourced municipalities or developing countries. Bridging this accessibility gap is crucial for ensuring that the advantages of ML for urban planning can be leveraged universally, fostering more inclusive and equitable urban development outcomes. This involves simplifying ML tools through user-friendly interfaces, providing comprehensive training and support to urban planners, and promoting open-source ML solutions that reduce the cost barriers associated with proprietary software. Additionally, encouraging collaborations between academia, industry, and government agencies can help develop tailored ML applications that meet the specific needs of diverse urban contexts.

Looking Ahead

The application of ML within urban planning will occur gradually as advancements in technology and research continue to unfold. The rapid pace of innovation in ML provides a preview into a future where urban planning is about managing physical spaces and designing and optimizing them harmoniously with digital innovations.

Generative design is one of the most promising areas, with algorithms generating various design solutions based on specified criteria and constraints. This method allows urban planners to explore numerous possibilities quickly, assessing the potential impacts of different design choices on urban livability, sustainability, and resilience. By using generative design, planners can make data-informed decisions that align with broader urban development goals, such as reducing carbon footprints or maximizing green spaces. GenAI is discussed in greater detail later.

Another emerging trend set to revolutionize urban planning is the development and implementation of digital twins—highly detailed digital models that mirror real-world cities. These models enable planners to simulate and analyze urban dynamics in real time, from traffic patterns and energy consumption to disaster response scenarios. The integration of ML with digital twins facilitates predictive modeling and scenario analysis at an unprecedented scale, providing insights that can preempt problems before they arise and identify opportunities for improving urban environments. Moreover, digital twins serve as a collaborative platform for stakeholders, including city officials, urban planners, and citizens, to engage with and understand the implications of planning decisions, thereby fostering more inclusive urban development processes.

The integration of ML with the concept of smart cities represents a pivotal shift in how urban environments are designed, managed, and experienced. At the heart of this integration lies the synergy between ML and the IoT, a network of interconnected devices and sensors that collect and exchange data in real time. This convergence sets the stage for a new era of urban infrastructure that is not only intelligent but also adaptive to the needs of its inhabitants and the environment. By analyzing data from IoT devices—from traffic sensors and waste management systems to energy grids and water supply networks—ML algorithms can uncover patterns, predict trends, and inform decision-making processes that enhance the efficiency and sustainability of city services.

This integration goes beyond optimizing urban infrastructure and opens new avenues for citizen engagement and participatory governance. ML can analyze data from social media, mobile applications, and feedback platforms to gauge public sentiment, identify community needs, and anticipate responses to policy changes. This allows city governments to adopt a more responsive and citizen-centric approach, tailoring services and initiatives to their communities' real-time needs and preferences. Furthermore, ML-driven urban data analysis can improve public safety, health, and well-being by predicting and mitigating risks from air pollution hotspots to areas prone to traffic accidents.

The potential of ML to transform smart cities extends to urban planning and development, where it can provide insights into land-use patterns, housing demands, and environmental impacts. This enables planners to make informed decisions that promote sustainable growth and equitable development. As cities continue to evolve, the integration of ML with IoT technologies is not just an option but a necessity for creating urban environments that are livable, resilient, and attuned to the digital age. This could redefine urban living, making cities more innovative, sustainable, and inclusive for future generations.

Chapter Summary

This chapter introduced ML approaches and potential applications in urban planning. It began by situating ML within the broader context of urban challenges, emphasizing its potential to analyze complex spatial, social, and economic data, leading to more informed and responsive planning decisions. The chapter outlined the fundamental differences between traditional computational approaches and ML, highlighting ML's ability to adapt and learn from data without explicit programming. This capability allows urban planners to shift from manual analysis of urban systems to automated, data-driven insights, potentially enhancing planning accuracy and efficiency. Key concepts such as supervised, unsupervised, and reinforcement learning were explained with urban planning analogies, illustrating how these methods could be applied to tasks like traffic prediction, land-use analysis, and resource optimization. The chapter emphasized the interdisciplinary nature of integrating ML into urban planning, requiring expertise from diverse fields to leverage ML's full potential.

The chapter also addressed the challenges and ethical considerations of using ML in urban contexts. Issues related to data privacy, security, and algorithmic bias were explored, underscoring the need for responsible and equitable use of ML technologies. The chapter advocated for transparency in ML models, the importance of diverse data sources to reduce bias, and the ethical imperative of ensuring that ML benefits all urban residents somewhat. Additionally, the chapter discussed the environmental implications of ML, emphasizing sustainable practices in data processing and the importance of making ML tools accessible to planners in various contexts. Looking ahead, the chapter highlighted emerging trends such as generative design and digital twins, which will further transform urban planning by enabling real-time simulations and collaborative, data-driven decision-making. Overall, the chapter underscored ML's potential to enhance urban planning processes but also calls for cautious, thoughtful implementation to maximize benefits while addressing inherent challenges.

References and Further Reading

Russell, S. J., & Norvig, P. (2021). *Artificial intelligence: a modern approach.* 4th edition. Pearson.

Sanchez, T. W., Brenman, M., & Ye, X. (2024). The ethical concerns of artificial intelligence in urban planning. *Journal of the American Planning Association,* 1–14.

Turing, A. M. (1950). Computing machinery and intelligence. Mind, 59(236), 433–460. https://doi.org/10.1093/mind/LIX.236.433

3

NEURAL NETWORKS FOR URBAN PLANNERS

Neural networks (NNs) are at the heart of many advancements in artificial intelligence (AI) and have revolutionized how we process and analyze data. Understanding NNs is important because they provide powerful tools for making sense of complex urban systems and decision-making processes. Understanding how they work enables better collaboration, informed discussions, and responsible implementation. For urban planners, a grasp of these processes ensures they can critically evaluate AI-driven planning tools, recognize their limitations, and apply them effectively to address urban challenges.

NNs consist of layers of interconnected neurons. Neurons are the fundamental units of an NN that receive input, process it using a mathematical function, and pass the output to the next layer. As will be discussed, these networks can learn from data through training, adjusting their internal parameters to recognize patterns and make predictions. This ability to learn and adapt makes NNs well-suited for tackling various

DOI: 10.4324/9781003476818-3

tasks, from image recognition and natural language processing (NLP) to predictive modeling and optimization.

One of the key reasons NNs are important to know about is their ability to handle vast amounts of data with high dimensionality and complexity. Traditional analytical methods can be less effective when dealing with such data, but NNs are better suited due to their architecture and learning capabilities. As cities generate increasing amounts of data from sensors, social media, and other sources, the capacity to process and interpret this information becomes crucial for effective urban analysis and management. Moreover, NNs have demonstrated high-performance levels in predictive tasks, which is valuable for planning and forecasting. Whether it is predicting the impact of new infrastructure projects, forecasting demographic changes, or anticipating the effects of climate change, NNs are used. This chapter discusses the fundamentals of NNs, exploring their architecture, training processes, and various applications in urban planning.

Historical Background and Development

The concept of artificial neural networks (ANNs or NNs) has its roots in the 1940s. Warren McCulloch and Walter Pitts were among the first to propose a mathematical model of an NN, demonstrating that simple NNs could compute logical functions. This laid the groundwork for significant contributions, including Frank Rosenblatt's perceptron, an algorithm for supervised learning of binary classifiers in the 1950s and 1960s. Rosenblatt's work demonstrated the potential of NNs for pattern recognition. Around the same time, Bernard Widrow and Marcian Hoff developed the Adaline (Adaptive Linear Neuron) model, which introduced the least mean squares (LMS) learning rule, further advancing the field.

However, the limitations of early NNs, particularly the inability of single-layer perceptrons to solve non-linear problems, led to a period of stagnation known as the "AI Winter" (McCorduck, 2004). Interest in NNs was revived in the 1980s with the development of the backpropagation algorithm. Popularized by researchers like Geoffrey Hinton, backpropagation enabled the efficient training of multi-layer networks, addressing many earlier limitations.

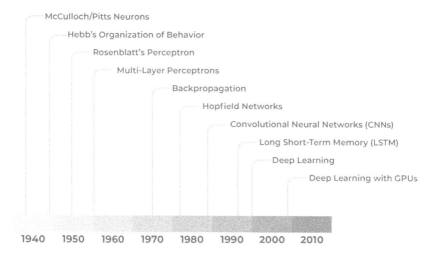

Figure 3.1 Neural network development timeline.

The advent of deep learning in the 2000s, characterized by NNs with many hidden layers (deep neural networks), revolutionized the field. This progress was driven by the availability of large datasets, increased computational power, and algorithm advances. Deep learning has enabled significant breakthroughs in various domains, including computer vision, natural language processing, and autonomous systems.

Introduction to Neural Networks

This section lays the foundation by defining NNs and how they differ from traditional computational approaches. These basic concepts and terminologies will help planners better understand how they function and better appreciate what is happening inside "the black box" process of neural networks.

> Neural Networks (NNs): Computerized systems based on how the brain processes information. They are a common approach used in ML to identify patterns, determine the likelihood of a specific outcome, and learn by using feedback loops. They can form connections between two items and learn to correlate them, which is the basis for making predictions.

Basic Concepts and Terminology

Understanding the core components of NNs is important for effectively constructing and applying these models. The key elements and mechanisms that underpin NNs are neurons, layers, and connections.

Neurons are the basic units of an NN, analogous to nerve cells in the human brain. Each neuron receives input, processes it, and produces an output.

The structure of a neural network is typically organized into layers. The input, hidden, and output layers are the primary building blocks of a neural network (Figure 3.2).

- **Input layer**: The input layer is the first NN layer responsible for receiving the raw input data. Each neuron in the input layer represents a feature of the input data. For example, in a network that predicts traffic flow, the input layer might receive data such as weather conditions, time of day, and current traffic density.
- **Hidden layers**: Hidden layers are the intermediate layers between the input and output layers. These layers perform the bulk of the computational work in an NN. Each hidden layer consists of neurons that apply weights to the inputs and pass them through an activation function. The number of hidden layers and neurons per layer can vary depending on the complexity of the task.

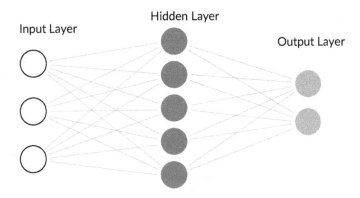

Figure 3.2 Basic structure of an artificial neural network (perceptron).
Source: Author.

- **Output layer**: The output layer is the final layer in an NN, producing the network's prediction or decision. The number of neurons in the output layer depends on the nature of the task. The output layer may have multiple neurons for classification tasks, each representing a different class. For regression tasks, a single neuron may represent a continuous value.

Edges (or lines) represent connections between neurons, each associated with a weight that adjusts as the network learns. These connections allow the network to propagate information from one layer to the next.

Activation functions are mathematical functions applied to each neuron's output. They determine whether a neuron should be activated (i.e., reach a threshold), influencing the network's ability to learn and make complex decisions.

Weights are parameters within the network that transform input data within the neurons. During training, the network adjusts the weights to minimize the prediction error. Each connection between neurons has an associated weight.

Biases are additional parameters that allow the model to better fit the data by shifting the activation function. Each neuron typically has one bias value. Adjusting weights and biases enables the network to learn from data.

Figure 3.3 illustrates how, compared to linear regression, NNs extend their analytical capabilities to encompass greater possibilities for interactions between variables (factors). Unlike linear regression, which is constrained to modeling straight-line relationships between inputs and outputs, NNs use a layered architecture composed of neurons, weights, and biases. This architecture enables them to capture intricate patterns and non-linear relationships in the data.

In the diagram, neurons are represented by circles, and lines and arrows represent connections. Each connection between neurons is associated with a weight, which adjusts the influence of one neuron on another, and each neuron has an associated bias that shifts the activation function. These parameters allow the network to model complex dependencies flexibly. For example, while linear regression might be able to model

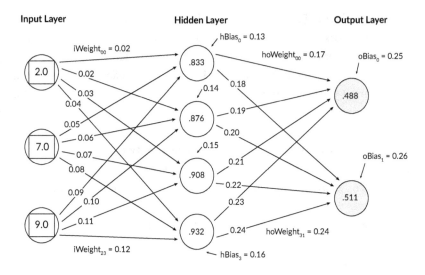

Figure 3.3 Example neural network with weights and biases.

the direct effect of a single variable on an outcome, an NN can model how multiple variables combine and interact subtly and nonlinearly to produce a result.

Additionally, through the activation functions applied at each neuron, NNs can transform inputs into nonlinear relationships that become more apparent. The multiple layers of an NN further amplify this capability, as they allow the model to identify hierarchical features, with earlier layers capturing basic patterns and deeper layers capturing increasingly abstract representations of the data. This capacity to learn and represent direct and interaction effects across multiple dimensions gives NNs power and distinguishes them from traditional linear models.

How a Neural Network Learns

The training process is the heart of developing an NN, transforming it from a simple structure of interconnected nodes into a powerful model capable of recognizing patterns and making accurate predictions. This process systematically teaches the network to map inputs to outputs by optimizing its internal parameters—weights and biases—based on the training data. The objective is to minimize the prediction error by iteratively refining the network's parameters, allowing it to generalize well to new data.

The NN training process comprises the following steps.

1. Initialization: The neural network's weights and biases are initialized, often with small random values.
2. Forward propagation: Input data is passed through the network, and each neuron's output is computed by applying the activation function to the weighted sum of its inputs plus the bias.
3. Loss calculation: The network's prediction is compared to the actual output using a loss function, quantifying any error.
4. Backward propagation (backpropagation): The error is propagated back through the network, and the weights and biases are adjusted to minimize the loss.
5. Iteration: Steps 2–4 are repeated for many iterations (epochs) until the network's performance stabilizes.

When an NN makes a prediction, it does not always get the answer right on the first try. The discrepancy between the predicted and target (or actual) values is measured using a loss function, which tells the network how far off its guess was (i.e., error). It is important to note that this means only supervised data can be used in an NN. The error is the starting point for a learning process called backpropagation, a feedback mechanism that allows the network to adjust and improve over time (Figure 3.4).

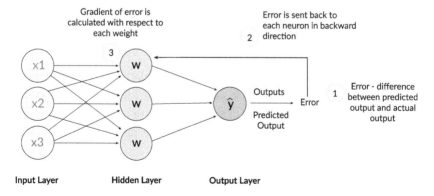

Figure 3.4 Example backpropagation process.

In backpropagation, the error from the output layer flows backward through the network, reaching the hidden layers that contribute to the prediction. At each step, the network determines how much each weight and bias influenced the final error. To do this, it uses the chain rule from calculus, calculating gradients (precise measures of how sensitive the loss is to changes in each weight and bias). Once the gradients are calculated, the network begins its adjustment process. It tweaks each weight and bias slightly, guided by an optimization algorithm. The adjustments are proportional to the gradients, scaled by a small factor called the learning rate. This learning rate ensures the changes are small enough to fine-tune the network without overshooting the optimal settings.

In other words, backpropagation helps the network learn by repeatedly adjusting its weights and biases to reduce errors and recognize patterns more accurately. Over time, this process fine-tunes the network's parameters, improving its predictions while maintaining a balance between learning speed and stability.

This process of error correction is not a one-time event. The network repeatedly cycles through its training data, making predictions, calculating errors, propagating them backward, and refining its parameters. Over many iterations, these incremental changes accumulate, allowing the network to hone in on patterns and relationships in the data gradually. Through this iterative process of learning from mistakes, the neural network becomes increasingly adept at capturing complex relationships and making accurate predictions, transforming raw data into meaningful insights.

Evaluating the performance of an NN is essential to ensure it makes accurate and reliable predictions. There are three key metrics for evaluation:

- **Accuracy** is the proportion of correct predictions from the total number of predictions. It is a standard metric for classification tasks.
- **Precision** is the proportion of accurate positive predictions out of all optimistic predictions made by the model. It indicates the accuracy of positive predictions.
- **Recall** is the proportion of true positive predictions out of all actual positive instances. It measures the model's ability to identify positive cases.

Figure 3.5 Examples of underfit, robust, and overfit training.

NN developers must also guard against overfitting and underfitting (Figure 3.5). **Overfitting** occurs when the model learns the training data too well, including its noise and outliers, leading to poor generalization of new data. Techniques to prevent overfitting include regularization methods, dropout, and early stopping. With underfitting, the model is too simple to capture the underlying patterns in the data, resulting in poor performance on training and new data. Increasing model complexity and ensuring sufficient training can help address underfitting.

Types of Neural Networks

NNs come in various architectures, each suited to different tasks and data types. The choice of architecture depends on the nature of the data input and the specific problem being addressed. Some networks are designed for structured, tabular data, while others are optimized for spatial patterns in images or sequential dependencies in time series and language data. Three fundamental types that illustrate these differences are feedforward neural networks (FNNs), convolutional neural networks (CNNs), and recurrent neural networks (RNNs), each with unique structural characteristics and applications.

Feedforward Neural Networks (FNNs)

FNNs are the simplest type of NN architecture. In FNNs, information moves in one direction—from the input layer through the hidden layers to the output layer. Each neuron in one layer is connected to every neuron in the next layer, and the primary goal is to map input data to the appropriate output.

Convolutional Neural Networks (CNNs)

CNNs are designed to process structured data, such as images. A CNN processes an image following a structured series of steps, as shown in Figure 3.6. Each step transforms the input data, gradually extracting and refining the information needed to classify the image.

The process begins by feeding a raw image into the network, represented as a grid of pixel values. For a color image, these pixels include three channels—red, green, and blue (RGB)—that carry the intensity information for each color. This raw data serves as the foundation for all subsequent processing.

Then, in a convolution layer, the network applies multiple small filters (or kernels) to the image, sliding them over the pixel grid to detect patterns like edges, textures, or shapes. Each filter produces a feature map highlighting specific features in the image, capturing diverse patterns critical for understanding the image. Next, the network applies a rectified linear unit (ReLU) activation function to the feature maps. This operation replaces negative values in the feature maps with zeros, introducing nonlinearity to the network. This step helps the CNN learn complex relationships and patterns that linear operations alone could not

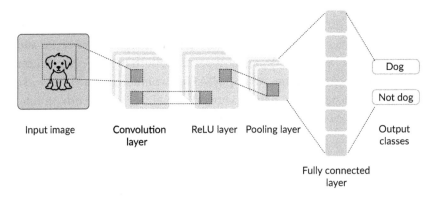

Figure 3.6 Example convolutional neural network.

capture. The resulting feature maps are then processed in a pooling layer that reduces their size while retaining the most essential information. Max pooling, a common pooling technique, selects the maximum value from each small region of the feature map. This step helps the network process information quickly and makes it reliable, even if the image has small changes like slight movements or noise.

After several rounds of convolution, ReLU, and pooling, the high-level features of the image are flattened into a one-dimensional vector to create a fully connected layer. This layer connects every neuron in the current layer to every neuron in the next, combining the extracted features to form complex relationships. The fully connected layer acts as the decision-making component, learning how these features relate to specific classes.

Finally, the network produces a set of probabilities corresponding to the possible categories for the input image. Using a softmax function, the network converts the output values into probabilities that sum to one. A softmax function is a mathematical formula that helps a computer decide between multiple options. It takes a list of numbers and converts them into probabilities, meaning that each number is transformed into a value between 0 and 1, and all the values add up to 1. This makes it useful for tasks like identifying objects in an image or classifying words in a sentence, where the computer needs to decide which category something belongs to. The higher the softmax value for an option, the more confident the computer is. For instance, if the network classifies animals, the output might indicate a 70% probability that the image is a cat, 20% a dog, and 10% a bird. The class with the highest probability is selected as the final prediction.

Together, these steps allow the CNN to transform raw image data into a meaningful classification, as the figure highlights at each stage, showing how features are progressively extracted, refined, and interpreted. This process makes CNNs effective for object detection, facial recognition, and more tasks.

Recurrent Neural Networks (RNNs)

RNNs are designed for sequential data (data for which the order of the data points is significant). RNNs have connections that loop back on themselves, allowing them to maintain a memory of previous inputs. RNNs are particularly effective for tasks involving time series or natural language processing.

An RNN processes sequential data, such as time series or text, by maintaining a memory of previous inputs. Figure 3.7 illustrates the architecture of an RNN with an input layer, two hidden layers, and an output layer. Each element of a sequence of data is fed into the input layer. In the case of a text sequence, these inputs might be words or characters turned into numbers, called embeddings, which help computers understand the meaning and relationships between words. The input is turned into a set of numbers (a vector) that describes its important features at each step.

The network passes the input to the first of two hidden layers, where the real power of the RNN lies. In addition to processing the current input, the hidden layer incorporates information from the previous time

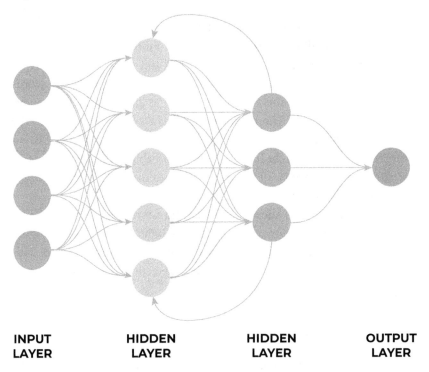

INPUT LAYER   **HIDDEN LAYER**   **HIDDEN LAYER**   **OUTPUT LAYER**

Figure 3.7 Example of recurrent neural network.

step. This is achieved through recurrent connections, represented in the figure as loops within the hidden layer. These loops enable the network to maintain a "memory" of past inputs, allowing it to recognize patterns that depend on the order or context of the data.

As the input progresses through the sequence, the first hidden layer passes its output to the next element of the sequence and the second hidden layer. The second hidden layer refines the information further, combining the contextual memory from the first hidden layer with the current input's features. The presence of two hidden layers, as depicted in the figure, allows the network to learn more complex and hierarchical relationships within the sequence.

Finally, the processed information reaches the output layer, which generates a prediction for each time step or the entire sequence, depending on the task. For instance, in language modeling, the output layer might predict the next word in a sentence. The output is typically passed through an activation function, such as softmax, to convert it into probabilities or other interpretable values.

In the RNN, each sequence element contributes to the network's understanding of the overall context. The RNN can model dependencies and patterns across time by using its recurrent connections and multilayer structure. It is well-suited for speech recognition, text generation, and time-series forecasting tasks.

Tools and Frameworks

NNs rely on specialized programming libraries that simplify their development, training, and deployment. Three of the most widely used frameworks are TensorFlow, PyTorch, and Keras, each with distinct strengths. TensorFlow, developed by Google, is a powerful open-source library designed for large-scale machine learning. It supports distributed training, works across different platforms, and includes tools like TensorBoard for visualization and TensorFlow Extended (TFX) for managing production pipelines. PyTorch, created by Facebook's AI Research lab, is favored for its dynamic computation graph and Python-like interface, making it highly flexible and user-friendly for research and prototyping. It also supports GPU acceleration for efficient training and is improving its production capabilities with tools like TorchScript and PyTorch Lightning. Keras, originally an independent project but now part of TensorFlow, provides a high-level API that allows users to build NNs with minimal code. Its simplicity makes it ideal for beginners and rapid prototyping, though it may be less suited for highly complex models.

Understanding the differences among these tools is important for choosing the proper framework based on the task. PyTorch is well-suited for research and experimentation due to its flexibility and ease of debugging, while TensorFlow excels in production environments where scalability and deployment across platforms matter. Keras, with its simple syntax, is ideal for those new to NNs or projects that require quick iterations. Recognizing these distinctions helps urban planners and other professionals select the best tool for their needs, whether they are testing new models, working on large-scale implementations, or focusing on user-friendly solutions.

Applications of Neural Networks in Urban Planning

NNs are powerful tools for addressing various challenges in urban planning. Their ability to analyze complex data and identify patterns can help urban planners make more informed decisions. Three key applications for neural networks in planning are traffic prediction and management, land use and zoning, and environmental impact assessment.

Traffic Prediction and Management

Traffic prediction is a critical component of urban planning, helping to alleviate congestion, improve road safety, and enhance the overall efficiency of transportation systems. NNs, with their ability to process vast amounts of data and recognize intricate patterns, are particularly well-suited for this task.

NNs can analyze historical traffic data, real-time sensor information, weather conditions, and social events to predict traffic flow. By identifying patterns and correlations within these data sets, NNs can provide accurate short-term and long-term traffic forecasts. These predictions can optimize traffic light timings, reroute traffic, and plan infrastructure improvements.

Example: A Neural Network Model for Real-Time Traffic Management in a Smart City

In Valencia, Spain, researchers developed an NN model to predict traffic flow and enhance real-time traffic management. This initiative aimed to address urban congestion by using deep learning techniques to forecast traffic patterns, thereby enabling proactive measures to alleviate congestion and reduce environmental impact.

Valencia faced significant traffic congestion, increasing travel times, and environmental concerns. Traditional traffic management systems struggled to adapt to the dynamic nature of urban traffic, necessitating a predictive approach to manage traffic flow effectively.

Researchers implemented an NN to address this challenge and predict traffic flux across the city's extensive sensor network (Folgado et al., 2022). The model was trained using historical traffic data from 2016 and 2017, enabling it to capture temporal patterns and forecast future traffic conditions. Valencia's traffic sensor system, comprising nearly 3,500 sensors, provided comprehensive coverage of the city's traffic flow. The dataset was processed to remove anomalies and increase accuracy, preparing it for practical model training.

Researchers chose a long short-term memory (LSTM) NN for its proficiency in handling sequential data and capturing long-term dependencies, making it suitable for modeling traffic patterns. An LSTM is a specialized type of RNN designed to handle sequential data, like time series or text, by maintaining a memory of past inputs, which is crucial for tasks involving order or context. Unlike FNNs, which process inputs independently and are better suited for tasks like image classification, LSTMs use feedback connections to remember information over time.

While CNNs effectively detect spatial patterns in grid-like data, such as images, LSTMs focus on temporal patterns in sequences. In practice, LSTMs are often combined with CNNs or FNNs for tasks like video analysis, where CNNs extract spatial features from frames, and LSTMs analyze the temporal sequence of those features. The model's architecture was optimized to balance complexity and performance, ensuring accurate predictions without overfitting. Researchers trained the model on the preprocessed dataset and employed validation techniques to assess the model's accuracy and generalization capabilities.

The LSTM model demonstrated high accuracy in predicting traffic flux, effectively capturing the temporal dynamics of urban traffic. This predictive capability allowed city planners to implement real-time traffic management strategies, such as adjusting traffic signals and providing driver route recommendations, thereby reducing congestion and improving urban mobility.

For Valencia, ensuring the accuracy and reliability of sensor data was critical for practical model training and prediction, and balancing the model's complexity to prevent overfitting while maintaining predictive accuracy required careful tuning. Building on this success, Valencia plans to integrate additional data sources, such as weather conditions and unique event schedules, to enhance the model's predictive capabilities. The city also aims to develop user-friendly applications to disseminate real-time traffic information to the public, promoting informed travel decisions and further alleviating congestion.

Land Use and Zoning

Accurate land-use classification is essential for effective urban planning. NNs can classify land-use types by analyzing high-resolution satellite images and geospatial data. This process involves identifying patterns and features distinguishing different land-use categories, such as residential, commercial, industrial, and agricultural areas.

By automating land-use classification, NNs enable urban planners to monitor urban sprawl, detect zoning violations, and plan new developments more efficiently. The ability to quickly and accurately process large volumes of satellite imagery makes NNs valuable for sustainable urban development.

Example: Neural Networks for Land-Use Classification

In San Francisco, California, researchers conducted a study using NNs to classify land use at the city scale. This approach aimed to overcome the limitations of traditional methods by using ground-level images to achieve detailed and accurate land-use mapping.

Traditional land-use classification methods often rely on overhead imagery, which can be insufficient for distinguishing between different land-use types, especially in urban environments where multiple activities occur nearby. The challenge was to develop a method capable of fine-grained classification to support urban planning and policy-making.

The researchers developed a CNN framework that integrated object and scene recognition to classify 45 distinct land use categories using georeferenced ground-level images from Flickr (Zhu, Deng, & Newsam, 2018). This method capitalized on the rich visual information available at the street level to enhance classification accuracy. The dataset comprised approximately 94,000 geotagged images of specific San Francisco land parcels, each labeled with one of the 45 land-use categories. It was curated to remove irrelevant or low-quality images, ensuring that the remaining data accurately represented the land-use categories.

Researchers employed a dual-stream CNN architecture, with one stream dedicated to object recognition and the other to scene recognition (Zhu, Deng, & Newsam, 2018). A dual-stream CNN is a deep neural network that processes two different aspects of an image simultaneously using separate but complementary convolutional streams. The model was trained as a whole, enabling it to automatically learn important patterns from ground-level images to classify different types of land use. Validation was performed to assess the model's performance. The model correctly identified more than 29% of land parcels, which is impressive considering how detailed and complex the classification task was. The CNN-based approach demonstrated the feasibility of using ground-level images for detailed land-use classification at the city scale. Integrating object and scene recognition enabled the model to capture nuanced differences between land-use types. For San Francisco, ensuring a diverse and representative dataset was crucial, as biases in the data could affect classification accuracy. Applying the model to other cities would require substantial data collection and potential retraining to account for different urban landscapes and land-use patterns.

Building on this study, future research could explore integrating additional data sources, such as social media check-ins or mobile phone data, to enhance classification accuracy further. Adapting the model to incorporate temporal dynamics could provide insights into how land use changes over time.

Environmental Impact Assessment

An environmental impact assessment is important for ensuring sustainable urban development. NNs can predict pollution levels and assess the ecological impact of new infrastructure projects by analyzing data from various sources, such as traffic patterns, industrial activities, and meteorological conditions. These predictions help urban planners identify potential environmental risks and develop strategies to mitigate negative impacts. By incorporating NNs into ecological monitoring systems, cities can proactively manage air quality, noise pollution, and other environmental factors.

Example: Using Neural Networks to Model the Impact of New Infrastructure on Air Quality

Researchers in Hong Kong developed a hybrid NN framework called Deep-AIR to model and predict air quality, focusing on pollutants like NO_2 and $PM_{2.5}$. The city's complex urban landscape, with its high-rise buildings and narrow streets, exacerbates air pollution through the street canyon effect, which traps pollutants at street level. Traditional air quality monitoring systems, relying on sparse sensor networks, struggled to provide accurate, fine-grained predictions for effective public health interventions. Deep-AIR combined CNNs and LSTM networks to address this challenge of capturing spatial and temporal air pollution dynamics. This hybrid approach incorporated urban features such as road density, building height, and meteorological data to enhance prediction accuracy (Han et al., 2021).

The study integrated air quality monitoring data, meteorological information, and urban structural data, including road networks and building geometries. After cleaning and preprocessing the data to remove anomalies and missing values, researchers trained the model using historical data, optimizing parameters to minimize prediction errors. The CNN component captured spatial features influencing pollutant dispersion, while the LSTM component modeled temporal sequences to track pollutant concentration trends over time. By combining outputs from both networks, Deep-AIR generated fine-grained, hourly air quality estimations and forecasts, achieving notable accuracy improvements over baseline models. The framework demonstrated superior performance, with 67.6% accuracy for fine-grained hourly estimations and 77.2% accuracy for one-hour forecasts, highlighting its ability to model urban air pollution effectively and provide valuable insights for urban planning and public health policy (Han et al., 2021).

Despite its success, implementing Deep-AIR required sophisticated data preprocessing to increase compatibility across diverse datasets and substantial computational resources for training and real-time predictions. Future research could enhance the framework by incorporating real-time traffic data and human mobility patterns, improving prediction accuracy. Applying Deep-AIR to other metropolitan areas with different urban morphologies could also validate its generalizability and robustness (Han et al., 2021).

NNs are transforming urban planning by enabling advanced predictive modeling across various domains. In traffic management, researchers in Valencia used an LSTM-based model to analyze historical and real-time sensor data, optimizing congestion control strategies. For land-use classification, a CNN model in San Francisco integrated object and scene recognition from ground-level images, enhancing zoning and development insights. In an environmental impact assessment, Hong Kong's hybrid CNN–LSTM model, Deep-AIR, combined spatial and temporal data to predict air pollution levels with high accuracy. These methods demonstrate how deep learning techniques process vast datasets, recognize complex patterns, and support data-driven urban planning decisions.

Challenges of Neural Networks

As NNs become more integrated into urban planning, it is essential to recognize the challenges that may arise. Their effectiveness depends on data quality, computational resources, and ethical considerations. Limited or biased datasets can reduce accuracy, while deep learning models require significant processing power, posing challenges for cities with limited infrastructure. Ethical concerns, including transparency and fairness, must also be addressed to increase responsible use. Understanding these limitations allows urban planners to make informed decisions and apply NNs effectively while mitigating potential risks.

Data Limitations and Quality

The effectiveness of NNs is directly tied to the quality and completeness of the data they are trained on. Urban data, while abundant, often comes with inherent limitations and inconsistencies that can hinder model performance and reliability. Addressing these data-related challenges is a technical task and critical for ensuring ethical and effective urban planning practices.

High-quality data is the backbone of any NN application. It enables the model to capture the intricate relationships between urban variables such as population density, land use, transportation patterns, and environmental factors. However, urban planners and data scientists frequently encounter significant hurdles in obtaining, processing, and safeguarding data. If not addressed, the following challenges can compromise the accuracy of predictions and undermine the trustworthiness of AI-powered urban planning solutions.

- **Incomplete data**. Datasets often suffer incompleteness, stemming from missing entries, unrecorded variables, or gaps in time-series data. For example, a dataset on public transportation usage might lack data for specific periods due to equipment failures or data collection errors. Missing information limits the model's ability to identify patterns and relationships, leading to suboptimal predictions or biased outcomes. Handling incomplete data requires sophisticated imputation techniques or supplementary data sources to fill gaps effectively.
- **Inconsistent data**. Data collected from multiple sources—such as municipal departments, private entities, and community sensors— may vary in format, measurement units, or categorization schemes. For instance, one dataset might record population density in people per square kilometer, while another uses people per square mile. Such inconsistencies can complicate data integration, requiring extensive preprocessing and standardization efforts. The NN may produce unreliable results without addressing these inconsistencies due to conflicting input features.
- **Data privacy**. Urban data frequently includes sensitive information, such as individual mobility patterns, income levels, or residential locations. The collection and use of such data raise significant privacy

concerns. Data privacy requires effective governance frameworks, anonymization techniques, and compliance with data protection regulations such as the General Data Protection Regulation (GDPR) and the California Consumer Privacy Act (CCPA). Striking a balance between using detailed data for model training and protecting individual privacy is a persistent challenge that demands technical solutions and ethical oversight.

Addressing these challenges requires a multi-faceted approach. Advanced data preprocessing techniques, standardized data collection protocols, and innovative privacy-preserving methods can help mitigate many of these issues. Additionally, fostering collaboration among urban planners, data scientists, and policymakers is critical for developing a shared understanding of data quality standards and ethical practices. By overcoming these obstacles, urban planning can fully harness the potential of NNs to create more innovative, efficient, and equitable cities.

DATA PREPARATION

Data preparation is one of the most critical steps in developing an NN model. It is the foundation upon which the entire model is built. The quality and suitability of the data directly affect model performance, accuracy, and reliability. Poorly prepared data can lead to unreliable models, biased predictions, and errors in analysis, regardless of how sophisticated the NN architecture is. Conversely, well-prepared data can enhance the model's ability to learn and generalize, making it effective across various applications.

The data preparation process typically includes three key stages: collection, cleaning, and transformation. Each is essential for ensuring the NN has the correct input to learn and make accurate predictions.

- **Data collection**: First, necessary data must be gathered from relevant sources. Data types may include demographic information, traffic patterns, land-use data, weather conditions, and economic indicators. Sources may include governmental databases, satellite imagery, sensors, and surveys.

- **Data cleaning**: Raw data often contains noise, missing values, and inconsistencies. Data cleaning involves addressing these issues by removing or imputing missing values, correcting errors, and filtering out irrelevant information.
- **Data transformation**: To make the data suitable for NN analysis, it must be transformed into a format the network can process. This includes normalizing or standardizing numerical features, encoding categorical variables, and creating new features that may enhance the model's performance.

For an NN designed to classify urban land use types based on satellite imagery, the data preparation process might look like the following:

- Obtaining high-resolution satellite images of the urban area and labeled data indicating different land-use types (e.g., residential, commercial, industrial).
- Remove images with poor resolution or significant occlusions (e.g., cloud cover) and address missing labels.
- Normalize the pixel values of the images to ensure they fall within a consistent range and convert the labeled land use types into numerical codes that the neural network can process.

Data preparation is essential for ensuring the accuracy and reliability of an NN model. High-quality data enhances the model's ability to learn and generalize, while poor data can lead to biased predictions and errors. This process involves gathering relevant information, refining it to eliminate inconsistencies, and converting it into a format suitable for analysis. In applications like urban land-use classification, proper data preparation ensures that inputs are structured and optimized for effective model training, ultimately improving predictive performance.

Computational Resources

NNs come with significant computational demands, presenting various challenges for those seeking to integrate AI into their workflows. The success of NNs hinges on the quality of data and algorithms and the availability of adequate computational resources. For urban planners in public agencies, many of whom operate within constrained budgets and infrastructure, this can be a significant barrier to adopting AI technologies effectively.

The computational demands of NNs stem from their architecture and training processes. Training large-scale models involves processing massive datasets, performing millions (or billions) of calculations, and optimizing numerous parameters. This requires specialized hardware, scalable systems, and considerable energy resources. As NN applications grow in size and complexity, urban planners must grapple with hardware access, system scalability, and sustainability challenges.

- **Hardware requirements**. NN training often necessitates high-performance hardware such as graphics processing units (GPUs) or tensor processing units (TPUs). These devices are designed to handle the parallelized computations required for training deep learning models. However, access to such specialized hardware can be a significant hurdle for urban planning organizations, particularly smaller municipalities or research teams operating on limited budgets. Cloud computing services such as Amazon Web Services (AWS), Google Cloud, or Microsoft Azure provide on-demand access to GPUs and TPUs. However, the associated costs can still be prohibitive for sustained use.
- **Scalability**. As datasets grow and models become more complex, the computational power required increases exponentially. This poses a scalability challenge, particularly for applications requiring real-time processing, such as dynamic traffic management systems or live environmental monitoring. Limited computational resources may force planners to simplify their models, compromising accuracy or utility. Moreover, deploying trained models across an entire city often requires adequate large-scale data processing and storage infrastructure.
- **Energy consumption**. Training deep neural networks is energy-intensive, with large-scale models consuming vast amounts of electricity during training. This raises environmental concerns, especially as urban planners strive to create sustainable, eco-friendly cities. For example, the energy footprint of training a

single large model can be equivalent to the annual electricity consumption of several households. These environmental implications highlight the need for more efficient algorithms, hardware, and practices that reduce the carbon footprint of AI applications.

Overcoming these challenges requires a multipronged approach. Using cloud-based platforms can provide access to advanced hardware as needed, while partnerships with tech companies or academic institutions may help offset costs. Optimizing models to balance complexity and efficiency, adopting lightweight (i.e., simple) neural architectures, and using pre-trained models can reduce computational requirements. AI practitioners should prioritize energy-efficient algorithms, green data centers, and renewable energy sources in training infrastructures to address sustainability. By addressing these computational resource challenges, urban planners can unlock the full potential of NNs, enabling innovative and sustainable solutions for managing urban growth, infrastructure, and quality of life.

Ethical Considerations

AI technologies can enhance decision-making, improve resource allocation, and enable innovative solutions to urban issues such as traffic congestion, housing shortages, and environmental sustainability. However, users of AI in urban contexts must navigate a complex web of ethical considerations to be sure that its use is fair, transparent, and beneficial to all.

The power of ANNs lies in their ability to learn patterns from data and make predictions or decisions based on that knowledge. However, this same strength introduces ethical concerns when the data used to train these models contains biases or when the inner workings of the models are not easily interpretable. When dealing with sensitive and impactful decisions—such as where to build affordable housing, how to allocate public resources, or how to design equitable transportation systems—these ethical considerations take on heightened importance. Planners and policymakers must address bias, transparency, accountability, and public trust issues to ensure that AI-driven urban planning serves the public good and upholds principles of equity and justice.

- **Bias and fairness**. NNs are only as unbiased as the data on which they are trained. The model may inadvertently perpetuate these biases in its predictions or recommendations if the training data reflects historical inequities or systemic discrimination. For instance, an AI system used to allocate funding for public transportation might prioritize wealthier neighborhoods if the training data heavily represents areas with existing infrastructure investments. Ensuring fairness requires rigorous auditing of training data, employing bias mitigation techniques, and involving diverse stakeholders in designing and deploying AI systems. Ethical AI in urban planning must actively counteract existing inequalities rather than reinforce them.
- **Transparency and accountability**. NNs are often criticized for being "black boxes," as their complex architectures make it difficult to interpret how decisions are made. This lack of transparency poses a challenge in urban planning, where decisions can impact communities. Planners and policymakers must strive to make AI models interpretable and explainable, ensuring that nonexperts can understand the rationale behind decisions. Accountability is equally important; urban planners must take responsibility for the outcomes of AI-driven decisions, ensuring that unintended consequences are identified and addressed.
- **Public trust**. Public trust is a cornerstone of successful AI implementation in urban planning. Communities are more likely to accept AI-driven decisions if they understand how and why the technology is being used and if they see tangible benefits. Transparent communication about the role of AI, its limitations, and its safeguards can help build trust. Communities should be involved in decision-making processes, such as through participatory planning workshops or public consultations, to ensure the technology aligns with the needs and values of the people it serves.

Addressing these ethical considerations requires a multidisciplinary approach, combining technical solutions such as bias detection and explainable AI with participatory planning practices and effective governance frameworks. By prioritizing fairness, transparency, and public trust, urban planners can harness the power of AI responsibly, creating more innovative, equitable, and inclusive cities. Through thoughtful and ethical integration, AI can become a transformative tool for addressing the complex challenges of modern urbanization.

Looking Ahead

As AI technology advances, the use of NNs in urban planning is expected to expand. These models will improve cities' management of transportation, land use, energy, and environmental challenges. However, their success will depend on continued innovation, ethical oversight, and collaboration between planners, policymakers, and data scientists.

One key development is the growth of hybrid models that combine different types of NNs to improve urban analysis. For example, CNNs can process spatial data from satellite images, while RNNs or transformers can track changes over time. Reinforcement learning could help optimize policies by simulating different urban scenarios. These combined approaches will improve the accuracy of urban predictions and decision-making.

Another important trend is federated learning, which allows AI models to learn from decentralized data sources while maintaining privacy. Since urban planning data is often spread across different agencies and departments, federated learning enables collaboration without requiring data to be stored in a single location. This reduces privacy risks and helps overcome data-sharing barriers.

NNs also raise concerns about energy consumption, as large AI models require significant computing power. To reduce their environmental impact, future efforts will focus on energy-efficient AI, including techniques like model compression and low-power hardware. At the same time, AI can contribute to sustainability by improving energy grids, reducing traffic congestion, and optimizing city resource use.

Ultimately, NNs' effectiveness in urban planning will depend on how well they are integrated into decision-making processes. Urban planners, data scientists, and policymakers should work together to ensure that AI tools are used responsibly and transparently. Public engagement will also build trust and ensure that AI-driven solutions address community needs.

Chapter Summary

This chapter explored NNs' role in urban planning, providing insights into their fundamental concepts, practical applications, and associated challenges. NNs have emerged as powerful tools for addressing the complexities of urban systems, providing planners with the capacity to analyze vast amounts of data, uncover hidden patterns, and make informed decisions. This concluding section synthesizes the key ideas discussed in the chapter, emphasizing their significance, limitations, and future directions in urban planning.

The chapter highlighted three primary types of NNs and their applications in urban planning. FNNs are well-suited for straightforward tasks such as classifying data or predicting future trends. CNNs are effective for analyzing spatial data like satellite imagery, making them useful for tasks such as land-use classification and infrastructure monitoring. RNNs, with their ability to process sequential data, are particularly effective for analyzing temporal patterns, such as traffic flow and energy consumption. Together, these architectures illustrate the adaptability and breadth of NNs in dealing with diverse urban challenges.

Several compelling case studies demonstrated that NNs have proven highly effective in real-world urban planning scenarios. In traffic management, NNs like LSTM models have been used to predict congestion patterns and optimize signal timings, exemplified by projects in Valencia, Spain. These models have enabled cities to address congestion in real time, improving mobility and reducing environmental impacts.

Land-use classification represents another area where NNs, particularly CNNs, have made significant contributions. In San Francisco, NNs have provided fine-grained analyses of urban land use by using ground-level imagery, overcoming the limitations of traditional overhead data. Such insights are invaluable for urban planners balancing development and conservation efforts.

NNs have also benefited environmental monitoring. In Hong Kong, a hybrid model combining CNNs and RNNs was used to predict air quality by integrating spatial and temporal data. This approach provided accurate pollution forecasts and offered actionable insights for public health interventions and sustainable urban planning.

Despite their potential, ANNs in urban planning face several critical challenges that must be addressed to ensure their effective and responsible use. One major obstacle is the limitation of data quality and availability. Urban datasets are often incomplete, inconsistent, or biased, which can compromise the reliability of NN predictions. Developing effective data governance frameworks and employing sophisticated preprocessing techniques are essential to overcoming these challenges.

The computational demands of NNs also pose significant hurdles. Training and deploying these models require access to high-performance hardware, such as GPUs or TPUs, which can be costly and resource-intensive. Additionally, the energy consumption associated with training large models raises concerns about sustainability and the environmental impact of AI applications in urban planning.

Ethical considerations further complicate the integration of ANNs into urban systems. NNs are often criticized for being "black boxes," making it difficult to interpret their decision-making processes. Transparency and accountability are important as urban planning decisions can have profound social and economic implications. Ensuring public trust requires engaging communities, clearly communicating the role of AI, and demonstrating its benefits while safeguarding individual privacy and equity.

References and Further Reading

Folgado, M. G., Sanz, V., Hirn, J., Lorenzo, E. G., & Urchueguia, J. F. (2022). Predicting the traffic flux in the city of Valencia with Deep Learning. arXiv preprint arXiv:2210.01630.

Han, Y., Zhang, Q., Li, V. O. K., & Lam, J. C. K. (2021). Deep-AIR: A Hybrid CNN-LSTM Framework for Air Quality Modeling in Metropolitan Cities. arXiv preprint arXiv:2103.14587.

McCorduck, P. (2004). *Machines who think: A personal inquiry into the history and prospects of artificial intelligence*. AK Peters/CRC Press.

Zhu, Y., Deng, X., & Newsam, S. (2018). Fine-Grained Land Use Classification at the City Scale Using Ground-Level Images. arXiv preprint arXiv:1802.02668.

4

NATURAL LANGUAGE PROCESSING FOR URBAN PLANNERS

Natural language processing (NLP) is at the heart of bridging the gap between human communication and machine understanding. Human language is complex, rich with nuance, and context-dependent, making it challenging for computers to manage. At its core, NLP seeks to enable machines to process, interpret, and generate human language in meaningful and practical ways. This requires breaking down language into structured components like words and sentences while understanding their deeper, contextual meanings.

Machines must recognize language structure and decode its meaning and intention, especially when faced with ambiguity or figurative expressions. Recent advances, particularly in machine learning (ML) and transformer-based models, have significantly improved a machine's ability to capture and utilize context, making NLP systems better at mimicking human-like understanding. However, to reach proper language comprehension, NLP systems must also integrate real-world

DOI: 10.4324/9781003476818-4

knowledge and reasoning, handling the literal meaning of words and the pragmatics—what is implied, inferred, or left unsaid. Combining all these elements, from syntax to semantics to context, defines the core of NLP's quest to enable machines to communicate in and understand human language while continually improving their ability to engage in increasingly complex and nuanced interactions.

NLP encompasses various techniques, from basic text processing like tokenization and part-of-speech tagging to advanced deep learning models that interpret context, semantics, and discourse. In the context of artificial intelligence (AI), NLP is crucial because it allows machines to interact with humans more naturally and intuitively. This capability is fundamental for developing applications such as virtual assistants, chatbots, and automated customer service, which rely on understanding and generating human language. These and related concepts will be discussed in this chapter.

A Brief History of Natural Language Processing

Early research on NLP began in the 1950s, paralleling the early developments of AI as researchers sought to understand how machines could process and replicate human cognition. The pioneering work of Alan Turing was particularly influential in laying the foundation for this field. In his seminal 1950 paper, "Computing machinery and intelligence," Turing introduced what is now known as the Turing Test, a thought experiment to assess whether a machine could exhibit intelligent behavior indistinguishable from a human. Because of language's inherent complexity, ambiguity, and context-dependence, the Turing Test proposed that if a machine could carry on a conversation with a human without the human realizing it was interacting with a machine, then that machine could be considered intelligent. This concept underscored the importance of language as a marker of intelligence. It established the groundwork for a central pursuit in AI research: developing systems capable of understanding, processing, and generating human language.

The development of NLP has progressed through several key milestones, each marked by advancements in computational methods and data availability. In the 1950s and 1960s, the first attempts at NLP were centered around simple rule-based systems. A landmark event during this period was the 1954 Georgetown-IBM experiment, where over 60 Russian sentences were successfully translated into English, demonstrating the potential of machine translation (Poibeau, 2017). These early systems relied on manually-crafted rules for processing language, which laid the foundation for future NLP advancements.

In the 1970s and 1980s, more sophisticated linguistic models began to emerge. Noam Chomsky's research on grammar provided a crucial theoretical framework for syntactic processing, allowing NLP systems to move beyond basic rules toward a deeper understanding of sentence structure. This period marked the rise of linguistic models, where theoretical linguistics significantly influenced how machines processed human language.

The 1990s saw a significant shift with the introduction of statistical methods and ML to NLP. Algorithms like the Hidden Markov Model (HMM) and the Maximum Entropy Model (MEM) became standard tools for various tasks such as speech recognition and part-of-speech tagging. HMMs represent sequential data by modeling hidden states and their transitions, making them effective for tasks like speech recognition and part-of-speech tagging. MEMs, based on the principle of maximum entropy, estimate the probability of linguistic structures using contextual features, enabling applications such as text classification and machine translation. This era moved NLP from rule-based systems to data-driven approaches in which statistical methods were used to model language more effectively.

The 2000s were defined by the explosion of the internet and the availability of massive text corpora (i.e., language-based datasets), which accelerated progress in NLP. ML techniques, especially supervised learning, gained prominence as they enabled more accurate and scalable language models. With the internet providing vast amounts of data, NLP systems have become more robust and capable of handling complex request tasks.

Since the 2010s, NLP has been revolutionized by deep learning and neural networks (NNs). Techniques such as Word2Vec, GloVe, and, more recently, transformers like BERT (Bidirectional Encoder Representations from Transformers) and GPT (Generative Pre-trained Transformer) (see Glossary) have dramatically improved NLP's ability to understand and generate human language with unprecedented accuracy. These neural models have shifted the field toward more sophisticated, context-aware systems, making it possible for machines to perform tasks such as language translation, sentiment analysis, and conversational AI with humanlike proficiency.

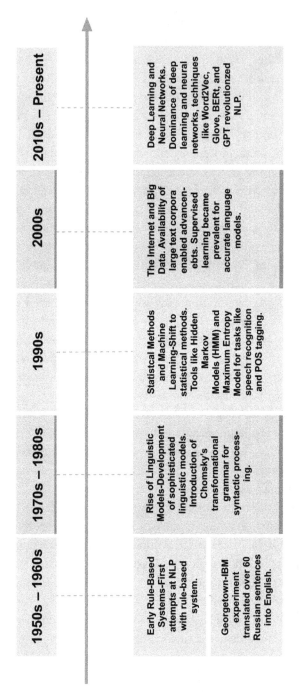

Figure 4.1 Evolution of natural language processing.

These milestones highlight the continuous evolution of NLP, driven by advancements in computational power, data availability, and improvements in algorithmic techniques. Understanding this historical context helps professionals, including urban planners, to appreciate the capabilities and limitations of modern NLP technologies and how they can be applied effectively in various fields.

Introduction to Natural Language Processing

> Natural language processing (NLP): A subfield of AI in which computer methods analyze human language, text, or verbal communication to derive meaning.

Basic Concepts and Terminology

NLP is a multidisciplinary field at the intersection of computer science, linguistics, and AI. It focuses on enabling machines to process, understand, and generate human language, making it a cornerstone of modern AI systems. NLP bridges the gap between human communication and machine interpretation, facilitating various applications from chatbots to machine translation and sentiment analysis.

NLP systems employ ML, statistics, and deep learning techniques to process and analyze large amounts of natural language data. These techniques enable computers to perform many tasks with high accuracy and efficiency. Some of the key functions in NLP include:

- **Language modeling** involves predicting the next word in a sentence or generating entire sentences based on a given prompt. Language models, such as GPT-4, are trained on vast text corpora (language data sets) to understand and generate human-like language.
- **Text classification**: This task involves categorizing text into predefined categories based on content. Applications include spam detection, sentiment analysis, and topic classification. ML algorithms, such as support vector machines (SVM) and NNs, are commonly used for text classification.

- **Entity recognition**: Also known as named entity recognition (NER), this task involves identifying and classifying entities (such as names of people, organizations, locations, dates, etc.) within a text. NER is crucial for information extraction, summarization, and question-answering systems.

NLP continues to evolve rapidly, driven by advancements in deep learning and the increasing availability of large datasets. As these technologies progress, NLP systems become more sophisticated and capable, enabling a deeper and more nuanced understanding of human language. This, in turn, opens up new possibilities for applications across various domains, making NLP an indispensable tool for a broad range of applications.

To manage the complexity of human language, NLP is divided into several subfields, each addressing a unique aspect of language structure and use. Together, these subfields allow the design of systems capable of comprehending and interacting with natural language. Below is a brief description of these core subfields.

Syntax: Syntax focuses on the rules and structures governing the arrangement of words in sentences. It is concerned with understanding how words combine to form phrases and sentences, the roles of different words within a sentence, and the hierarchical structure inherent in language. Syntactic analysis often employs techniques such as parsing, which involves breaking down a sentence into its components according to a set of grammatical rules. Parsing enables machines to discern the grammatical relationships within sentences, facilitating tasks such as machine translation, grammar checking, and text generation.

Semantics: Semantics involves the meaning of words, phrases, and sentences. It aims to capture how individual words combine to form meaningful expressions and how context shapes interpretation. While syntax provides the form, semantics provides the substance of language, and both are essential for comprehensive language understanding. Tasks in semantic analysis include word sense disambiguation—determining the specific meaning of a word based on its context—and semantic role labeling, which identifies the relationships between verbs and associated nouns (e.g., identifying the "agent" or "object" in a sentence). These techniques are integral to applications such as information retrieval, question answering, and knowledge representation. Recent advancements, including vector-based word representations such as Word2Vec and contextual embeddings such as BERT, have revolutionized semantic analysis by enabling machines to capture nuanced meanings.

Pragmatics: Pragmatics extends beyond syntax and semantics to explore how context influences the interpretation and use of language. It considers the situational and cultural factors that affect communication, focusing on how meaning is constructed in specific interactions. Pragmatic analysis includes understanding implicatures (implied meanings), speech acts (e.g., requests, commands, or questions), and the intentions behind utterances. This subfield is vital for building systems such as dialogue managers, context-aware text generators, and conversational agents, where understanding user intent and context is paramount. Pragmatics enables machines to generate appropriate and contextually relevant responses, enhancing the naturalness of interactions.

Morphology: Morphology studies the internal structure of words and their formation from smaller units called morphemes—the most minor meaningful elements in a language. It involves analyzing how prefixes, suffixes, roots, and stems combine to form words and convey grammatical features such as tense, number, or case. Morphological analysis is important for tasks like stemming, which reduces words to their root form (e.g., "running" to "run"), and lemmatization, which identifies the base form of words while considering context (e.g., "better" to "good"). Morphology is critical in languages with rich inflectional systems, supporting tasks such as text normalization, spell-checking, and machine translation.

By addressing these distinct but interrelated aspects of language, NLP subfields provide the theoretical and practical tools necessary to decode the complexities of human communication. Each subfield contributes to a deeper understanding of language, enabling the creation of systems that are not only syntactically correct but also semantically meaningful, pragmatically aware, and morphologically precise. These advancements allow machines to interact with humans increasingly naturally and intuitively.

Key Natural Language Processing Techniques and Models

NLP employs a variety of techniques to analyze and process text data effectively. These techniques range from simple statistical methods to advanced NN models, each with strengths and applications. They equip machines with the tools to understand, analyze, and generate human language.

One of the primary techniques in NLP is tokenization, the process of breaking down text into smaller units called tokens. These tokens can be words, parts of words, phrases, or even characters, depending on the specific application. For instance, the sentence "Urban planning is essential for sustainable cities" can be tokenized into individual words: ["Urban," "planning," "is," "essential," "for," "sustainable," "cities"]. Tokenization is a crucial step in text preprocessing, allowing NLP algorithms to analyze and process language effectively.

Part-of-speech (POS) tagging assigns grammatical categories (noun, verb, adjective, etc.) to each word in a text. POS tagging helps understand the syntactic structure of sentences and is an essential step for many NLP tasks. For example, in the sentence "An efficient public transportation system is crucial," POS tagging would label "The" as a determiner, "efficient" as an adjective, "public transportation system" as a noun phrase, "is" as a verb, and "crucial" as an adjective.

Named entity recognition (NER) is a technique used to identify and classify named entities in text into predefined categories, such as names of people, organizations, locations, dates, and more. For example, in the sentence "The new park in San Francisco will open next summer," NER would recognize "San Francisco" as a location and "next summer" as a date. NER is particularly useful in extracting structured information from unstructured text, which can benefit urban planning tasks such as identifying key stakeholders or locations in planning documents. Unstructured text refers to freeform text like reports or articles. At the same time, structured information is organized data that can be easily analyzed, such as names, dates, or locations in a database. The structured information lets planners quickly navigate the document and focus on the most relevant sections.

Text summarization is a technique that condenses long documents into shorter, more manageable summaries without losing the key points.

There are two primary approaches to text summarization: extractive and abstractive. Extractive summarization works by selecting and extracting the most important sentences from the original text, while abstractive summarization generates a more concise version of the content, rephrasing and condensing ideas. In urban planning, summarization tools can be applied to large policy documents or project proposals to create executive summaries, helping planners and stakeholders get an overview of the document's main points before delving deeper into specific sections.

A bag of words (BoW) is a model that counts how often each word appears in a document, disregarding grammar, word order, or syntactic structures. This makes BoW a simple and effective tool for tasks like text classification, sentiment analysis, document categorization, and information retrieval, where capturing the presence or absence of particular words is sufficient. However, because BoW ignores word order, context, semantics, and syntactic relationships, it cannot capture the meaning conveyed by sentence structure or distinguish between different uses of the same word in other contexts. In modern NLP, BoW has mainly been superseded by more sophisticated models that capture context and meaning, such as word embeddings (e.g., Word2Vec, GloVe) and transformer-based models (e.g., BERT, GPT). However, BoW remains an essential technique that is beneficial for understanding the basics of text representation in ML. It is still employed in various scenarios where simplicity, speed, and interpretability are more critical than deep semantic understanding.

Term frequency-inverse document frequency (TF-IDF) is a BoW model that incorporates a measure of how rare or common a word is across an entire corpus. This allows the model to count the frequency of words within a document (term frequency) and discount words ubiquitous across all documents (inverse document frequency), thus highlighting words that are more unique or specific to a particular text. In information retrieval, such as search engines, TF-IDF helps identify which documents are most relevant to a user's query, making it an important element of many search algorithms and document classification systems. TF-IDF also plays a crucial role in text mining and document clustering. By weighting words according to their importance in each document, TF-IDF enables more accurate classification and clustering, as it helps differentiate between documents that share a common language but are about different subjects by focusing on the terms that are unique to each article rather than standard terms that appear across the corpus.

TF-IDF improves upon BoW by considering word rarity. Still, like BoW, it cannot capture the meaning conveyed by sentence structure or distinguish between different uses of the same word in other contexts. While more advanced methods like word embeddings and deep learning models have gained popularity in recent years for capturing context and meaning, TF-IDF remains one of the most widely used techniques in information retrieval, document classification, and natural language processing due to its simplicity, interpretability, and effectiveness in highlighting the essential terms in a document.

Word embeddings are a significant advancement in NLP. Unlike BoW and TF-IDF, word embedding models capture semantic relationships between words, enabling models to understand and process language to reflect the meanings and relationships between words rather than just their raw occurrences. This approach allows word embeddings to model how words are used in context and how they relate to one another, making them far more effective for complex language tasks.

One of the most popular models for generating word embeddings is Word2Vec, which was introduced by Google researchers in 2013. Word2Vec uses NNs to learn to predict a target word based on its surrounding context and the context given a target word. This ability to capture semantic similarity enables it to perform advanced NLP tasks like solving analogies. Another widely used word embedding model is GloVe (Global Vectors for Word Representation), which learns word representations by using global statistics about how often words appear together throughout the entire corpus (hence "global"), as well as the local context in which each word occurs (similar to Word2Vec). This hybrid approach allows GloVe to balance a more global understanding of word relationships while preserving the local context in which words appear. As a result, GloVe is particularly effective at capturing subtle semantic relationships between words, such as analogies and word associations, in a computationally efficient manner.

Word embedding enables NLP models to perform tasks like synonym detection, semantic search, and document clustering much more effectively. Because they provide richer representations of language, they can improve the performance of models that understand context, meaning, and relationships between words. For instance, in sentiment analysis, word embeddings help models capture the subtle differences in word usage that indicate whether a text expresses a positive or negative sentiment. In machine translation, word embeddings improve the model's ability to understand and generate language that accurately reflects the semantic relationships between words in different languages.

One limitation of traditional word embedding models is that they do not distinguish between different uses of the same word in other contexts. More recent models, such as contextualized word embeddings generated by models like BERT and GPT, dynamically adjust word representations based on the context in which the word is used. Word embeddings significantly improve NLP, providing a deeper understanding of language and enabling more nuanced language processing tasks. They have formed the foundation for many modern NLP systems, from search engines to chatbots, and continue to evolve as new techniques like contextual embeddings further refine the ability of machines to comprehend and generate human language.

Transformer models are deep learning architectures designed for processing and understanding sequential data, mainly text. They use self-attention, which allows them to weigh the importance of different words in a sentence regardless of their position. This makes them highly effective for translation, text generation, and question-answering tasks. Two widely known transformer models are BERT and GPT. BERT is designed to understand text by analyzing words in context from both directions, making it useful for tasks like sentiment analysis and named entity recognition. In contrast, GPT focuses on generating coherent and contextually relevant text by predicting the next word in a sequence, which benefits applications such as chatbots, summarization, and composition. Transformer models have revolutionized NLP by enabling more accurate and flexible language understanding and generation.

LDA (Latent Dirichlet Allocation) topic modeling is a text analysis method for uncovering hidden thematic structures within a collection of documents, enabling the automatic discovery of topics based on word patterns. Developed by David Blei, Andrew Ng, and Michael Jordan in 2003, LDA is a generative probabilistic model that assumes each document is a mixture of several topics, and a distribution of words characterizes each topic (Blei, Ng, & Jordan, 2003). This allows LDA to identify the underlying issues that best explain the observed content in a corpus, making it a highly effective tool for text analysis, information retrieval, and organizing large-scale textual data.

LDA works by modeling each document as a combination of multiple topics, where each topic is a probability distribution over words. LDA assumes that documents are not limited to one topic but instead contain a mix of topics, with some more dominant topics. Each word in the document contributes to this distribution, and LDA iteratively refines its estimates of both the word distributions for each topic and the topic proportions for each document. It is unsupervised and does not require labeled data or predefined topic categories. This makes it highly flexible and scalable to various applications, such as analyzing extensive document collections, mining research papers, categorizing customer reviews, or summarizing news archives. It allows users to discover patterns and structure in data that would otherwise remain hidden, providing insights into the main themes without needing prior knowledge about the content.

One limitation of LDA is that the number of topics must be specified in advance, but choosing the correct number of issues can be challenging as selecting too few might result in overly broad topics, while selecting too many might lead to fragmented or incoherent topics. Additionally, LDA does not capture word order or context, or distinguish between different uses of the same word in other contexts. LDA may also struggle with very short documents (such as tweets) or highly diverse corpora, as the lack of sufficient word co-occurrence can lead to less meaningful topic distributions.

Despite its limitations, LDA remains a widely used and effective technique for topic modeling, particularly in situations where little is known about the underlying structure of a text corpus. Topic models are unsupervised ML techniques that uncover hidden themes within a collection of text documents. They analyze word patterns and co-occurrences to group words frequently appearing together, forming clusters representing distinct topics. It has been applied in numerous domains, including journalism, digital humanities, business intelligence, and scientific research, helping users gain insights into extensive collections of unstructured text. As NLP has evolved, LDA remains relevant, often used in conjunction with other models like word embeddings or neural networks to enhance the depth of text analysis.

Applications in Urban Planning

For urban planners, using NLP can lead to more efficient data processing, insightful analysis, and enhanced decision-making in planning projects. Understanding and applying these techniques can significantly improve the ability to extract valuable information from vast amounts of text data, ultimately contributing to more informed and effective urban planning strategies. Three key applications for NLP in planning are sentiment analysis of public opinion, information extraction from planning documents, and chatbots for customer service.

Sentiment Analysis of Public Opinion

Urban planners are increasingly using sentiment analysis to assess public opinion on urban projects, policies, and services. Sentiment analysis uses NLP techniques to detect and quantify the emotional tone conveyed in written text. Social media platforms, such as Twitter and Facebook, provide rich sources of public feedback, as users frequently share opinions on urban developments, transportation initiatives, and other community projects. By analyzing large volumes of social media data, planners can gain real-time insights into how the public feels about ongoing or proposed projects, which can help inform decisions and shape more responsive urban policies.

Processing social media content allows urban planners to detect patterns of public sentiment and identify trends. For instance, planners can analyze public reactions to a new park development to see whether the project is viewed positively, as an improvement to public space, or negatively, perhaps due to construction disruptions. This information provides a valuable layer of public engagement that traditional methods, such as surveys or public meetings, might miss. Additionally, sentiment analysis helps planners understand how different communities or regions respond to projects, which is critical for ensuring that underrepresented voices are heard.

Tools and Methods for Sentiment Analysis

Sentiment analysis of social media data typically involves three key stages: data collection, data preprocessing, and sentiment analysis using NLP models.

The first step, data collection, involves gathering relevant social media data using APIs from platforms like Twitter (now X) and Facebook. These APIs allow developers to access a wide range of public content, such as tweets, posts, and comments, based on specific keywords, hashtags, or geolocation. Tools like Tweepy or Scrapy can be used to automate the data collection process. The goal is to build a dataset that reflects various public opinions on urban projects and policies.

Once the data is collected, it must undergo data preprocessing. Social media data is often noisy, containing irrelevant content such as URLs, emojis, hashtags, and special characters. Preprocessing involves cleaning the data to improve its quality for analysis. This includes removing unwanted elements, tokenization (breaking text into individual words or tokens), and lemmatization (reducing words to their root forms to increase consistency). By cleaning the data, the sentiment analysis tools can focus on meaningful content, leading to more accurate sentiment detection.

The final step is sentiment analysis, where NLP models are applied to analyze the emotional tone of the text. Several tools and libraries are available, ranging from fundamental sentiment analysis to more advanced, context-aware models. Popular libraries like NLTK and spaCy provide straightforward tools for classifying text as positive, negative, or neutral. Models like VADER (Valence Aware Dictionary and sentiment Reasoner) and TextBlob are commonly used for more nuanced sentiment analysis. VADER, in particular, is designed for analyzing social media text, accounting for informal language, slang, and emoticons often found in tweets or posts. It assigns a sentiment intensity score, providing a more detailed understanding of the public's emotional response. TextBlob also provides sentiment scoring with polarity (negative or positive) and subjectivity scores in order to measure whether the content expresses an opinion or fact. For deeper contextual understanding, BERT can be used to analyze more complex sentence structures and detect subtle shifts in sentiment.

Applications and Benefits for Urban Planning

Social media sentiment analysis provides a range of benefits for urban planning. First, it can give real-time feedback, allowing planners to assess public reactions to new initiatives, such as transit expansions or housing developments. With real-time sentiment insights, planners can respond more quickly to public concerns, improving transparency and trust in the planning process. This immediacy is particularly useful for managing large-scale or controversial projects, where public opinion may shift rapidly as new information becomes available.

Another advantage is the ability to conduct localized sentiment analysis. Planners can track how specific neighborhoods or communities respond to urban projects by analyzing sentiment data with geolocation tags. This enables a more granular understanding of local sentiment, which is essential for ensuring that community-specific needs and concerns are addressed. For instance, a transportation project that receives positive feedback citywide might still face resistance in specific neighborhoods due to localized disruptions or unequal access to benefits.

In addition to real-time feedback and localized insights, sentiment analysis can enhance public engagement. Traditional forms of public engagement, such as surveys or town hall meetings, often capture a limited subset of the population. In contrast, social media provides a broader range of voices. By tapping into social media conversations, planners can better understand the opinions of younger or more digitally connected residents who may not participate in conventional forums. This expanded reach helps create more democratic and representative urban planning processes.

Lastly, sentiment analysis helps planners predict future outcomes by analyzing historical sentiment data related to similar projects. For example, if a previous urban renewal project generated negative sentiment due to community displacement concerns, planners can preemptively use that insight to address similar problems in upcoming projects. This predictive capacity allows planners to be more proactive, anticipating challenges and mitigating potential public resistance before it escalates.

Example: Sentiment Analysis of Tweets about Public Transportation

A notable real-world example of sentiment analysis applied to public transportation is a study in which researchers developed an NLP framework to analyze user feedback on the New York City (NYC) subway system by using Twitter (now X) data. Traditional user feedback collection methods through transit surveys are often time-consuming, resource-intensive, and costly. In contrast, social media platforms like Twitter provide vast, abundant, and inexpensive data that can be harnessed to understand users' perceptions of various service issues.

Researchers gathered tweets about the NYC subway system over a specified period. The collected tweets underwent cleaning to remove noise, such as URLs, emojis, and special characters, and tokenization and lemmatization were applied to prepare the text for analysis. The model classified tweets into predefined categories, effectively identifying the issues described in tweets. Sensitivity analysis was then used to assess the intensity and polarity of the tweet sentiments, distinguishing between positive, negative, and neutral tweets.

The framework accurately classified tweets related to the safety, reliability, and maintenance of the subway system, and it effectively measured sentiment intensities within each category, providing insights into public perceptions. The general findings were corroborated by comparing them with an agency-run customer survey conducted in the same year, highlighting the framework's effectiveness in gauging user feedback through inexpensive social media data.

This study demonstrates the potential of using social media data to perform sentiment analysis on public transportation services. The NLP framework provided a cost-effective and efficient alternative to traditional survey methods, enabling transit authorities to understand public sentiment and plan targeted improvements based on real-time user feedback.

Information Extraction from Planning Documents

Urban planners are frequently tasked with analyzing extensive documentation, such as policy papers, environmental impact assessments, and planning proposals. These documents are often dense and filled with technical jargon, making it challenging and time-consuming to extract the most relevant information manually. With the increasing scale of urban development and the growing complexity of regulations and policies, planners need more efficient ways to process and digest these large volumes of text. Fortunately, NLP techniques provide powerful tools for automating this process, significantly improving efficiency while ensuring accuracy in identifying critical details. Using NLP techniques such as NER and text summarization, described earlier in this chapter, planners can quickly extract key information, saving time and effort that would otherwise be spent manually reviewing lengthy documents.

Tools and Methods for Automating Information Extraction

The first step in applying NLP for document analysis is gathering and preprocessing the relevant planning documents for analysis. Documents can be sourced from government repositories, project proposals, or legal frameworks. Preprocessing is crucial because planning documents often contain various formatting styles, tables, and diagrams, which must be cleaned to provide smooth text analysis. Preprocessing includes removing non-text elements (like images and tables), standardizing the text, and tokenizing (breaking down the text into individual words or phrases for easier processing).

Once the text is preprocessed, NER can identify and classify specific entities within a document, such as geographic locations, organizations, legal statutes, or project names. For example, in a policy paper discussing a significant transportation development, NER can extract references to critical stakeholders like government agencies, the names of impacted neighborhoods, deadlines for project phases, and laws that govern the approval process. This structured data allows planners to quickly extract relevant information, reducing the time spent scanning through irrelevant sections.

Alternatively, text summarization can condense long documents into shorter, easily digestible summaries. Tools like spaCy or Gensim provide extractive summarization techniques, where the most important sentences from the original document are compiled into a summary. These tools can help planners review the most critical sections of a 100-page environmental report or a lengthy urban development proposal in minutes. For more advanced applications, abstractive summarization models such as Bidirectional and Auto-Regressive Transformer (BART) and Text-to-Text Transfer Transformer (T5) can generate shorter, more coherent summaries that capture the essence of the document in fewer words—for example, providing a high-level overview of a project without technical detail.

Applications and Benefits for Urban Planning

NLP's ability to automate the extraction of key information provides several clear benefits for urban planners. First, it saves time and resources. Manually reviewing long documents, especially those filled with technical language or legal jargon, can take days or even weeks, delaying project decisions. NLP tools can drastically reduce the time spent on this process by quickly identifying important content and summarizing the main points.

Second, NLP tools provide consistency and accuracy in document analysis. Human review is subject to fatigue and error, mainly when dealing with repetitive or dense material. NLP algorithms can analyze documents highly, ensuring that critical details are not overlooked. This consistency is particularly valuable when comparing multiple documents, such as reviewing different versions of a policy paper or analyzing reports from various stakeholders on the same project.

Moreover, NLP techniques enable planners to prioritize the most critical information. For instance, planners can focus on sections related to legal compliance, geographical impacts, or key stakeholder feedback when reviewing an environmental impact report rather than wading through less relevant data. This prioritization improves decision-making by bringing essential details to the forefront.

In addition, NLP facilitates collaboration among planners and stakeholders by generating summaries that can be easily shared and discussed. Executive summaries of large documents allow stakeholders to engage with the content without reading the entire report. For example, a city council meeting might focus on a transportation development proposal summary, with the detailed full report available for deeper analysis when necessary.

Finally, NLP aids in the standardization of document analysis. When planners need to compare multiple reports or proposals, NLP tools can automatically extract similar categories of information (such as costs, timelines, or environmental impacts), making comparing and contrasting different projects easier. This is especially useful in large-scale urban planning projects that require reviewing dozens of documents with overlapping or conflicting information.

Example: Text Classification for Urban Planning Documents

An example of the practical application of NLP in urban planning was demonstrated when researchers developed an urban analytics approach using planning application (PA) data and NLP techniques to forecast the housing supply pipeline in Australia. By automating the classification of planning documents, they aimed to provide planners and policymakers with timely information to understand future urban development trends and related infrastructure requirements.

The researchers scraped, geocoded, and filtered PA data from council websites and planning portals to create a nationally available daily dataset of PAs under consideration. They then classified the collected PAs into four distinct urban development categories, selected based on infrastructure planning provisioning requirements.

The researchers applied the model to classify and map urban development trends in Australia's two largest cities, Sydney and Melbourne, from 2021–2022 and 2023–2024. The NLP framework accurately classified planning documents into relevant urban development categories, providing planners with timely insights into development trends.

This example illustrates the potential of NLP to enhance urban planning processes by automating the classification of planning documents, allowing previously inaccessible planning text data to be integrated into planning analysis and decisions. The developed approach enables planners to process large volumes of textual data efficiently, facilitating data-driven decision-making and improving information management in urban development contexts.

Chatbots for Customer Service

Chatbots have the potential to significantly enhance urban services by providing residents with instant, accessible information and facilitating a wide range of topics and transactions. These AI-driven systems use NLP to understand user inputs and respond in natural, conversational language, making it easier for residents to get answers to common questions, request services, or access important information about their city. Chatbots can be deployed across various platforms, from city websites to mobile apps, providing real-time information on public transportation, explaining local regulations, guiding residents through administrative procedures, and even assisting with emergencies.

One of the main advantages of chatbots in urban services is their ability to provide 24/7 support, reducing the need for human-operated customer service centers and ensuring that residents can get assistance at any time. For example, a chatbot could help residents locate nearby recycling centers, report infrastructure issues such as potholes, or check the status of building permit applications. By automating these interactions, chatbots can improve the efficiency of public services, reduce waiting times for residents, and free up human resources for more complex tasks.

Tools and Methods for Building Chatbots

The architecture typically consists of several key components to implement a chatbot that provides urban services: a user interface, an NLP engine, and backend integration with municipal services.

The user interface is the platform through which residents interact with the chatbot. This can be a web-based interface integrated into a city's website, a chatbot embedded in a mobile app, or a voice assistant. It allows residents to ask their questions or input their requests in natural language, which are then processed by the chatbot. Some advanced implementations also allow multimodal interaction, enabling users to type or speak their queries and receive responses in text or audio form. The user interface plays a crucial role in ensuring a smooth and intuitive interaction, which is especially important for residents who may not be tech-savvy.

The NLP engine is at the core of the chatbot's functionality, which processes user input, interprets its meaning, and generates an appropriate response. The NLP engine is responsible for understanding the user's wants (intent recognition) and extracting relevant information, such as addresses or dates, from their input (entity extraction). The NLP model can be customized and trained to understand the specific language used in urban services, such as terms related to public transportation, waste management, or city regulations (dialogue management). Popular frameworks for building chatbot NLP engines include Rasa, an open-source platform; Dialogflow, a Google cloud-based model that can understand multiple languages and integrate with Google Assistant, WhatsApp, and Facebook Messenger; and Microsoft's Bot Framework, which integrates with Azure services.

Backend integration connects the chatbot to city databases, APIs, and services to retrieve or update information in real time. This facilitates transactions such as bill payments, service requests, or permit applications, making the chatbot a transactional tool that enables users to complete tasks that would otherwise require navigating multiple departments or websites. It also allows the chatbot to pull up a resident's previous requests or current service statuses, creating a more seamless and user-friendly experience.

Applications and Benefits for Urban Services

By integrating NLP-powered chatbots into urban services, cities can improve the accessibility and efficiency of their operations. One primary application is public service information dissemination. Rather than browsing multiple web pages or waiting in line to speak to a representative, residents can ask the chatbot questions like "What are the hours for the local waste disposal site?" or "How do I apply for a building permit?" The chatbot provides immediate, accurate responses based on up-to-date information from the city's backend databases.

Chatbots can also facilitate service requests. For example, residents can use the chatbot to report infrastructure problems such as potholes, graffiti, or streetlight outages. The chatbot collects the necessary details, logs the request in the city's maintenance system, and provides the resident with a confirmation or reference number. Furthermore, the chatbot can update residents on the status of their requests, ensuring transparency and reducing the burden on city employees who would otherwise need to handle such inquiries manually.

Another key application is in public transportation. Chatbots can provide real-time updates on bus and train schedules, delays, or service disruptions. Residents can ask questions like "When is the next bus to downtown?" and receive instant, location-specific answers. This type of service dramatically enhances the commuter experience, especially in large cities with complex public transportation networks.

Chatbots can also be employed for emergency services by providing residents with information on evacuation routes, emergency shelters, and updates during natural disasters or public health crises. Chatbots can be essential for disseminating critical information quickly and efficiently, ensuring that residents remain informed and safe.

Challenges in Natural Language Processing

As NLP technologies evolve, urban planners must understand the field's challenges. These insights are crucial for anticipating the limitations and opportunities of NLP applications in urban development, ensuring that planners can effectively leverage the technology.

Understanding these challenges and trends helps urban planners make informed decisions about adopting NLP technologies. By recognizing potential limitations, such as data biases or interpretability issues, planners can implement safeguards and best practices to mitigate risks. Effective use of NLP in urban development ultimately depends on a proactive and informed approach, integrating technical expertise with a deep understanding of planning contexts and ethical considerations.

Ambiguity and Context Understanding

One of the primary challenges in NLP is dealing with the inherent ambiguity of human language. Many words and sentences can have multiple meanings depending on the context in which they are used. For example, "park" could refer to a public green space or vehicle parking. This ambiguity poses significant difficulties for NLP models, as accurately resolving these nuances requires a deep understanding of context that is often beyond the capabilities of current systems.

In addition to word-level ambiguity, NLP models must also grasp the broader context within conversations or documents. Understanding elements such as sarcasm, irony, or implied meanings presents an even more significant challenge, especially in the informal or colloquial language commonly found in public discourse. While advanced models like transformers (e.g., BERT, GPT) have made notable progress in understanding context, accurately capturing these subtleties in complex interactions still requires further advancements.

Processing Multilingual Data

Urban planners often operate in multilingual environments where data is available in multiple languages. Processing multilingual data introduces several challenges, including differences in grammar, syntax, and idiomatic expressions. Developing NLP models capable of seamlessly processing and understanding multiple languages is a complex task that demands both extensive linguistic knowledge and significant computational resources.

Moreover, high-quality training data for many languages is often scarce, especially for less commonly spoken or regional dialects. This data scarcity limits the ability of NLP models to generalize effectively across languages, hindering their performance in multilingual contexts. Urban planners working in diverse cities may struggle to analyze or extract insights from multilingual documents, surveys, and community feedback without practical NLP tools to bridge this gap.

Ethical Considerations

Urban planners using NLP must consider several ethical challenges for responsible and equitable applications in planning processes. One primary concern is bias in data and models, as NLP systems learn from existing text data, which may contain historical and systemic biases related to race, gender, socioeconomic status, or geography. If these biases go unchecked, they can reinforce discrimination in planning decisions, perpetuating inequalities rather than addressing them. Ensuring transparency and explainability is another key issue, as many NLP models, particularly deep learning-based ones, function as "black boxes," making it difficult to understand how they generate insights. Planners should prioritize tools that provide interpretability, particularly when NLP is used in decision-making or policy formulation.

Another critical consideration is privacy and data protection, as NLP systems often analyze vast amounts of text, including sensitive planning documents, public feedback, and social media discussions. Urban planners must be conscious of compliance with data privacy regulations and protect personally identifiable information, mainly when working with government records or community-generated content. Additionally, misinformation and accuracy pose significant risks, as NLP-generated text, summaries, or insights are unreliable. Planners should critically assess the validity of NLP outputs, mainly when using them to inform policy, public communications, or decision-making.

Ensuring equitable access and representation is also vital, as NLP models trained predominantly on dominant languages or mainstream sources may fail to capture the perspectives of marginalized communities. This limitation can lead to underrepresenting certain voices in urban planning discussions. Planners should strive to use diverse and representative datasets to ensure inclusivity in their analysis. Lastly, there is the issue of automation versus human oversight. While NLP can automate many tasks, such as analyzing planning documents and summarizing stakeholder feedback, it should not replace human expertise. Urban planners must remain actively involved in interpreting findings and contextualizing results within the complexities of urban development.

By addressing these ethical considerations, urban planners can harness NLP as a powerful tool for more informed, inclusive, and responsible decision-making. Thoughtful integration of NLP can enhance planning processes, but it must be accompanied by safeguards to mitigate risks and uphold ethical standards.

Looking Ahead

The field of NLP is rapidly advancing, with new methodologies and technologies poised to overcome current limitations and expand its capabilities. Planners can use these tools to enhance decision-making, foster public engagement, and streamline workflows by keeping up with recent advances and improvements.

Deep learning has revolutionized NLP, leading to the development of effective models such as BERT, GPT, and T5. These models have demonstrated remarkable proficiency in understanding and generating human language, and future advancements in deep learning are expected to enhance their capabilities further. Ongoing research into developing more significant, more sophisticated models aims to capture the intricacies of language more effectively, improving the accuracy and versatility of NLP applications.

One direction is the exploration of techniques like transfer learning and few-shot learning, which enable models to perform well with limited training data. These methods are particularly beneficial for languages with fewer resources, helping address the challenges that multilingual contexts pose. As deep learning evolves, NLP models will become more efficient, scalable, and adaptable, opening new possibilities for urban planners to apply NLP across diverse projects.

One promising trend in NLP is its integration with other AI technologies, such as computer vision and geographic information systems (GIS). Urban planners can extract valuable insights from visual and textual data sources by combining NLP with computer vision. For example, analyzing social media images alongside posts can provide a more comprehensive understanding of public sentiment toward urban spaces or infrastructure projects.

Integrating NLP with GIS can enhance spatial analysis by providing richer contextual information. Textual data from policy documents, community feedback, or news articles can be analyzed to extract insights that complement geographic data, providing a more holistic view of urban challenges. This integration allows planners to make more informed decisions by understanding urban development's social and geographic dimensions.

Chapter Summary

This chapter discussed NLP and how it can be valuable for urban planning. NLP, a subfield of AI, enables machines to interpret and analyze human language. For urban planners, it provides tools to process large volumes of text data, extract insights, and support decision-making. The chapter also covered text analysis techniques that allow planners to organize and extract meaning from large datasets. Methods like a BoW, TF-IDF, and word embeddings help quantify and analyze text efficiently. BoW and TF-IDF are simple approaches for measuring word importance, while word embeddings capture deeper semantic relationships between words. Libraries like NLTK, spaCy, and Gensim provide frameworks to implement these techniques in real-world urban planning applications.

NLP has several practical applications in urban planning. Sentiment analysis can help planners gauge public opinion on policies or projects by analyzing social media and other text sources. Text classification and NER assist in processing planning documents by categorizing them by topic and extracting key details such as locations, dates, and stakeholders, helping planners navigate large amounts of information efficiently. Additionally, AI-powered chatbots using NLP can improve public engagement by answering questions, providing real-time information, and streamlining communication between planners and the public.

Despite its benefits, NLP comes with challenges. Human language is ambiguous, and words or phrases can have multiple meanings depending on context, requiring more advanced models to improve accuracy. Multilingual data processing is another issue, particularly in diverse urban environments where planners must analyze information in multiple languages. However, advancements in deep learning and transformer models like BERT and GPT are improving NLP's ability to handle complex language tasks.

As NLP technology evolves, urban planners will benefit from its increasing accuracy and efficiency. Transfer learning and few-shot learning help address limitations related to training data, particularly in multilingual contexts. NLP is also being integrated with other AI technologies, expanding its capabilities. For example, combining NLP with computer vision allows planners to analyze visual and text-based data, such as using social media images alongside text to assess public sentiment. Similarly, integrating NLP with GIS enables richer spatial analysis by linking geographic data with insights from community feedback, policy documents, and news articles. These advancements will continue to enhance how planners use NLP in decision-making and urban analysis.

References and Further Reading

Blei, D. M., Ng, A. Y., & Jordan, M. I. (2003). Latent Dirichlet Allocation. *Journal of machine Learning research*, 3(Jan), 993–1022.

Poibeau, T. (2017). *Machine translation*. MIT Press.

Turing, A. M. (1950). Computing machinery and intelligence. *Mind*, 59(236), 433–460. https://doi.org/10.1093/mind/LIX.236.433

5

COMPUTER VISION FOR URBAN PLANNERS

By mimicking the complexity of human vision, computer vision (CV) systems can analyze images and videos to extract meaningful information, which can be used in various applications. Its importance in artificial intelligence (AI) stems from its ability to automate tasks that require visual perception and incorporate them into analytical processes.

Integrating CV technologies into urban planning potentially enhances planners' ability to make informed, data-driven decisions by automating the analysis of large amounts of visual information. CV combines AI and machine learning (ML) to process images, videos, and geospatial data in real time, allowing for more precise detection and mapping of urban features. This technology can generate highly detailed 3D models of urban areas, assisting planners in better understanding spatial relationships and infrastructure needs. Additionally, it enables the detection of patterns—such as traffic congestion, pedestrian flows, or environmental changes—that might go unnoticed through traditional methods. These insights can help to optimize land use, mobility networks, and public services.

DOI: 10.4324/9781003476818-5

CV also plays a vital role in monitoring and proactively managing urban areas. In real-time, CV can identify problems such as illegal dumping, parking violations, overcrowding, and potholes through video systems, drones, and sensors embedded in public spaces. This allows city officials to address issues promptly, preventing them from escalating into more significant problems. For example, traffic cameras powered by CV can monitor road conditions and provide predictive analytics, allowing cities to adjust traffic lights or reroute public transit to prevent bottlenecks. Moreover, CV aids in disaster preparedness and resilience by monitoring flood-prone areas, identifying structural weaknesses in buildings, and helping design safer evacuation routes.

CV technologies can also improve citizen engagement by generating immersive visualizations, like augmented reality (AR) models, which enable residents to experience proposed developments and provide input on future projects. As urban environments become increasingly complex, CV allows planners to visualize scenarios better and share them with stakeholders. This chapter explores how these applications make CV valuable for a variety of planning activities.

Historical Background and Development

CV, which enables machines to interpret and analyze visual data, is rooted in the 1960s when early AI researchers tried to understand human vision more deeply. One of the first significant milestones came in 1966 at MIT when Marvin Minsky assigned a summer project to a student, Gerald Sussman, to develop a system to segment objects in images (Sejnowski, 2018). This problem turned out to be far more complex than anticipated. This realization led to decades of research into image processing, feature extraction, and pattern recognition. In the 1970s and 1980s, David Marr at MIT significantly advanced the field by introducing computational vision models, emphasizing that visual perception occurs in stages, from essential edge detection to complex object recognition.

During the 1990s and early 2000s, the field saw breakthroughs with the rise of statistical methods, such as support vector machines (SVMs) and feature-based recognition techniques like scale-invariant feature transform (SIFT) by David Lowe. However, the real revolution came in the

2010s with the resurgence of deep learning, particularly convolutional neural networks (CNNs). In 2012, the AlexNet model, developed by Alex Krizhevsky, Ilya Sutskever, and Geoffrey Hinton, won the ImageNet competition by a wide margin, demonstrating the power of deep learning for object recognition. Since then, CV has advanced rapidly, enabling applications such as facial recognition, autonomous vehicles, and urban planning tools for analyzing satellite imagery, detecting infrastructure conditions, and observing activity patterns.

Today, CV continues to evolve with self-supervised learning, transformer-based models like Vision Transformers (ViTs), and multimodal AI systems that integrate vision with other data sources. With ongoing improvements in real-time processing and AI-driven spatial analysis, CV is becoming a very useful tool for urban planners, allowing for automated mapping, smart city monitoring, and enhanced decision-making based on vast visual datasets.

Introduction to Computer Vision

This section lays the foundation by defining CV and describing key concepts and terms essential for understanding its applications in urban planning. It explores how computers process and analyze visual data, covering fundamental techniques such as image segmentation, feature extraction, object detection, and deep learning-based recognition. Key terms like CNNs, edge detection, and semantic segmentation are introduced to provide a clear framework for understanding how visual data is transformed into actionable insights. By establishing this groundwork, the section prepares readers to explore real-world CV applications in urban analysis, transportation systems, and infrastructure monitoring.

> Computer vision (CV): A subfield of AI that enables machines to see, interpret, and analyze the visual world like humans do. CV algorithms and models can process and analyze visual data, such as images and videos, to identify objects, track movements, and generate insights, transforming raw visual data into structured information.

Basic Concepts and Terminology

At the heart of CV lies the fundamental concept of the **pixel**, the smallest unit of a digital image. Each pixel represents a single point in the image and holds a value corresponding to the light intensity. When combined, millions of pixels form a complete picture, capturing the visual information that the CV systems analyze.

An image can be considered a grid or matrix of pixels, where each pixel's value can vary depending on the type of image. For example, in a grayscale image, each pixel value represents light intensity, ranging from black to white. In a color image, each pixel's value consists of multiple channels that define the color. Because CV algorithms analyze these pixels to extract meaningful information, understanding pixels and their representation is an important part of visual data.

Color spaces are systems used to represent colors in a standardized format so that CV systems can accurately process, interpret, and analyze color information in digital images. These systems provide a structured way to translate visual data into numerical values that computers can manipulate. Different color spaces serve distinct purposes depending on the type of analysis required, with some focusing on color intensity while others capture brightness or luminance variations. One of the most commonly used color spaces in CV is the RGB color space, which represents colors through the combination of three primary color channels—red, green, and blue. Each pixel in an RGB image contains three values, one for each channel, determining the amount of red, green, and blue light at that pixel.

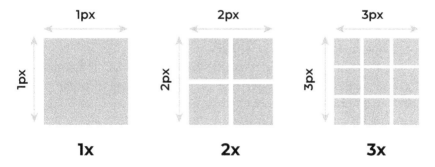

Figure 5.1 Pixel and grids.

For example, a pixel with the values (255, 0, 0) represents pure red because the red channel is at its maximum intensity, while the green and blue channels are at zero intensity. Similarly, a pixel with the values (0, 255, 0) represents pure green, and (0, 0, 255) represents pure blue. The RGB color space is widely adopted because of its straightforward representation of colors and its compatibility with most digital devices, such as cameras, monitors, and scanners. Through various combinations of these three-color channels at different intensities, an extensive range of colors can be produced, making this space ideal for applications where accurate color reproduction is essential.

In some CV tasks, however, the full range of color information is not always necessary. In such cases, images can be converted to **grayscale**. A grayscale image uses only a single channel to represent the light intensity at each pixel. Each pixel in a grayscale image is assigned a value between 0 and 255, where 0 corresponds to black, 255 represents white, and the values in between indicate varying shades of gray. Grayscale images reduce computational complexity and are particularly useful in tasks where color is not the primary feature of interest, such as edge detection, texture analysis, or shape recognition.

By simplifying visual data representation, grayscale images make it easier for algorithms to focus on key structural or intensity patterns, significantly when color does not add significant information to the task at hand. While the RGB color space is adequate for applications that require detailed color information, such as object detection in complex scenes or color-based segmentation, grayscale images provide advantages when processing speed and simplicity are priorities. In CV workflows, both color spaces play complementary roles, and the choice between them depends on the task's specific requirements.

Understanding these color spaces and image channels is important when selecting the appropriate image data type for specific analyses. For instance, traffic analysis might rely on grayscale images for simplicity, while land-use classification might require RGB images to distinguish between different types of surfaces.

Image processing techniques allow CV algorithms to extract meaningful features and patterns from raw visual data. At their core, these techniques allow computers to transform, enhance, and analyze images in order to make it easier to identify objects, detect boundaries, or understand visual scenes. Among the many image processing methods, filtering and edge detection are two of the most widely used techniques, each serving distinct but complementary purposes.

Filtering involves the application of a filter, which is a small matrix or kernel, to an image. The process, known as convolution, involves sliding the filter across the image to produce a modified version of the original (see example in Figure 5.2). Filters perform various operations, including noise reduction, image smoothing, and sharpening. For example, applying a Gaussian filter to an image introduces a blur effect that smooths the image by averaging pixel values within a specific neighborhood (surrounding cells). A Gaussian filter is used in image processing to smooth an image by reducing noise and detail. It applies a mathematical function (the Gaussian function) that averages pixel values to give more weight to pixels near the center of the considered area. This is particularly useful in reducing noise and eliminating minor, irrelevant variations that could interfere with further processing. Applying a Laplacian filter enhances edges by amplifying regions of rapid intensity change. Unlike the Gaussian filter, it does not smooth the image but enhances transitions between different areas. Such sharpening filters are helpful when the goal is to highlight structural elements, such as object outlines, in preparation for further analysis.

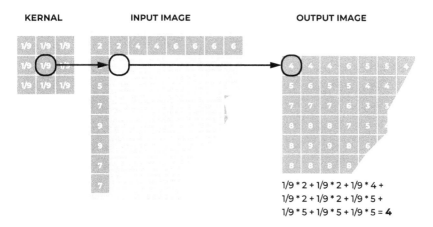

$$1/9 * 2 + 1/9 * 2 + 1/9 * 4 +$$
$$1/9 * 2 + 1/9 * 2 + 1/9 * 5 +$$
$$1/9 * 5 + 1/9 * 5 + 1/9 * 5 = 4$$

Figure 5.2 Image filtering.

Edge detection is a technique used to identify the outlines of objects in an image by finding areas where colors or brightness change sharply. This helps computers understand the structure of a scene. Different methods for detecting edges exist, ranging from simple approaches that highlight changes in brightness to more advanced techniques that refine the details. These methods are widely used in CV to help with tasks like recognizing objects, dividing an image into meaningful parts, and tracking movement.

Filtering and edge detection often work in tandem. Before applying edge detection, an image might be preprocessed using smoothing filters to reduce noise, ensuring that only meaningful edges are detected. For example, the Canny edge detector includes a step where a Gaussian filter is applied before detecting edges, ensuring that minor noise does not result in false edge detection. Similarly, edge-enhancing filters like Laplacian can make object boundaries more prominent, making it easier for algorithms to recognize and segment distinct objects. By carefully applying these image-processing techniques, CV systems can identify patterns, detect objects, and understand scenes efficiently and accurately.

Image processing techniques form the foundation for the more advanced operations of image classification, object detection, and image segmentation.

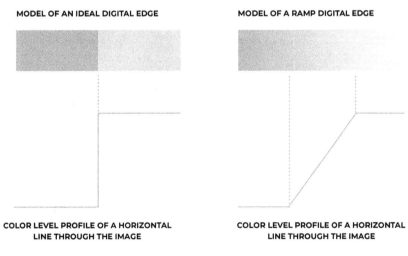

MODEL OF AN IDEAL DIGITAL EDGE

MODEL OF A RAMP DIGITAL EDGE

COLOR LEVEL PROFILE OF A HORIZONTAL
LINE THROUGH THE IMAGE

COLOR LEVEL PROFILE OF A HORIZONTAL
LINE THROUGH THE IMAGE

Figure 5.3 Edge detection.

Image classification is a core technique in CV that enables the automatic categorization of images into predefined classes or categories. This process involves training a model on a dataset containing labeled images, where each image is tagged with a specific category (i.e., supervised learning). During training, the model learns to recognize visual patterns and associate them with the appropriate class. Once trained, the model can predict the class of new, unseen images by identifying these learned features.

These applications rely heavily on deep learning models, particularly CNNs, which are optimized for analyzing image data (see Chapter 3). CNNs automatically extract hierarchical features, starting with low-level patterns like edges and progressing to more complex shapes and objects. This automated feature recognition makes CNNs particularly effective for large-scale classification tasks. As high-resolution satellite imagery becomes more accessible and ML algorithms continue to advance, the accuracy and efficiency of image classification models will improve.

Object detection builds on image classification by identifying the presence of objects and locating them within an image. This process involves classifying objects and drawing bounding boxes around each detected item, allowing the simultaneous recognition and localization of multiple objects. Models for object detection are trained using annotated datasets, where each object is labeled and its exact position specified. An annotated dataset refers to a collection of images with objects of interest

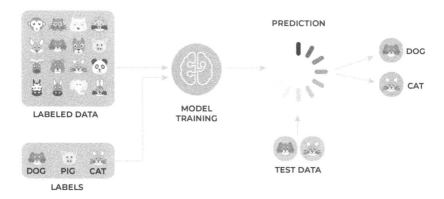

Figure 5.4 Image classification process.

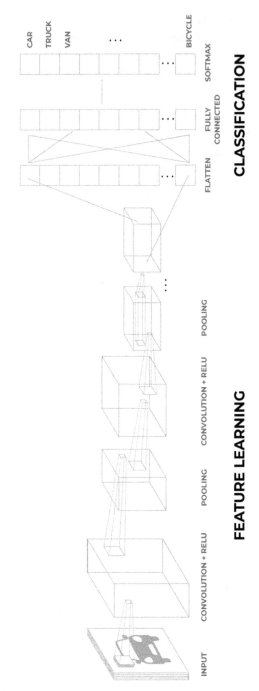

Figure 5.5 Convolutional neural network showing key layers.

labeled with specific information, such as their category (e.g., car, building, pedestrian) and position within the image (usually represented by bounding boxes, masks, or key points). These annotations provide the training data that helps object detection models learn to recognize and locate objects in new images.

Advanced algorithms are at the core of successful object detection in CV. YOLO (you only look once) is known for its speed and ability to analyze entire images in a single pass, making it ideal for real-time applications such as traffic monitoring and public safety. YOLO's ability to detect multiple objects with minimal delay promotes seamless tracking in dynamic environments. Faster R-CNN (region-based convolutional neural network) provides another popular approach, achieving high accuracy by focusing on regions of interest within images. Although it operates slower, Faster R-CNN is well-suited for tasks requiring detailed analysis, such as infrastructure inspection.

Image segmentation divides an image into distinct regions or segments, each representing different objects or parts of objects. While image classification and object detection provide higher-level information

Figure 5.6 Bounding boxes around vehicles, cyclists, and pedestrians.

about the presence or location of objects, image segmentation provides pixel-level precision by labeling every pixel in an image according to its class. This detailed labeling allows for a more granular understanding of visual data, making it particularly useful for applications that require nuanced spatial analysis.

There are two primary types of image segmentation. Semantic segmentation assigns a class label to each pixel in the image, grouping all objects of the same class as a single entity. For example, in an image containing several trees, all the trees would be labeled "trees" without distinguishing between individual trees. Instance segmentation labels each pixel and identifies individual instances of the same class. In this case, each tree in the image would receive a unique label, allowing the segmentation to differentiate between individual trees even if they belong to the same category.

Advanced models like U-Net and Mask R-CNN have become the standard for image segmentation tasks. These models provide high accuracy and can manage complex scenes with overlapping objects. By accurately identifying and segmenting different components within an image, these models allow for precise visual analysis that would otherwise be time-consuming and labor-intensive.

Training Computer Vision Models

The quality and preparation of image data play an important role in the success of any CV analysis or application. Since AI models learn from data, the accuracy and reliability of their outputs depend heavily on the quality of the images they are trained on. Image data acquisition involves collecting images from various sources, such as cameras, satellites, drones, or publicly available datasets. These images may vary in resolution, lighting conditions, or clarity, affecting how well a model learns to recognize patterns.

Before analysis, images must go through preprocessing, a critical step leading to the best possible condition for accurate interpretation. This process may include adjusting brightness and contrast, resizing images, removing noise, and normalizing color values. Just as clean and well-structured data is essential for any AI method—whether in natural

Figure 5.7 Segmented output image after applying FCN ResNet model.

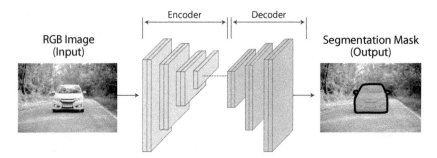

Figure 5.8 Image segmentation process.

language processing (NLP), predictive modeling, or ML—properly prepared image data is fundamental for achieving reliable CV results. High-quality, well-preprocessed images improve model performance, reduce errors, and enhance the overall effectiveness of AI-driven urban planning applications.

DATA SOURCES FOR COMPUTER VISION

CV draws on many image data sources. Three primary sources are satellite imagery, drone footage, and street-level imagery.

• Satellite imagery provides high-resolution images covering extensive urban areas. These images are critical for large-scale analysis, such as monitoring land-use patterns, infrastructure development, and environmental changes over time. Satellite imagery is particularly valuable for long-term urban monitoring and strategic planning efforts.

• Drone imagery comes from drones equipped with high-definition cameras. Drones have the flexibility to capture detailed aerial views of specific areas, making them helpful in obtaining up-to-date images of construction sites, disaster-affected regions, or other areas that require focused attention.

• Street-level imagery is collected from cameras mounted on vehicles or positioned in fixed locations, such as traffic cameras or closed-circuit television (CCTV) systems, both public and private.

It provides a ground-level perspective of the urban environment and helps analyze the condition of pedestrian infrastructure, roadways, and public spaces.

Several publicly available datasets provide valuable image data for urban planning. They provide standardized, high-quality visual information that supports a variety of analyses.

- **Google Street View** has extensive street-level imagery from around the world, captured by cameras mounted on vehicles or placed in specific locations. This resource provides detailed ground-level views, making it ideal for assessing road conditions, public spaces, pedestrian infrastructure, and urban aesthetics. Planners can use Google Street View to conduct virtual site visits, eliminating the need for costly fieldwork. It is also valuable for identifying the placement and condition of street furniture, such as benches and signage, and for examining accessibility features like curb cuts or crosswalks.
- **OpenStreetMap (OSM)** is primarily known as a crowdsourced mapping platform, but it also provides a wealth of imagery and map data that can be integrated with other datasets. OSM provides detailed street maps, building footprints, and land-use information contributed by volunteers. This highly flexible platform enables urban planners to overlay OSM data with satellite images, demographic data, or traffic models for comprehensive urban analysis. It supports various applications, from transportation planning to zoning analysis, and is especially useful in areas where proprietary data may be limited or outdated.
- **Sentinel-2 and Landsat** datasets provide satellite imagery invaluable for environmental monitoring and land-use analysis. Sentinel-2, operated by the European Space Agency (ESA), captures high-resolution optical imagery frequently, enabling real-time monitoring of urban expansion, vegetation health, and environmental changes. Landsat, managed by NASA, provides a more extended historical archive of satellite images, making it ideal for studying long-term trends in land use, deforestation, or climate-related changes. These datasets are particularly useful for

monitoring urban sprawl, identifying green space availability, and evaluating the impact of development on ecosystems.

- **Mapillary** is a platform that provides crowdsourced street-level imagery contributed by individuals using smartphones, action cameras, or vehicle-mounted devices. Mapillary provides up-to-date and diverse visual data, which makes it valuable for urban planners working on projects that require the most current imagery. Because the platform relies on crowdsourcing, it captures images from locations not always covered by commercial services, filling critical gaps in coverage. Urban planners use Mapillary to analyze infrastructure conditions, identify maintenance needs, and monitor urban development in areas where traditional datasets might lag.

These publicly accessible datasets provide diverse and complementary sources of imagery that enable planners to carry out detailed urban analyses efficiently. By integrating data from multiple sources, urban planners can comprehensively understand complex urban systems. The availability of such datasets also democratizes access to critical information, allowing government agencies and independent planners to leverage high-quality data for sustainable urban development. With advances in data integration and visualization tools, these datasets will play an essential role in shaping the future of urban planning and management.

Preprocessing Techniques

Preprocessing techniques prepare image data to increase consistency and high quality, improving the performance of CV models. These methods make images consistent, augment data, and address different resolutions and aspect ratios.

Image resizing and normalization ensure that images from various sources are consistent and ready for analysis by ML models. Image resizing is needed for uniform dimensions across images. Without resizing, differences in resolution between different images could cause errors. For example, when analyzing satellite data from multiple sources, inconsistent sizes between images could cause the model to misinterpret key features, such as vegetation areas or road networks. Normalization adjusts pixel values to fall within a standard range. For example, images from different cameras may have varying brightness levels due to lighting changes. Normalizing the pixel values helps the model interpret the data consistently regardless of whether the image was captured on a cloudy day or under bright sunlight.

Data augmentation techniques artificially increase the size and diversity of a dataset by applying transformations to existing images, helping models generalize better to new scenarios. Rotating images by random angles can make the model less sensitive to orientation changes. This helps the model to correctly classify or detect objects regardless of their alignment in an image. Flipping horizontally or vertically introduces symmetry and variety into the dataset. This technique helps the model to detect objects irrespective of image orientations, such as left or right-hand perspectives. Scaling zooms in or out on images, making the model more resilient to scale variations. This enables models to correctly classify objects that may appear larger or smaller depending on their proximity to the camera.

Images collected from multiple sources often vary in resolution and aspect ratio, posing challenges for analysis. The proper handling of these differences ensures that model predictions remain accurate. Aspect ratio preservation prevents distortion when resizing images by maintaining their original proportions. This is typically achieved by adding padding or borders to the image to fit the desired dimensions without altering its content. Multiresolution processing involves designing models to process images at multiple scales, ensuring that the model can detect objects regardless of their size within the image. This is particularly useful for applications where objects appear at varying distances from the camera.

Training Techniques

The two methods most commonly used for training CV models are supervised learning and transfer learning.

Supervised learning is the most common approach for training CV models. It uses a labeled dataset where each image is associated with a corresponding label or annotation. The model learns to map input images to their labels by minimizing the error between its predictions and the actual labels. Labeled datasets are typically created through manual annotation, which can be time-consuming but is essential for achieving high accuracy.

Transfer learning uses models pre-trained on large, diverse datasets such as ImageNet, one of CV's most influential image datasets. Created in 2009 by Fei-Fei Li and her team at Stanford University, ImageNet contains millions of labeled images spanning thousands of object categories. It is a benchmark for training and evaluating CV models, particularly for object recognition tasks. By being exposed to such a vast and varied dataset, pre-trained models develop a strong ability to recognize fundamental visual patterns. This enables them to learn various visual features, such as shapes, edges, textures, and colors. Transferring this prior knowledge to new applications significantly reduces the time and computational resources required to train a model from scratch. There are two primary approaches to transfer learning: feature extraction and fine-tuning.

In **feature extraction**, the early layers of the pre-trained model, which have already learned generic visual patterns, are kept intact. In contrast, the final classification layer is replaced and retrained on the new dataset to fit the specific task. This approach is highly efficient as it requires retraining only a tiny portion of the model to provide accurate results with minimal computational effort. For example, in a land-use classification task, a model might be trained on ImageNet to extract relevant visual features from satellite imagery, with the final classification layer replaced and trained to categorize land-use types— such as residential, commercial, and industrial areas—using a smaller, labeled dataset.

Fine-tuning is a more advanced approach that involves retraining some or all layers of the pre-trained model on the new dataset. This allows the model to adapt to the specific characteristics and patterns of the latest data. Fine-tuning is especially useful when the target dataset differs significantly from the original benchmark dataset, requiring more tailored adjustments across multiple layers. For example, fine-tuning a pre-trained infrastructure monitoring model allows it to recognize specific urban features that may not be present in the original training dataset, such as damaged roads or aging bridges. Adjusting several model layers helps the system accurately detect and classify infrastructure conditions unique to their region.

Transfer learning is helpful for its ability to perform well with limited labeled data. In many urban planning applications, it is not easy to collect and label large datasets due to the complexity, cost, and time-intensive nature of the task. Transfer learning addresses this challenge by providing a strong starting point through models already learned from extensive datasets. This advantage allows urban planners to achieve high levels of accuracy even when their datasets are small or sparsely labeled. Transfer learning is likely to become even more impactful as new pre-trained models become available, trained on increasingly diverse datasets that are more relevant to urban planning.

Evaluation Metrics

It is important to evaluate CV models' performance using appropriate metrics. Each metric provides different insights into understanding how well the model will perform in real-world applications, as other tasks may prioritize various aspects of performance. Key metrics for CV models are accuracy, precision, recall, and F1 score.

Accuracy is the ratio of correctly predicted instances to the total number of cases in the dataset. It measures how often the model's predictions align with the ground truth.

$$\text{Accuracy} = \frac{\text{True Positives} + \text{True Negatives}}{\text{Total Instances}}$$

While accuracy is intuitive and easy to interpret, it can be misleading in datasets with imbalanced classes. For example, if only 10% of an area is classified as industrial land and the remaining 90% as residential, a model that predicts "residential" for every pixel may achieve high accuracy without correctly identifying any industrial areas.

Precision focuses on the positive predictions made by the model. It measures the proportion of true positive predictions relative to the total positive predictions, indicating how many predicted positive instances are correct.

$$\text{Precision} = \frac{\text{True Positives}}{\text{True Positives} + \text{False Positives}}$$

High precision is essential in tasks where false positives (incorrect positive predictions) can lead to costly or disruptive actions. A highly precise model means that it will likely be correct when it predicts a particular class (such as "damaged infrastructure").

Recall (also known as **sensitivity**) measures the model's ability to identify all relevant instances within the dataset. It is the proportion of true positives relative to the actual positives, focusing on how well the model captures all the appropriate instances.

$$\text{Recall} = \frac{\text{True Positives}}{\text{True Positives} + \text{False Negatives}}$$

High recall is crucial when missing positive instances, which could have serious consequences. For example, if a model fails to detect damaged infrastructure, it could lead to repair delays, posing safety risks.

The **F1 score** provides a balanced measure by combining precision and recall into a single metric and giving equal weight to both metrics. It is beneficial when the importance of precision and recall needs to be balanced, especially in tasks where false positives and false negatives can have negative consequences.

$$\text{F1 Score} = 2 \times \frac{\text{Precision} \times \text{Recall}}{\text{Precision} + \text{Recall}}$$

For example, a public safety monitoring model used to detect unauthorized access to restricted areas must balance precision (avoiding false alarms) and recall (capturing all unauthorized entries). The F1 score helps the model perform reliably by considering both aspects.

These metrics can provide important insights into the reliability and effectiveness of CV models. Choosing the right metric depends on the specific urban planning task and the consequences of false positives and false negatives. The selection of metrics should align with the goals of a particular project.

Applications in Urban Planning

For urban planners, CV provides practical applications that enhance decision-making and operational workflows. Key applications include land-use classification, infrastructure monitoring, traffic management, and public safety and security.

Land-Use Classification

Image classification techniques are beneficial for land-use classification, where satellite or aerial imagery is analyzed to categorize areas into residential, commercial, industrial, or green spaces. This helps planners monitor urban development, assess zoning compliance, and identify potential areas for future growth. Image segmentation techniques are well suited for providing several valuable applications. One key use is land cover analysis, where satellite images are segmented into vegetation, water bodies, and built-up areas. This supports environmental monitoring, urban growth assessments, and ecological research. Another important application is detailed infrastructure mapping, where roads, sidewalks, buildings, and parks are segmented to create precise maps that aid urban planning and resource allocation. During natural disasters, segmented images help assess damage to infrastructure, facilitating efficient response and recovery strategies.

Monitoring Urban Growth with Computer Vision—Denmark Case Study

Process

The study used Landsat satellite imagery from 1985 to 2018 to analyze urban growth in Denmark, focusing on both horizontal expansion (e.g., compact, open, and sparse urban development) and vertical densification (e.g., high-rise and low-rise development) (Chen et al., 2020). The researchers employed semantic segmentation using a deep learning model (DeepLab) to classify urban areas at a 30-meter resolution. The methodology involved:

1. **Data Collection and Preprocessing**: Using Google Earth Engine to compile cloud-free Landsat images spanning 33 years.
2. **Model Training and Classification**: Comparing three models— DeepLab, a fully convolutional network (FCN), and a texture-based Random Forest (RF).
3. **Validation and Generalization**: Testing model performance across different years and cities to seek **spatial and temporal transferability**.
4. **Mapping Urban Growth**: Generating annual maps of urban density and analyzing how growth patterns correlate with population trends (Chen et al., 2020).

Objectives

The study's primary objective was to develop an automated, scalable method for long-term urban growth monitoring using freely available satellite data. By applying deep learning techniques, the researchers sought to determine whether semantic segmentation models could accurately classify urban form and track spatial changes over multiple decades. Additionally, the study aimed to compare urban growth patterns across Danish cities, particularly Copenhagen and Aarhus, to understand how planning policies and population growth influenced densification over time. Another key goal was to test the spatial and temporal transferability of the models, assessing whether a deep learning model trained on Danish data could be applied to cities in other European countries.

Outcomes

The study demonstrated that DeepLab performed best, improving classification accuracy by 4–10% compared to traditional methods like Random Forest. The analysis revealed diverse urban growth trends: while Copenhagen's central areas experienced a decline in density, its suburbs saw significant vertical expansion as new developments focused on high-rise structures. In contrast, Aarhus displayed a different growth pattern, with expansion occurring in lower-density areas. The study also confirmed that models trained on Danish data could be successfully applied to ten other European cities, highlighting the transferability of the approach. By providing high-resolution, long-term data, this method enables urban planners to monitor densification trends, track zoning compliance, and inform future development strategies with a data-driven approach (Chen et al., 2020).

Infrastructure Monitoring

Another practical application is infrastructure monitoring, where classification models detect and categorize urban assets, such as roads, bridges, and public buildings. This allows cities to maintain an accurate infrastructure inventory, plan upgrades, and schedule maintenance more efficiently. For example, identifying and classifying road conditions from images can help prioritize repairs for high-traffic areas.

Urban infrastructure monitoring also benefits significantly from object detection. The ability to automatically detect construction activities ensures compliance with safety standards and regulations. Similarly, identifying infrastructure damage—like cracks in bridges or potholes—enables cities to prioritize repairs and maintain public assets efficiently. Object detection also assists in monitoring the presence and condition of street furniture, including benches, streetlights, and signage, helping urban maintenance teams keep public spaces in good condition.

Monitoring Bridge Conditions with Computer Vision— Turkey Case Study

Process

In Turkey, researchers applied CV-based structural monitoring to assess the health of three landmark long-span suspension bridges: the First Bosphorus Bridge, the Second Bosphorus Bridge, and the Osman Gazi Bridge. These bridges, with main spans ranging from 1074 m to 1550 m, were monitored using high-resolution cameras positioned at 600 m to 1350 m. The researchers used CV algorithms to track displacements and vibrations of the bridge decks by analyzing video sequences. The collected data were then compared with finite element models and existing literature to validate the accuracy of the CV-based measurements (Öztürk et al., 2023).

Objectives

The primary objective of this study was to demonstrate the feasibility of using CV techniques for non-contact, long-distance monitoring of structural displacements in large-scale bridges. By comparing CV measurements with traditional monitoring approaches and finite element analyses, the researchers aimed to validate the accuracy and reliability of this method. Additionally, the study sought to identify challenges associated with environmental factors, such as camera positioning, weather conditions, and image distortions, and to propose considerations for future applications in similar contexts (Öztürk et al., 2023).

Outcomes

The study successfully achieved non-contact displacement measurements from significant distances. The discrepancies between CV results and finite element models were minimal—approximately 5% for displacement and 2% for dynamic frequencies on the First Bosphorus Bridge. These findings indicate that CV-based monitoring can provide accurate assessments of bridge behavior while reducing the need for costly and invasive physical inspections. However, the research also highlighted limitations, such as the impact of environmental conditions on measurement accuracy, emphasizing the need for optimized camera placement and protective measures in future implementations. This case study demonstrates how CV technology can enhance structural health monitoring, providing an efficient, scalable, and non-invasive approach to assessing bridge conditions (Öztürk et al., 2023).

Traffic Management

Object detection is helpful in managing and optimizing city operations. One important application is traffic management. Real-time detection and tracking of vehicles, pedestrians, and cyclists using traffic camera footage enables planners to optimize traffic flow, reduce congestion, and enhance road safety. Adaptive traffic signals can adjust timing based on real-time vehicle and pedestrian counts, improving the efficiency of intersections. Object detection also plays a critical role in accident prevention by identifying potential hazards, such as a pedestrian crossing unexpectedly, allowing immediate alerts or interventions. Over time, the data collected from these systems helps planners analyze traffic patterns and design more efficient road networks.

Monitoring Pedestrian and Bicyclist Activity—San Francisco Case Study

Process

The San Francisco County Transportation Authority (SFCTA) developed a smartphone application called CycleTracks to collect data on bicyclist travel patterns in San Francisco. The app uses GPS tracking to record cyclists' routes and travel times, enabling planners to analyze real-world cycling behavior. Users voluntarily download the app and consent to share their anonymized travel data, which is then aggregated to increase privacy. This data helps transportation officials understand route choices, peak travel periods, and the effectiveness of existing bicycle infrastructure. Insights gained from the program have informed bike lane expansions, safety improvements, and broader transportation planning initiatives (SFCTA, 2011).

Objectives

The primary objective of the CycleTracks initiative was to gather detailed, real-time data on bicyclist movements to support evidence-based infrastructure development. By using smartphone technology, the SFCTA aimed to collect accurate and comprehensive information on cycling routes, travel durations, and usage frequencies. The goal was to identify high-demand corridors, assess gaps in the cycling network, and prioritize investments in safer, more accessible bike infrastructure. Additionally, the program aimed to enhance public engagement by encouraging cyclists to actively contribute data to improve their city's transportation system (Schneider et al., 2013).

Outcomes

The implementation of CycleTracks provided critical insights into bicyclist behavior in San Francisco. The data revealed popular routes, highlighted areas where infrastructure improvements were needed, and supported the strategic expansion of bike lanes and safety measures. This information allowed city planners to prioritize investments based on real-world cycling patterns rather than assumptions. Moreover, the success of CycleTracks demonstrated the effectiveness of using mobile technology for transportation data collection, leading to its adoption in other cities looking to improve their pedestrian and bicyclist monitoring strategies (SFCTA, 2011; Schneider et al., 2013).

This case study highlights how local governments can utilize innovative technology to enhance pedestrian and bicyclist infrastructure, promoting safer and more efficient urban mobility.

Public Safety and Security

Public safety and security are other key areas where object detection is useful. Video surveillance systems equipped with object detection algorithms can monitor public spaces, identifying suspicious behavior, unauthorized access, or abandoned objects that might pose risks. For example, the technology can track crowd density at events, allowing authorities to manage large gatherings safely. It can also detect unusual patterns—such as unattended bags or erratic behavior—enabling timely interventions by security personnel. By automating these processes, urban environments become safer and more responsive to emerging risks.

Monitoring Crowd Density Using Computer Vision—Hamburg Case Study

Process

In response to the COVID-19 pandemic, a team of researchers in Hamburg developed a CV-based system to analyze crowd density in public spaces. Using strategically placed surveillance cameras throughout the city, the system captured real-time video footage of high-traffic areas such as public squares, transportation hubs, and shopping districts. These video streams were processed using deep learning algorithms, which could detect, count, and track individuals to assess crowd density dynamically. The system was designed to identify patterns of crowd formation and issue alerts when social distancing measures were not being followed, allowing authorities to respond proactively to potential health risks (TechLabs Hamburg, 2020).

Objectives

The primary objective of this initiative was to enhance public health and safety by ensuring compliance with social distancing guidelines during the pandemic. By implementing an automated, real-time monitoring system, the project aimed to reduce reliance on manual observation, which is labor-intensive, costly, and prone to human error. The system sought to provide accurate and timely data on crowd densities, enabling city officials to make data-driven decisions regarding public space management, event planning, and emergency response measures. Additionally, the researchers aimed to explore how CV technologies could be integrated into long-term urban planning strategies to manage pedestrian flow in busy areas beyond the pandemic (Khan et al., 2020).

Outcomes

The deployment of the CV-based crowd monitoring system in Hamburg significantly improved the city's ability to manage public spaces during the pandemic. The real-time data allowed authorities to swiftly identify and address overcrowded areas, reducing the risk of virus transmission. The system's ability to track trends over time also provided valuable insights for transportation planning, urban design, and public safety improvements. Additionally, this initiative demonstrated how AI-driven crowd monitoring can serve broader purposes, such as optimizing traffic flow, improving emergency evacuation procedures, and enhancing event management strategies. The success of the Hamburg system underscored the potential of integrating CV technologies into urban governance, providing a scalable, adaptable solution for managing public spaces beyond health-related applications.

These case studies highlight various applications of CV in urban planning, illustrating how AI-powered image analysis supports decision-making and operational efficiency. As seen in Denmark's urban growth study, land-use classification utilizes satellite imagery and deep learning models to track urban expansion, assess zoning compliance, and inform sustainable development strategies. Similarly, infrastructure monitoring, exemplified by Turkey's bridge condition study, shows how high-resolution cameras and CV algorithms can detect structural issues in bridges, reducing the need for costly manual inspections while ensuring public safety. In San Francisco, the CycleTracks program demonstrates how smartphone-based data collection and CV help planners analyze bicyclist travel patterns, leading to improved cycling infrastructure and safer, more efficient transportation networks.

Beyond transportation and infrastructure, CV can be applied to traffic management and public safety efforts. Real-time object detection allows cities to optimize traffic flow, reduce congestion, and improve road safety, ensuring smoother urban mobility. Hamburg's crowd density monitoring system illustrates how AI-powered surveillance can track pedestrian movement, issue real-time alerts, and assist in emergency response planning, particularly in high-traffic areas. By integrating CV into urban governance, planners can make data-driven decisions that enhance sustainability, safety, and resilience.

Challenges of Computer Vision

While CV holds great potential for augmenting urban planning, several challenges must be addressed to realize its capabilities appropriately. These challenges include data management, computational demands, privacy concerns, and ethical issues.

Data Storage and Management

CV draws upon extensive visual data from satellites, drones, and street-level cameras. These datasets are often massive, containing high-resolution images, traffic surveillance video, and other inputs that require significant computational resources for analysis. Managing such data at scale presents several challenges. Data storage solutions are critical for handling large datasets while ensuring quick retrieval for real-time analysis. Proper data management includes organizing datasets systematically and maintaining data integrity over time, which is particularly important for historical analyses in which planners compare visual data across different timeframes to monitor urban growth or environmental changes.

Computational Resources

Computational resources are essential for training and deploying deep learning models. Models such as CNNs, used for object detection and image segmentation tasks, require powerful hardware such as GPUs (graphics processing units) or distributed computing environments. Smaller planning departments or municipalities with limited budgets may find it challenging to access the necessary infrastructure, which can slow the adoption of advanced CV technologies.

Cloud computing platforms provide a scalable solution to these challenges, enabling planners to store, process, and analyze large datasets without relying on local hardware. Distributed processing frameworks can also help spread computational workloads across multiple machines, ensuring faster processing times and enabling planners to work with complex models even on limited budgets.

Privacy Concerns

Using surveillance cameras, drones, and other imaging technologies in urban planning raises significant concerns about individual privacy and the ethical implications of data collection and usage. These tools provide valuable insights for traffic monitoring, land-use analysis, and public safety improvements, but they also present risks of misuse, surveillance overreach, and unintended consequences. Without proper safeguards, such technologies can infringe on personal privacy rights, facilitate mass surveillance, or contribute to biased decision-making, especially if data collection disproportionately targets specific communities. The potential for discriminatory practices, such as the over-policing of specific neighborhoods or biased algorithmic interpretations of urban activity, further underscores the ethical challenges in using such data.

To address these concerns, data anonymization is a critical technique that enables urban planners to utilize visual data while safeguarding individual privacy. Techniques such as face blurring, license plate masking, pixelation of identifiable features, and generalization of sensitive data points help ensure that personally identifiable information is not misused. Advanced privacy-preserving methods, such as differential privacy and homomorphic encryption, can further protect individuals while maintaining the integrity of large-scale urban analyses. By integrating these privacy safeguards, planners can extract meaningful insights from surveillance and imaging technologies without compromising public trust.

Striking a balance between data utility and privacy protection is essential for ethical urban planning. Transparent policies on data governance, public consent, and accountability mechanisms should accompany the use of these technologies to prevent misuse and foster public confidence. As urban environments become increasingly digitized, ensuring that privacy considerations are embedded into data-driven decision-making will be crucial for responsible and equitable urban development.

Ethical and Legal Considerations

Ethical guidelines are necessary to be sure that CV applications in urban planning are deployed responsibly. These guidelines should cover informed consent for data collection, transparency about how data will be used, and limitations on the scope of data usage. For example, surveillance footage intended for traffic analysis should not be repurposed for unrelated purposes without public approval. Developing ethical frameworks is important to deploying CV technologies that align with public trust and community values.

Another critical consideration is regulatory compliance with data protection laws. Urban planners must ensure that their data collection and analysis efforts comply with legal frameworks such as the General Data Protection Regulation (GDPR) in the European Union, which governs the handling of personal data. This includes obtaining consent when necessary, securely storing data, and limiting access to authorized personnel. Compliance with such regulations fosters public trust and leads to the responsible use of visual data.

Looking Ahead

Integrating CV into planning practice can lead to new and effective ways to observe and analyze urban places. Several key trends are expected to drive future developments in this field.

Unlike traditional cloud-based models, edge computing processes data locally, near the collection source (e.g., on cameras or drones). This approach reduces latency (or time delay), enabling real-time decision-making for applications like traffic monitoring or public safety systems. Automated data annotation will further streamline the development of CV models. Manually labeling images is time-consuming and labor-intensive, especially for large datasets. Advances in semi-supervised and active learning will allow models to self-annotate data with minimal human input, accelerating the development of urban planning tools.

The combination of NLP and CV enables the analysis of textual and visual data in tandem. NLP extracts meaning from unstructured text, such as reports, policy documents, or planning regulations, while CV analyzes images, video footage, and other visual inputs. This allows planners to correlate policies and regulations with real-world developments. This integration also supports automated compliance monitoring. NLP identifies specific regulatory requirements, while CV monitors whether new developments align with those policies. This cross-technology application reduces manual workload, enhances urban governance, and provides a more comprehensive view of urban planning efforts.

The integration of geographic information systems (GIS) with CV enables spatial analysis of visual data, providing deeper insights into how physical spaces evolve. GIS stores and analyzes location-based data, while CV automates the interpretation of large volumes of imagery. This combination facilitates the development of dynamic, real-time maps that reflect the current state of urban infrastructure, land use, and environmental conditions. Digital twin technology will be another transformative trend, with cities developing virtual replicas of urban environments. Digital twins allow planners to simulate the impact of various planning scenarios, monitor infrastructure in real time, and predict future changes. CV will provide the visual data needed to keep digital twins up to date, ensuring they reflect the current state of the city.

Addressing the current challenges of CV in urban planning, such as managing large datasets, ensuring computational efficiency, and safeguarding privacy, will provide new opportunities for the field. By adopting cloud computing, edge processing, and data-sharing frameworks, planners can overcome technological and resource constraints. Developing robust ethical guidelines and complying with regulatory frameworks will lead to the responsible and trustworthy use of CV technologies. Looking to the future, advancements in interdisciplinary AI integration, automated annotation, and digital twin technology will drive significant progress in urban planning.

Chapter Summary

This chapter discussed the fundamentals of CV and some of its applications in urban planning. CV can help urban planners process and analyze vast amounts of visual data efficiently, making it a valuable tool in the planning and management of urban environments. This technology enhances data analysis, facilitates real-time monitoring, and automates traditionally labor-intensive tasks, thereby increasing efficiency and accuracy in urban planning processes.

Understanding the core concepts of CV, including image representation, color spaces, and essential image processing techniques such as filtering and edge detection, is helpful for understanding and applying more advanced

CV methods, including image classification, object detection, and image segmentation. For instance, image classification techniques can identify different land uses from satellite imagery. Object detection techniques can be used to analyze traffic patterns from camera footage, enabling optimized traffic management. Image segmentation could help in assessing the extent and health of urban green spaces using drone imagery. These techniques demonstrate the diverse applications of CV for urban planning.

Current challenges in CV include the issues of handling large datasets and computational requirements, ensuring data privacy, and ethical and legal considerations. Large datasets, such as high-resolution satellite images and extensive traffic footage, demand significant storage and computational power. Techniques like data augmentation and the use of advanced sensor technologies can help mitigate these challenges. Robust algorithms and ethical guidelines are essential for ensuring data privacy and responsible use of data.

Looking to the future, advances in deep learning promise to enhance the accuracy and efficiency of CV applications. Techniques like self-supervised learning and the use of generative models can reduce the reliance on large labeled datasets and improve model performance. The integration of CV with other AI technologies, such as NLP and GIS, will create more powerful tools for urban planning, enabling comprehensive analysis and potentially better decision-making.

References and Further Reading

Chen, T. H. K., Qiu, C., Schmitt, M., Zhu, X. X., Sabel, C. E., & Prishchepov, A. V. (2020). Mapping horizontal and vertical urban densification in Denmark with Landsat time-series from 1985 to 2018: A semantic segmentation solution. *Remote Sensing of Environment, 251*, 112096.

Khan, K., Khan, N., Ullah, R., Ahmad, W., & Qureshi, A. M. (2020). *Advances and Trends in Real-Time Visual Crowd Analysis*. Sensors, 20(18), 5201. https://doi.org/10.3390/s20185201

Öztürk, B., Kaya, Y., Bilgin, M., & Soyluk, K. (2023). Long-distance structural health monitoring of large-scale suspension bridges using computer vision-based techniques. *Sensors, 23*(19), 8161. https://www.mdpi.com/1424–8220/23/19/8161

San Francisco County Transportation Authority (SFCTA). (2011). *CycleTracks: Using smartphones to improve bicycle planning*. Retrieved from https://onlinepubs.trb.org/onlinepubs/circulars/ec183.pdf

Schneider, R. J., Arnold, L. S., & Ragland, D. R. (2013). *Methodology for bicycle and pedestrian data collection: A case study in San Francisco.* Transportation Research Record, 2339(1), 36–45. https://doi.org/10.3141/2339–05

Sejnowski, T. J. (2018). *The deep learning revolution.* MIT press.

TechLabs Hamburg. (2020). *COVID-19 Crowd Analysis: Analyzing Crowd Density Using Computer Vision.* Retrieved from https://medium.com/@TechLabs_Hamburg/covid-19-crowd-analysis-analyzing-crowd-density-using-computer-vision-31ae45d6f08

6

GENERATIVE AI FOR URBAN PLANNERS

Generative AI (GenAI) represents a significant leap in artificial intelligence (AI) with its ability to create new content by learning patterns from existing data. Unlike traditional AI models, which primarily focus on classification, prediction, or optimization tasks, GenAI relies on algorithms that learn the patterns and structures within input data, enabling it to generate new data that closely resembles the input data it was trained on. This content can take various forms, including text, images, videos, or fully simulated environments. This capability opens up numerous opportunities for urban planners, providing innovative solutions for designing, analyzing, and visualizing urban spaces.

The primary difference between GenAI and other types of AI, which can be categorized as discriminative, lies in their objectives and outputs. Discriminative AI models focus on distinguishing between classes or categories in the data. For instance, a discriminative model used in computer vision could determine whether an image contains a tree or

DOI: 10.4324/9781003476818-6

not by learning to classify objects based on labeled data. In contrast, GenAI models aim to produce entirely new content. Instead of classifying images, a generative model would create new images, such as realistic-looking trees, based on its understanding of what trees typically look like.

To illustrate this distinction in an urban planning context, imagine a city planner using AI to address zoning issues. A discriminative model might assess zoning compliance by analyzing satellite images and determining whether buildings in a particular area conform to zoning regulations, such as identifying whether residential, commercial, or industrial zones are correctly designated. A generative model, on the other hand, could be used to simulate potential future urban developments both visually and descriptively through text generation. For example, it might generate new land-use scenarios by creating virtual models of what an area could look like if repurposed for mixed-use development. This helps urban planners visualize potential changes and explore a variety of development possibilities, enabling better decision-making for future city planning projects.

The significance of GenAI lies in its ability to produce content that is not only realistic but also highly adaptable, with applications spanning numerous application areas. In design and urban planning, it generates conceptual layouts and visualizations and can simulate different scenarios to predict policy or regulatory outcomes and test system solutions. GenAI is being used more and more to generate text as part of reports and other documentation. These capabilities underscore a profound shift as generative models extend AI's reach beyond analytical tasks into the realm of creativity and innovation—areas historically regarded as uniquely human domains.

This chapter will discuss GenAI, exploring its underlying mechanisms, strengths, and wide-ranging applications in urban planning, as well as its broader implications for the future of the field. It will explain how GenAI differs from traditional AI, which focuses on classification, prediction, and optimization, by instead learning patterns and structures from existing data to generate new content, including text, images, videos, and simulations. This capability enables planners to visualize alternative zoning configurations, simulate urban growth patterns, and generate detailed textual descriptions for reports, streamlining workflows and expanding the range of possibilities for urban design and policy evaluation. As GenAI pushes AI's role beyond data analysis into creative problem-solving, it raises new opportunities and challenges, including questions about interpretability, reliability, and the evolving role of human expertise in planning. Ethical concerns, such as the potential reinforcement of biases in AI-generated outputs and the need for transparency in AI-assisted decision-making, also require careful consideration.

A Brief History of Generative AI

The history of GenAI began with early methods that relied on probability and statistical models to create new data based on patterns found in existing examples. Two primary approaches were Gaussian Mixture Models (GMMs) and Hidden Markov Models (HMMs), both of which were widely used in tasks like speech synthesis, handwriting generation, and pattern recognition. GMMs worked by combining multiple statistical distributions to model complex data, while HMMs helped predict sequential patterns over time, making them useful for applications involving spoken or written language. These models allowed AI to generate structured outputs that mimicked real-world patterns, but their capabilities were limited to relatively simple and predefined tasks. As AI research advanced, deep learning techniques replaced these early models, leading to the more sophisticated and creative GenAI systems we see today.

The development of artificial neural networks (ANNs) marked a significant turning point in GenAI, significantly expanding its potential. One of the early breakthroughs was the autoencoder, a type of neural network (NN) that used unsupervised learning to compress data into a more straightforward form and then reconstruct it back to its original state. This process helped AI learn essential patterns in data without needing explicit labels. Autoencoders showed that AI could discover hidden structures within data, making it possible to generate more flexible and realistic outputs. This advancement laid the foundation for more powerful generative techniques, enabling AI to create increasingly complex and expressive content.

In 2013, the introduction of variational autoencoders (VAEs) marked a critical advancement. VAEs combined autoencoder representation learning with probabilistic modeling, enabling data generation by sampling from a learned latent space. This probabilistic integration allowed for greater flexibility, producing diverse and novel outputs while maintaining statistical coherence with the input data. VAEs became an essential tool in applications such as image synthesis, anomaly detection, and data interpolation.

The field of generative modeling underwent a groundbreaking transformation in 2014 with the introduction of Generative Adversarial Networks (GANs) by Ian Goodfellow and his colleagues. Goodfellow, a computer scientist specializing in machine learning (ML), developed GANs during his doctoral research at the University of Montreal. His work built on earlier advancements in NNs but introduced a completely new approach to training AI models to generate realistic data.

GANs work by using two competing NNs—a generator, which creates new data, and a discriminator, which evaluates whether the generated data is real or fake. This setup, often described as a zero-sum game, forces both networks to improve over time, leading to highly realistic outputs. This adversarial process solved key challenges in GenAI, particularly in producing sharper and more detailed images and videos. GANs quickly became one of the most important tools in AI, influencing fields such as artificial image synthesis, video generation, and deepfake technology and solidifying Goodfellow's reputation as a pioneer in deep learning.

In subsequent years, advancements in NN architectures and training techniques led to the development of even more sophisticated generative models. StyleGAN, introduced in 2018, refined the GAN framework to produce high-resolution, photorealistic images with unprecedented control over style and features. In parallel, the rise of autoregressive models, such as GPT (generative pre-trained transformer), brought generative capabilities to text and sequential data. Models like OpenAI's GPT-3 and GPT-4 demonstrated the ability to generate coherent, contextually-rich text, pushing the boundaries of natural language generation and interaction.

Today, generative models continue to evolve, integrating advances in computing power, data availability, and algorithmic innovation. These models are now being applied to a diverse range of fields, including creative industries, scientific research, urban planning, healthcare, and beyond. The trajectory of generative modeling underscores the fusion of statistical rigor, NN advancements, and computational creativity, propelling the field into an era where machines are not just tools for analysis but collaborators in creation.

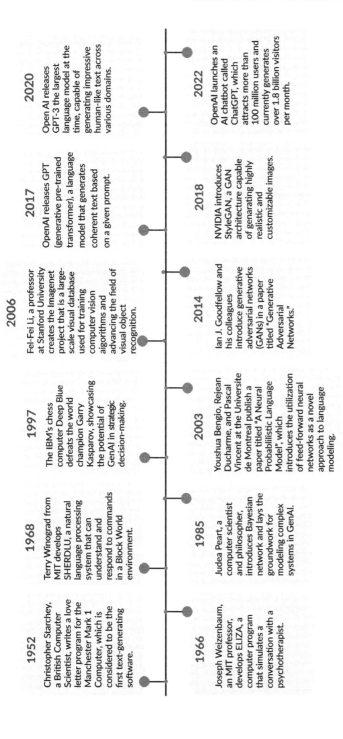

1952

Christopher Starchey, a British Computer Scientist, writes a love letter program for the Manchester Mark 1 Computer, which is considered to be the first text-generating software.

1968

Terry Winograd from MIT develops SHERDLU, a natural language processing system that can understand and respond to commands in a Block World environment.

1966

Joseph Weizenbaum, an MIT professor, develops ELIZA, a computer program that simulates a conversation with a psychotherapist.

1985

Judea Peart, a computer scientist and philosopher, introduces Bayesian network and lays the groundwork for modeling complex systems in GenAI.

1997

The IBM's chess computer Deep Blue defeats the world champion Garry Kasparov, showcasing the potential of GenAI in strategic decision-making.

2003

Youshua Bengio, Rejean Ducharme, and Pascal Vincent at the Universite de Montreal publish a paper titled "A Neural Probabilistic Language Model", which introduces the utilization of feed-forward neural networks as a novel approach to language modeling.

2006

Fel-Fei Li, a professor at Stanford University creates the Imagenet project that is a large-scale visual database used for training computer vision algorithms and advancing the field of visual object recognition.

2014

Ian J. Goodfellow and his colleagues introduce generative adversarial networks (GANs) in a paper titled "Generative Adversarial Networks."

2017

OpenAI releases GPT (generative pre-trained transformer), a language model that generates coherent text based on a given prompt.

2018

NVIDIA introduces StyleGAN, a GAN architecture capable of genarating highly realistic and customizable images.

2020

Open AI releases GPT-3 the largest language model at the time, capable of generating impressive human-like text across various domains.

2022

OpenAI launches an AI chatbot called ChatGPT, which attracts more than 100 million users and currently generates over 1.8 billion visitors per month.

Figure 6.1 Generative AI evolution.

Introduction to Generative AI

This section lays the foundation by defining GenAI and introducing the key concepts and terms essential for understanding how these models work. GenAI has rapidly evolved into a powerful tool capable of creating realistic images, synthesizing human-like text, composing music, and even generating lifelike videos. However, to fully grasp its potential and limitations, it is important first to understand the fundamental principles behind it.

This section explores core ideas such as probabilistic modeling, NNs, and adversarial training and provides a structured introduction that will help readers navigate more advanced topics later. Understanding these basics is crucial not only for those developing AI models but also for policymakers, urban planners, designers, and other professionals looking to integrate GenAI into their work. With a solid foundation, readers will be better equipped to evaluate AI-generated outputs, recognize biases, and apply generative models responsibly in real-world applications.

Generative AI (GenAI): A subfield of AI using algorithms that learn the patterns and structures within input data, enabling it to generate new data that closely resembles the input data it was trained on.

Basic Concepts and Terminology

At its core, GenAI models learn the underlying distribution of the training data and use this knowledge to generate new, similar types of data. This process involves two key steps: understanding the data distribution and developing new samples that follow this distribution. This capability opens up a wide range of applications, particularly in fields where data is scarce or costly to obtain or where creativity and innovation are paramount.

One of the key ideas in GenAI is the concept of latent space, which helps AI create new variations of data. Latent space is a simplified representation of information that a generative model learns from its training data. Instead of storing every detail, the model captures essential patterns and relationships in a compressed form, allowing it to generate new versions of the data based on these learned patterns.

Think of latent space as a map of possibilities. By adjusting different points on this map, the AI can create slightly different versions of an image, a city layout, or other types of generated content. This ability is useful in urban planning, where exploring different designs, layouts, or zoning scenarios can help planners visualize many options before making decisions.

To measure how realistic and practical the generated data is, researchers use evaluation metrics such as the Inception Score (IS) and Fréchet Inception Distance (FID). These tools compare the AI-generated results to real-world data, checking for quality and diversity. In urban planning, additional customized evaluation methods may be needed to be sure that AI-generated maps, building layouts, or infrastructure models are both realistic and practical for real-world use.

Generative AI Models

GenAI uses multiple models to carry out its two-part process of learning data distributions and generating new samples that follow this distribution. The models used to achieve these aims have evolved. Today, advanced AI models equip machines with the tools necessary to analyze content and create new content based on that analysis.

GenAI learns from existing data and then uses that knowledge to create new content following the same patterns. This process involves two main steps: first, the AI analyzes and learns the structure of the data; and second, it generates new examples that look similar to what it has learned. Over time, the models used for this process have improved, allowing AI to produce increasingly realistic text, images, speech, and even urban planning simulations.

Early Generative AI Models: Probabilistic Approaches

The first GenAI models were based on probability and statistics— mathematical methods that estimate patterns in data. Two primary models that helped shape the field were GMMs and HMMs. These models were widely used in areas like speech synthesis, handwriting recognition, and predicting sequences of data.

Gaussian Mixture Models

A GMM is a statistical technique that represents complex data by breaking it down into multiple simpler patterns called Gaussian distributions (which are bell-shaped curves used in statistics). Instead of treating all data as one large pattern, GMMs combine several smaller patterns to create a more accurate model of real-world data.

For example, in speech generation, GMMs were used to capture the natural variations in human speech, such as differences in pronunciation between speakers. By analyzing how sounds change, GMMs could generate realistic speech patterns. In handwriting synthesis, GMMs helped AI learn the shapes of letters and words, allowing it to create synthetic handwriting that closely mimicked different human writing styles.

Hidden Markov Models

A HMM is a method that helps AI understand and generate sequences of data over time. It assumes that every data point (such as a spoken word or a written letter) is influenced by hidden states—patterns that are not directly visible but can be inferred.

In speech synthesis, HMMs helped AI predict the order and flow of sounds by modeling how phonemes (units of sound) transition from one to another in natural speech. This allowed AI to create coherent, flowing speech patterns rather than isolated sounds. Similarly, in handwriting generation, HMMs captured the movement of a pen as it formed letters, helping the AI generate continuous and realistic handwriting instead of drawing disconnected shapes.

The Impact and Limitations of Early Models

GMMs and HMMs were significant breakthroughs because they allowed AI to learn from data and generate realistic outputs with variation.

However, they also had limitations. These models struggled to capture complex relationships in data, especially when patterns were nonlinear or highly detailed. As AI research advanced, newer models, such as NNs and deep learning, were developed to overcome these challenges.

Despite their limitations, GMMs and HMMs remain influential in AI and continue to be used in unsupervised learning and sequence prediction. They also provided the foundation for today's advanced GenAI techniques, which are now used for tasks like text generation, image synthesis, and urban planning simulations.

Probabilistic Models

The origins of modern generative models can be traced to two primary probabilistic frameworks: GMMs and HMMs. Both were essential tools for generating data in fields like speech synthesis, handwriting recognition, and sequential data modeling. These early models laid the groundwork for many of the sophisticated generative methods used in AI today.

GMMs use a probabilistic approach to model data as a combination of multiple Gaussian distributions. A combination of various Gaussian distributions means that instead of using a single Gaussian distribution (a bell-shaped curve) to represent a dataset, multiple overlapping Gaussian distributions are used to better capture the complexity and variability in the data. This approach is commonly used in GMMs to describe data that may have multiple clusters or patterns. Each Gaussian component captures a distinct aspect of the dataset, and together, these components approximate complex real-world data distributions. In speech generation, GMMs help AI understand how speech sounds (phonemes) vary between different speakers and situations. A phoneme is the smallest unit of sound in speech, like the "p" in "pat" or the "b" in "bat." Since people pronounce words differently based on accent, tone, and speaking speed, GMMs analyze these differences and learn the patterns. Once trained, the model can predict and generate realistic speech sounds by naturally combining these patterns.

In handwriting generation, GMMs help AI learn the shapes and styles of letters and words by analyzing how real people write. Everyone's handwriting is slightly different—some letters are taller, more curved, or written faster than others. GMMs capture this variation and use it to create synthetic handwriting that looks like a real person wrote it. This technique is helpful for applications like digital handwriting simulation and signature generation.

In contrast, HMMs are sequence-based models that assume data is produced by a series of hidden states, with each state emitting observable outputs. The power of HMMs lies in their ability to generate and predict sequential patterns. For speech, HMMs model the transitions between phonemes, allowing the generation of coherent speech patterns by simulating how sounds evolve. Similarly, in handwriting synthesis, HMMs capture the temporal sequence of pen strokes, enabling the generation of continuous handwriting that reflects the dynamics of human writing.

The generative power of GMMs and HMMs lies in their ability to learn from data and reproduce patterns with a high degree of variability. However, these models have limitations, such as their inability to capture more complex dependencies in data or handle nonlinear patterns efficiently. Despite their limitations, GMMs and HMMs remain influential. Their probabilistic principles continue to underpin many modern approaches in AI and ML, especially in unsupervised learning and sequence modeling. They also served as conceptual stepping stones for more advanced frameworks, contributing to today's progress in GenAI, including text generation, image synthesis, and urban planning simulations.

Standard Autoencoders

Autoencoders, a class of NNs used for unsupervised learning, have played an important role in the development of more advanced generative models. Their architecture enables them to learn latent spaces (described on p. X). Autoencoders consist of two main components: an encoder and a decoder. The encoder compresses input data (such as images or text) into a latent space representation, capturing only the most essential features of the input. The decoder, in turn, reconstructs the original data from this compressed latent space, learning to generate outputs that closely match the original input.

The value of autoencoders lies in their ability to represent complex, high-dimensional data in a lower-dimensional space. This makes them practical for tasks like image compression, noise reduction, and anomaly detection. Unlike supervised models, autoencoders do not rely on labeled data; instead, they learn to reconstruct inputs by minimizing the difference (or reconstruction loss) between the original and reconstructed data.

There are different types of autoencoders, each designed for specific tasks. Convolutional Autoencoders (CAEs) are especially effective for working with images because they use convolutional layers, which help the model recognize patterns such as edges, shapes, and textures. This makes them useful for applications like image compression and enhancement. Another type, Denoising Autoencoders (DAEs), is trained to fix and reconstruct data that has been damaged or altered. For example, if an image has noise or missing parts, a DAE can learn to restore it, helping the AI focus on the most important features while ignoring irrelevant details. Meanwhile, Sparse Autoencoders introduce constraints that limit how much information the model can store in its latent space (a hidden, compressed version of the data). By forcing the model to learn only the most essential patterns, Sparse Autoencoders are helpful in reducing unnecessary details and uncovering hidden structures in data.

Variational Autoencoders

VAEs, introduced by Diederik P. Kingma and Max Welling in 2013, represented a breakthrough in generative modeling by adding probabilistic principles to the traditional autoencoder structure. Kingma, a researcher in deep learning and probabilistic modeling, and Welling, a professor specializing in ML, developed VAEs as a way to improve unsupervised learning by making the latent space more flexible and capable of capturing richer variations in data. Their work built on previous autoencoder designs but introduced a probabilistic framework that allowed for more realistic and diverse data generation.

Unlike standard autoencoders, which encode input data into fixed representations, VAEs treat the latent space as a probability distribution, typically using Gaussian distributions (bell-shaped curves that describe data variability). Instead of mapping each input to a single point in this space, VAEs learn a range of possible values, allowing them to sample new variations rather than just reconstructing exact copies. This approach makes VAEs especially useful in image generation, anomaly detection, and other GenAI tasks, as they can create highly realistic and diverse outputs while maintaining control over the variations they generate.

One of the hallmark features of VAEs is their ability to generate smooth interpolations between data points. Since the latent space is continuous and follows a well-defined probability distribution, interpolating between two points in the latent space produces gradual, realistic transitions. For instance, VAEs trained on images can smoothly transition between different objects or facial expressions, providing advanced capabilities for artificial creativity, image morphing, and data augmentation. This property makes VAEs invaluable in creative industries, urban simulations, and even biomedical research, where generating synthetic yet realistic data is critical.

Artificial creativity refers to the ability of AI models to generate new, innovative, or unexpected content by learning patterns from existing data. Unlike traditional AI systems that follow strict rules or pre-defined outputs, generative models like VAEs, GANs, and diffusion models can create unique images, music, text, or even design ideas by sampling from a learned probability space. These models do not simply replicate past data but can blend, transform, and innovate, allowing for novel outputs that resemble human creativity.

For instance, VAEs trained on images can smoothly transition between different objects or facial expressions, providing advanced capabilities for artificial creativity, image morphing, and data augmentation. By manipulating the latent space, VAEs can generate interpolated variations, such as transitioning between different architectural styles, merging artistic styles, or altering human expressions in a natural, fluid manner. This ability is widely used in artistic AI, concept design, and synthetic media, where AI assists in creating new visuals, enhancing artistic workflows, and expanding creative possibilities beyond traditional human imagination.

Generative Adversarial Networks

GANs, introduced by Ian Goodfellow and colleagues in 2014, have revolutionized generative modeling by using a novel game-theoretic framework. The core idea behind GANs is the interplay between two NNs, the generator and the discriminator, which are trained simultaneously in a competitive setup. The generator creates synthetic data, such as images or text. At the same time, the discriminator evaluates whether the generated data is real or fake, attempting to distinguish between actual data and the generator's output. This adversarial process continues iteratively, pushing both networks to improve, resulting in the generation of increasingly realistic data.

The generator's goal is to fool the discriminator by producing outputs that are indistinguishable from accurate data, while the discriminator is trained to identify fake examples correctly. Over time, both networks improve: the generator produces more lifelike data, and the discriminator becomes better at detecting subtle inconsistencies. This dynamic process resembles a minimax game in which each network optimizes its strategy in response to the other's performance. The result is that GANs generate highly realistic data across domains such as image synthesis, video generation, text creation, and audio production.

Since their introduction, GANs have become one of the most popular and widely used generative models across multiple fields. Their capacity

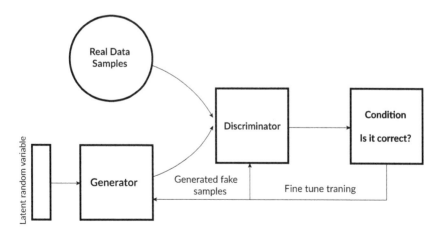

Figure 6.2 Generative adversarial network.

to generate photorealistic images has had a profound impact on the creative industries, powering applications in deepfakes, virtual clothing design, and video game development. GANs are also widely used for data augmentation in ML, where they generate additional training samples to improve the performance of models in fields like medical imaging or autonomous driving. In scientific research, GANs are used to simulate physical processes, create synthetic datasets for urban planning simulations, and enhance satellite imagery resolution. Their versatility and potential to create highly realistic synthetic data make them essential tools in both academic research and industry.

Another challenge is that training GANs is complex—they require precise adjustment of settings (called hyperparameters) and can take a significant amount of time to train. This makes them computationally expensive, meaning they need a lot of computer power to work well. However, researchers have worked on improving GANs by developing new versions, like Wasserstein GANs (WGANs) and StyleGAN, which help make training more stable and increase the variety and quality of the generated outputs.

In particular, StyleGAN—developed by NVIDIA—has become a leading architecture for generating high-resolution, photorealistic images by incorporating control over image styles at different levels. It builds on the original GAN architecture, introducing new techniques for controlling the style of generated images at multiple levels of abstraction. This allows StyleGAN to create photorealistic images that can be manipulated with precision, such as by altering facial expressions or creating seamless transitions between different image styles. StyleGAN has become widely used in creative industries for virtual try-on applications, video game character design, and even art creation. Its outputs are so realistic that they are frequently used in deepfake content, raising both creative opportunities and ethical challenges. GANs will continue to evolve with improvements in architecture and training methods, cementing their role as one of the most influential innovations in modern AI.

Large Language Models

Large language models (LLMs) are an AI technology that generates text by identifying patterns in massive datasets. They rely on deep learning techniques to analyze, predict, and generate text that reflects real-world language use. They are designed to handle a wide range of natural language tasks, including text completion, summarization, translation, and conversational interaction. LLMs represent a significant advancement in GenAI, providing powerful tools for urban planners to improve processes, engage with communities, and make data-driven decisions.

The LLM training process typically involves two stages. Pre-training teaches the model general language patterns by predicting missing words or phrases across a massive dataset, often consisting of public text from books, websites, news articles, technical reports, and social media corpus. The model contains billions or trillions of parameters—weights that adjust during training—allowing it to capture the subtleties and nuances of human language. Fine-tuning refines the model on specific datasets to adapt it for certain tasks, such as technical jargon related to urban planning. This fine-tuning phase may also include reinforcement learning with human feedback (RLHF) to align the model's outputs more closely with real-world expectations. These stages require high computational power, typically using GPU clusters or TPUs, which makes the development of LLMs both expensive and energy-intensive.

A GPU (Graphics Processing Unit) is a specialized computer chip designed to handle many tasks at once, making it ideal for processing large amounts of data in parallel. Initially developed for rendering graphics in video games, GPUs are now widely used in AI because they can speed up complex tasks like training deep learning models. A TPU (Tensor Processing Unit) is a type of AI-specific processor developed by Google. Unlike more general-purpose GPUs, TPUs are custom-built for ML and optimized for TensorFlow, a popular AI framework. TPUs are even faster and more energy-efficient for training large AI models, making them valuable for developing robust AI systems like LLMs.

The architecture of LLMs is based on transformers, which rely on self-attention mechanisms to understand the relationships between words and phrases, not just locally within sentences but across entire documents. This is important for capturing the larger context. Perhaps the most well-known transformer model is the GPT (generative pre-trained transformer) family developed by OpenAI, which powers models like ChatGPT. GPT-4, for example, contains 1.76 trillion parameters (compared to 175 billion for GPT-3), allowing it to write essays, answer questions, generate code, summarize texts, and carry on conversations, powering chatbots, automated content generation tools, and language-based interfaces.

While LLMs provide numerous benefits, they also present significant challenges. Because LLMs are trained on publicly available data, they can inherit biases related to race, gender, and socioeconomic status. Their use may also raise privacy issues if sensitive data is involved, requiring strict data governance policies. Another limitation is that LLMs are not always accurate; they sometimes generate text that sounds plausible but is factually incorrect ("hallucinations"). LLMs also struggle with domain-specific knowledge; although they are highly proficient in general language tasks, they may misunderstand or misuse technical terms without additional fine-tuning. The computational costs associated with LLMs are another concern, as running and maintaining these models requires significant resources. These models' reliance on massive datasets and computational power reflects the direction of modern AI, and their considerable leap forward in generative capabilities has the power to reshape industries and challenge traditional notions of creativity, design, and content creation.

GENERATIVE AI TOOLS AND PLATFORMS

Several tools and platforms make it easy for urban planners to start using GenAI without needing extensive technical expertise. These tools often come with intuitive interfaces, prebuilt models, and comprehensive documentation, making them accessible even to those with limited experience in AI.

- **Runway ML**: This popular platform allows users to experiment with GenAI models through a simple visual interface. It has a variety of pre-trained models that can be used for tasks such as image generation, style transfer, and data augmentation. Urban planners can use Runway ML to create realistic visualizations of urban projects or generate synthetic data to enhance their datasets.

- **Google Colab**: This is a free, cloud-based platform that provides access to powerful computing resources and allows users to run Python code in Jupyter notebooks. It is an excellent tool for experimenting with GenAI models and includes numerous tutorials and sample notebooks. Urban planners can find prebuilt scripts for tasks such as generating urban layouts or simulating environmental impacts.
- **Hugging Face**: This platform has an extensive library of pre-trained AI models and provides models for a wide range of generative tasks. While it is more commonly associated with natural language processing, it also supports generative models for images and other data types. The platform provides easy-to-use APIs that can be integrated into urban planning projects.
- **DALL·E**: Developed by OpenAI, this model is specifically designed for generating images from textual descriptions. Urban planners can use DALL·E to create visual representations of proposed projects by simply describing the desired outcomes. This tool is handy for generating conceptual images and visual aids for community engagement.
- **ChatGPT**: Developed by OpenAI, this is an advanced conversational AI tool that provides text-based generative capabilities. It can assist urban planners by summarizing reports, drafting project proposals, or brainstorming ideas. With its ability to generate coherent and context-aware text, ChatGPT supports a variety of planning tasks, such as creating community outreach materials, simulating public feedback, or drafting zoning regulations. Planners can also use it to translate technical concepts into layperson's terms for effective community engagement.

Applications in Urban Planning

GenAI has numerous real-world applications, including urban planning. Notable applications include data augmentation, urban design and visualization, community engagement, scenario generation, and communications. Understanding GenAI and its capabilities is important for urban planners looking to enhance their work creatively. As this technology continues to evolve, its potential applications in urban planning are likely to expand, providing even more innovative solutions to complex challenges.

Data Augmentation

Data can be scarce in urban planning for various reasons. For example, detailed traffic patterns or specific demographic information might be difficult or expensive to collect. Historical datasets may also be incomplete due to inconsistent record-keeping practices or rapid changes in the urban environment. These limitations can hinder the development of accurate models and simulations, ultimately impacting the quality of planning and decision-making.

Data augmentation addresses these issues by artificially expanding the available dataset. Generating synthetic data that mimics the actual data enriches datasets, providing more comprehensive inputs for training models. This process helps in creating more reliable and generalizable models that can perform well even in diverse and previously unseen scenarios. This, in turn, supports better analysis, decision-making, and planning, ultimately contributing to more efficient and effective urban development.

GenAI, with its ability to learn from and replicate data distributions, is a powerful tool for data augmentation. GANs and VAEs, in particular, understand the underlying patterns and structures of the original dataset and generate new data samples that fit these patterns, creating synthetic data that closely resembles real-world data. In GANs, the generator creates synthetic data samples, while the discriminator evaluates them against actual data. Through an iterative process, the generator improves its ability to produce realistic data that the discriminator cannot easily distinguish from actual data. This adversarial training results in high-quality synthetic data that can be used to augment the original dataset. VAEs' probabilistic approach encodes the input data into a latent space. Then, it decodes it back into new data samples, generating diverse and realistic synthetic data points that can enhance the original dataset.

Consider a scenario where urban planners are working on a traffic management project in a city with limited traffic data. The existing data might only cover certain times of the day or specific areas of the city, making it challenging to develop comprehensive traffic models. Planners can use GANs to generate realistic traffic flow patterns based on the available data, simulating traffic conditions during different times of the day, across various parts of the city, and under different scenarios, such as special events or road closures. By incorporating this augmented data into their models, planners can achieve more accurate traffic predictions and develop better traffic management strategies.

Similarly, demographic data augmentation can enhance urban planning projects focused on population growth, housing needs, or social services. If planners have limited demographic data, GenAI can create synthetic demographic profiles that reflect the diversity and distribution of the population. This enriched dataset can improve the accuracy of models predicting future population trends, housing demand, or the need for public services, leading to more effective and targeted planning initiatives.

Case Study: Enhancing Urban Landscape Design with Conditional Generative Adversarial Networks

In urban planning, data scarcity often makes it challenging to develop accurate models and efficient design processes. A notable example is rendering detailed landscape designs from basic sketches, which traditionally requires significant time and manual effort. To address this issue, researchers have developed a system utilizing conditional GANs to automate and enhance the design process.

A recent study introduced a system that uses conditional GANs to transform black-and-white park sketches into fully rendered color designs. This approach streamlines the urban ecological development process by reducing the workload required in the early design stages. The system is trained on a dataset of existing park designs, allowing the model to learn patterns and color schemes associated with different landscape elements. Once trained, the generator network creates detailed color renderings from simple sketches, while the discriminator network evaluates their realism and quality. This adversarial training process increases the chances that the generated designs are both aesthetically accurate and practical for urban development (Zhao et al., 2024).

Additionally, the study highlights the role of data augmentation in enhancing model performance. By increasing the diversity and volume of training data, planners can improve the GAN's ability to generate a broader range of realistic urban landscape designs. The system allows urban planners to visualize and refine design concepts quickly, making urban development more efficient, data-driven, and adaptable to different scenarios (Zhao et al., 2024).

This case study exemplifies how GenAI, particularly GANs, can help overcome data limitations in urban planning by producing synthetic data that mimics real-world patterns. With these AI-driven tools, urban planners can explore a broader range of scenarios and solutions, ultimately leading to more informed and effective decision-making.

Design, Visualization, and Engagement

Urban design and visualization are critical aspects of urban planning as they help planners and stakeholders envision potential development scenarios and make informed decisions. By using models such as GANs, urban planners can create accurate and lifelike visualizations of proposed projects that include detailed renderings of buildings, parks, streetscapes, and other urban elements.

These realistic visualizations are valuable for assessing the feasibility and impact of urban projects. Planners can explore different design options, evaluate their potential effects on the urban environment, and make data-driven decisions to optimize outcomes. For example, AI-generated visualizations can help identify potential issues, such as shading effects from new buildings or the visual impact of proposed infrastructure on the surrounding area.

Moreover, GenAI enhances community engagement by providing clear and compelling visuals that communicate design ideas effectively. When communities can see realistic images of proposed developments, they are better able to understand and provide feedback on the projects. This transparency fosters trust and collaboration between planners and community members, leading to more inclusive and accepted urban planning processes.

Consider a scenario where urban planners are tasked with designing a new park in a residential neighborhood. Traditional methods might involve creating sketches or digital renderings, which can be time-consuming and may not fully capture the park's potential impact. By using GenAI, planners can quickly generate realistic visualizations of the park's design, showing detailed elements such as walking paths, playgrounds, landscaping, and seating areas. These AI-generated images can be displayed at community meetings, shared on social media, or included in interactive online platforms where residents can explore the proposed changes from different angles and perspectives. The visualizations can illustrate different design options, such as variations in plantings or the layout of recreational areas, enabling planners to gather valuable feedback and preferences from the community.

For instance, an AI-generated visualization could show how the park would look at different times of the day or in various seasons, helping residents understand the full impact of the redesign. It could also simulate the broader impact of the park redesign on the neighborhood by showing how increased green space might affect local air quality, property values, and community well-being. This level of detail makes it easier for community members to provide informed feedback, suggest modifications, and express their support or concerns. It also allows planners to collect valuable input that can be used to refine and improve the project. This collaborative approach ensures that the final design aligns with the needs and desires of the residents, enhancing the park's success and acceptance.

Similarly, for more significant urban developments, GenAI can produce comprehensive visualizations that include new buildings, streetscapes, and public spaces. These images can be used in public meetings, planning documents, and promotional materials to convey the project's vision and benefits clearly. By providing a realistic and immersive view of the proposed development, planners can facilitate better understanding, support, and engagement from stakeholders and the public.

AI-Driven Urban Design and Visualization in Aljezur, Portugal, and Jakarta, Indonesia

A notable example of GenAI in urban planning is the UrbanGenoGAN project conducted in Aljezur, Portugal. This innovative approach integrates GANs, genetic optimization algorithms, and Geographic

Information Systems (GIS) to create optimized urban plans. By learning from existing urban layouts, UrbanGenoGAN generates realistic visualizations of proposed developments, including detailed renderings of buildings, parks, and streetscapes. These AI-generated designs allow urban planners to assess the feasibility and potential impact of projects more effectively, enabling data-driven decision-making and fostering community engagement through clear and compelling visuals (Cheng et al., 2023).

Another practical application is the Urban Massing Generator, which has been utilized in Jakarta, Indonesia to automate the massing configuration process for high-density urban housing. Jakarta, known for its rapid urbanization, faces significant challenges in optimizing land use while maintaining livability. The Urban Massing Generator uses AI-driven tools to generate different design options rapidly. It allows planners to explore various configurations, assess their impact on the built environment, and make informed decisions that optimize space and accessibility. This AI-driven approach streamlines the urban planning process and enhances efficiency in massing studies, making it an important tool for urban development in densely populated areas (Wibowo & Soedarsono, 2021).

These case studies illustrate how AI-powered visualization tools are transforming urban planning by generating realistic and adaptable designs, improving stakeholder communication, and enabling planners to better anticipate challenges and community needs. By integrating GANs and optimization techniques, cities like Aljezur and Jakarta are using AI to create more sustainable, efficient, and inclusive urban spaces.

Generating Scenarios for Environmental Impact Assessments

Environmental planning is an essential aspect of urban planning, aimed at assessing whether new developments are sustainable and do not adversely impact the environment. GenAI can play an important role in this domain by enabling planners to generate detailed and realistic scenarios for environmental impact assessments (EIAs). These scenarios help planners understand the potential environmental consequences of their projects and make informed decisions to mitigate negative impacts.

GenAI models such as GANs and VAEs can simulate a wide range of environmental conditions based on historical data and predictive algorithms. These simulations provide valuable insights into how urban developments might affect factors like air quality, water resources, and ecosystem health. By using these AI-generated scenarios, planners can conduct comprehensive EIAs that consider various environmental variables and their interactions.

One of the key advantages of using GenAI for environmental planning is its ability to model complex systems and predict outcomes under different conditions, providing planners with a powerful tool for scenario analysis and decision-making. Unlike traditional methods of environmental impact assessment, which are often constrained by the availability and granularity of data, GenAI can synthesize diverse datasets, identify hidden patterns, and generate high-resolution simulations to fill in data gaps. For example, in coastal resilience planning, GenAI can integrate satellite imagery, climate models, and land-use data to simulate the effects of rising sea levels on urban infrastructure. Generating detailed flood risk maps under different climate scenarios allows planners to evaluate potential mitigation strategies, such as the placement of flood barriers, wetland restoration, or adaptive zoning regulations. This ability to create data-driven projections enhances the accuracy and comprehensiveness of environmental assessments, ultimately leading to more informed and proactive planning decisions.

Communications

LLMs, in particular, can significantly enhance urban planning practices by automating labor-intensive processes and supporting communication between planners and the public. They can assist in drafting proposals, policy briefs, and zoning documents, saving time while ensuring consistency in language and structure. This is particularly useful for urban planning offices with limited staff or resources. LLMs can also analyze public feedback collected through surveys or public meetings, identifying recurring themes and summarizing citizen input in clear, actionable terms. This enables planners to engage communities more effectively by quickly processing large volumes of unstructured feedback.

Another important application of LLMs is chatbot integration for community engagement. LLM-powered chatbots can answer residents' questions about zoning, permitting, and public events, providing real-time, accessible information. These chatbots help bridge communication gaps between city officials and the public, especially in large cities where direct interaction with every resident is impractical. In multicultural cities, LLMs can provide real-time translations of planning documents and public notices, ensuring equitable access to critical information for non-English-speaking residents. They also aid knowledge management by summarizing technical documents and organizing urban planning archives, making it easier for planners to access and apply relevant data.

LLMs can also play a critical role in intercity collaboration. By summarizing best practices and lessons learned from different municipalities, LLMs enable planners to exchange knowledge efficiently. This is particularly valuable for cities working on common challenges, such as affordable housing, green infrastructure, and public transportation.

Case Study: Large Language Models Enhancing Urban Planning and Community Engagement

A notable real-world application of LLMs in urban planning is the UrbanLLM project, which focuses on autonomous urban activity planning and management. This innovative approach integrates LLMs so as to enhance urban planning processes by automating complex tasks and improving communication between planners and the public. By using LLMs' natural language processing capabilities, UrbanLLM can analyze large urban datasets, optimize resource allocation, and generate policy recommendations. These features enable planners to draft proposals, policy briefs, and zoning documents efficiently, ensuring consistency, accuracy, and efficiency. This is particularly beneficial for urban planning offices with limited staff or resources. Additionally, UrbanLLM can process public feedback from surveys or meetings, identifying recurring themes and summarizing citizen input into clear, actionable insights, thereby enhancing community engagement and data-driven decision-making (Cheng et al., 2024).

Another practical application is the use of AI-powered chatbots to enhance citizen engagement in city services. For instance, the city of Lansing, Michigan, has implemented AI-based chatbots on municipal websites to assist residents with zoning, permitting, and public service inquiries. These chatbots provide real-time, accessible information, effectively bridging communication gaps between city officials and the public. This approach is especially advantageous in large cities where direct interaction with every resident is impractical. Additionally, in multicultural communities, LLMs provide real-time translations of planning documents and public notices, ensuring equitable access to critical information for non-English-speaking residents. By automating routine inquiries, these AI chatbots free up municipal staff to focus on more complex planning tasks, ultimately improving the efficiency and responsiveness of city services (Michigan Municipal League, 2024).

These case studies illustrate how LLMs are transforming urban planning by automating labor-intensive processes, improving accessibility, and facilitating better communication between planners and the public. By integrating LLMs into planning workflows, municipalities can improve efficiency, foster greater community engagement, and make more informed, data-driven decisions.

ESSENTIAL STEPS TO IMPLEMENT GENERATIVE AI IN URBAN PLANNING PROJECTS

Implementing GenAI in urban planning projects involves several basic steps, from understanding the project requirements to deploying the AI-generated outputs. Here is a step-by-step guide to help urban planners navigate this process.

1. **Identify the project goals**. Start by clearly defining the project goals. Determine what you aim to achieve with GenAI, whether it is enhancing datasets, creating visualizations, simulating scenarios, or engaging with the community. Clear objectives will guide the selection of appropriate tools and models.
2. **Select the right tools and models**. Based on your project goals, choose the tools and platforms that best suit your needs.

Platforms like Runway ML and Google Colab are excellent starting points for beginners. Ensure that the chosen models are appropriate for the specific tasks, such as GANs for image generation or VAEs for data augmentation.

3. **Gather and prepare data.** Collect the necessary data for training and input it into the generative models. This might include images, urban layouts, environmental data, or textual descriptions. Ensure that the data is clean, relevant, and well-organized.

4. **Experiment and iterate.** Use the selected tools to experiment with GenAI models. Start with pre-trained models and gradually fine-tune them to better suit your specific needs. Iterate the models by adjusting parameters, incorporating feedback, and refining the outputs.

5. **Integrate and visualize.** Once you have generated the desired outputs, integrate them into your urban planning project. This might involve creating visualizations, augmenting datasets, or developing interactive models. Use the generated data to enhance analysis, presentations, and decision-making processes.

6. **Engage stakeholders.** Share the AI-generated outputs with stakeholders, including community members, decision-makers, and collaborators. Use realistic visualizations and interactive models to facilitate discussions, gather feedback, and build consensus.

Getting started with GenAI in urban planning involves selecting the right tools, following a straightforward implementation process, and using AI-generated outputs to enhance planning projects. By using accessible platforms and following these basic steps, urban planners can effectively integrate GenAI into their workflows, leading to more informed decisions, better visualizations, and increased community engagement.

Challenges of Generative AI

GenAI has the potential to transform the urban planning process, but it also comes with significant technical challenges that must be addressed for successful implementation. These challenges include training instability, the need for large datasets, and high computational demands. If not properly managed, these issues can limit the accuracy and reliability of AI-generated urban models and insights. However, with the right strategies, urban planners can overcome these hurdles and maximize AI's benefits.

One of the most significant difficulties in GenAI, particularly with GANs, is the instability of the training process. As discussed, GANs use two competing NNs: the generator, which creates synthetic data such as maps, zoning layouts, or traffic patterns; and the discriminator, which evaluates whether the generated data looks real or fake. Since these networks are constantly learning and adjusting, training can sometimes fail to reach a balance. A common issue is mode collapse, where the generator only produces a narrow range of outputs instead of diverse, realistic samples. Another challenge is oscillation, where the two networks struggle to settle, leading to inconsistent results. To improve stability, researchers have developed more advanced versions of GANs, such as WGANs, which modify how differences between actual and generated data are measured to create a smoother training process. Other techniques, such as the gradient penalty, help regulate training and prevent extreme fluctuations. These improvements result in more reliable models that generate high-quality urban planning outputs.

For GenAI to be effective in urban planning, large, high-quality datasets are required, but obtaining this data can be difficult. Privacy concerns may limit access to detailed urban records, some cities may lack comprehensive datasets, and collecting new data—such as satellite imagery, sensor readings, or traffic surveys—can be costly. Without enough training data, GenAI models may struggle to produce accurate and meaningful results. To address this, planners can use data augmentation, a technique that generates synthetic variations of existing data to expand the dataset without additional real-world data collection. This is especially useful for simulating different urban scenarios, such as alternative zoning plans or changes in traffic patterns. Another solution is transfer learning, where AI models that have already been trained on large, general datasets—such as global satellite images—can be fine-tuned using smaller, more specific datasets for a particular city or region. This reduces the need for extensive data collection while making AI models more applicable to local urban planning needs.

Another major challenge is the computational power required to train GenAI models. Large AI models can take days or weeks to process, making them impractical for planners who need timely results. Since not all planning offices have access to high-performance computing systems, cloud-based AI solutions can help. Platforms such as Google Colab, Amazon Web Services (AWS), and Microsoft Azure provide on-demand access to powerful computing resources, allowing planners to train models without needing to invest in expensive hardware. Cloud computing also enables scalability, meaning planners can adjust computing power based on project needs, making AI more accessible and cost-effective.

While GenAI presents challenges, the right approaches can manage these obstacles. By improving GAN stability, using data augmentation and transfer learning, and utilizing cloud-based computing solutions, urban planners can effectively integrate AI into their workflows. This will allow them to generate more accurate urban models, improve community engagement, and optimize planning processes in practical and scalable ways.

Looking Ahead

The future of GenAI in urban planning is quite promising, with several emerging trends set to revolutionize the field further. As technology continues to advance, urban planners can expect GenAI to become even more integrated into their workflows, providing new capabilities and efficiencies.

One significant trend is the increasing use of multimodal generative models. These models, which can handle multiple types of data simultaneously (such as text, images, and spatial data), will allow for more comprehensive and nuanced urban planning analyses. For example, a multimodal model could generate detailed urban landscapes by combining textual descriptions, geographic information, and visual data, providing a richer context for planning decisions.

Another trend is the improvement in AI's ability to simulate complex urban systems. As models become more sophisticated, they will be able to simulate a broader range of urban scenarios with greater accuracy. This includes not only environmental impacts but also social and economic dynamics. These advanced simulations can help planners anticipate and mitigate potential issues, leading to more resilient and adaptable urban designs.

The integration of GenAI with other emerging technologies, such as the Internet of Things (IoT) and augmented reality (AR), is also on the horizon. IoT devices can provide real-time data streams that GenAI models can use to update simulations and visualizations dynamically. Meanwhile, AR can enhance community engagement by allowing residents to experience proposed changes in their environment through immersive, interactive visualizations.

Ethical AI is another critical area of focus, particularly as AI systems become more embedded in urban planning and decision-making processes. Future developments will likely include more effective frameworks for ensuring fairness, accountability, and transparency in AI applications, addressing concerns about biased data, opaque decision-making processes, and unintended consequences. One key advancement will be the development of AI models that can actively detect and mitigate biases in urban datasets, ensuring that predictions and recommendations do not disproportionately favor certain demographic groups over others. For example, AI-driven housing policy tools could be designed to analyze historical zoning decisions and identify patterns of exclusion, enabling planners to counteract discriminatory practices proactively. Additionally, explainable AI (XAI) techniques will become more sophisticated, providing planners with clear, interpretable justifications for AI-generated recommendations rather than relying on black-box models. Accountability mechanisms, such as audit trails and regulatory oversight, will also be crucial, ensuring that AI applications in urban planning align with ethical standards and legal requirements.

GenAI provides significant potential for urban planning, enhancing efficiency, fostering community engagement, and supporting data-driven decision-making. However, to fully realize their benefits, planners must apply these tools thoughtfully. With the right approach, GenAI models can become indispensable tools in shaping inclusive, sustainable, and responsive urban environments.

Chapter Summary

GenAI represents a transformative technology with vast potential to enhance urban planning processes and outcomes. This chapter has explored GenAI's fundamental concepts and various applications in urban planning, highlighting its importance and practical benefits.

GenAI, through models like GANs and VAEs, allows urban planners to create synthetic data, realistic visualizations, and simulations that significantly improve the planning process. This technology can address the common challenge of limited or incomplete datasets by generating additional, high-quality data, leading to more effective and accurate predictive models.

In urban design and visualization, GenAI enables planners to produce detailed and lifelike representations of proposed projects. These visualizations enhance community engagement by making it easier for residents to understand and provide feedback on potential developments. They also help planners and stakeholders assess the feasibility and impact of different design options more effectively.

GenAI benefits environmental planning by providing simulations of various environmental scenarios. These simulations can predict pollution levels, climate impacts, and other environmental factors, helping planners develop strategies to mitigate negative effects and promote sustainability.

AI-generated interactive and realistic visualizations greatly enhance community engagement. These tools facilitate better communication and collaboration between planners and the public, ensuring that community members can actively participate in the planning process and that their voices are heard.

Collaboration with AI experts is crucial for the successful implementation of GenAI in urban planning projects. By working closely with data scientists and AI specialists, urban planners can leverage technical expertise to overcome challenges, promote the ethical use of AI, and integrate AI-generated insights into their workflows.

Ethical and practical considerations are paramount when using GenAI. Ensuring data privacy, mitigating biases, fostering transparency, and evaluating social impacts are essential steps to harnessing AI's power in urban planning responsibly.

References and Further Reading

Cheng, L., Chu, X., Xia, Y., Zhang, J., Chen, Y., Jia, Y., & Wang, S. (2023). UrbanGenoGAN: Pioneering urban spatial planning using the synergistic integration of GAN, GA, and GIS. *Frontiers in Environmental Science*, 11, 1287858. https://www.frontiersin.org/articles/10.3389/fenvs.2023.1287858/full

Cheng, L., Wang, X., Liu, J., & Xia, Y. (2024). UrbanLLM: Enhancing Urban Planning with Large Language Models. *Findings of the 2024 Conference on Empirical Methods in Natural Language Processing (EMNLP)*. Retrieved from https://aclanthology.org/2024.findings-emnlp.98.pdf

Michigan Municipal League. (2024). AI in Action: Case Studies from Michigan Communities. Retrieved from https://blogs.mml.org/wp/events/files/2024/09/AI-in-Action-Case-Studies-from-Michigan-Communities.pdf

Wibowo, A., & Soedarsono, J. W. (2021). A Study of Concept Design Massing Generator for Urban Houses in Jakarta. *Proceedings of the 4th International Conference on Sustainable Innovation 2020—Technology, Engineering and Agriculture (ICoSITEA, 2020)*, 192–198. https://www.researchgate.net/publication/353651142_A_Study_of_Concept_Design_Massing_Generator_for_Urban_Houses_in_Jakarta

Zhao, L., Wang, X., Chen, Y., & Liu, J. (2024). *Enhancing Urban Landscape Design with Conditional GANs: A Data-Augmented Approach*. Land, 13(2), 254. https://www.mdpi.com/2073-445X/13/2/254

7

CHALLENGES TO ADOPTING AI IN URBAN PLANNING

Adopting artificial intelligence (AI) tools in urban planning presents a host of exciting opportunities, but also significant challenges that must be carefully navigated to achieve practical and ethical outcomes. AI technologies are already transforming the planning and management of urban environments, enabling the analysis of vast datasets, the simulation of complex urban systems, and the generation of innovative solutions. However, as these technologies are integrated more deeply into urban planning processes, they bring with them complexities that require deliberate attention. Proactively identifying those challenges and understanding potential adverse disruptive effects will be important for effective adoption.

Some of the anticipated challenges urban planners face when adopting AI technology are technical. These include bias in AI systems, error and misapplication of AI tools, poor data quality and availability, and ensuring that new AI tools are integrated with existing systems. Other anticipated challenges relate to organizational and practitioner needs.

DOI: 10.4324/9781003476818-7

These include unclear goals for AI adoption and use, fear and uncertainty that can fuel resistance to change, the need for new skills to understand and optimize the use of new AI tools, and the costs of procuring AI tools, training staff, and maintaining the necessary infrastructure.

Significant challenges also exist regarding the legality and ethics of data collection and AI use. These include data privacy and confidentiality, data security, legal and regulatory barriers, and ethical use of data and AI. Addressing stakeholder concerns and developing public trust through transparency is also key to the successful adoption of these technologies.

Understanding these challenges provides a foundation for strategic action. By identifying barriers early, planners can develop targeted strategies to mitigate them. Acknowledging public concerns fosters trust and affirms that AI initiatives align with community values. Furthermore, these challenges highlight areas for future research and innovation, driving the development of tools and frameworks tailored to the unique needs of urban planning.

In navigating these complexities, urban planners have added responsibilities that may not be the case with other analytical tools. By addressing these challenges thoughtfully and proactively, the profession can ensure that AI technologies are not only powerful tools for innovation but also catalysts for effective plan-making.

Technical Challenges

As urban planners increasingly integrate AI technologies into their practices, several technical challenges must be navigated so that these tools are effective, fair, and reliable. Key issues include bias, error and misapplication, and poor data quality and availability. This section highlights these challenges, their impact on urban planning, and strategies for mitigation.

Bias

The extent to which human biases can infiltrate AI systems and cause detrimental outcomes has become a topic of significant discussion in recent years (Roselli et al., 2019). As artificial intelligence becomes more deeply embedded in decision-making processes across industries—ranging from

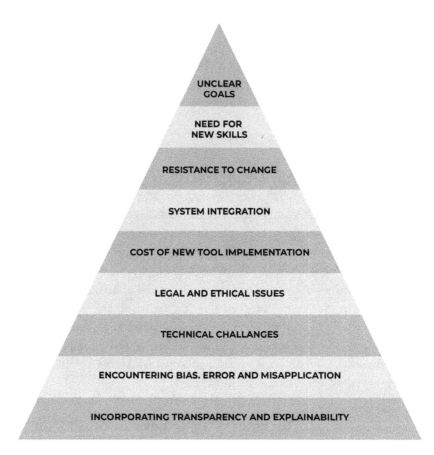

Figure 7.1 Challenges involved with AI adoption.

healthcare and finance to urban planning and criminal justice—concerns about the fairness, accountability, and transparency of AI systems have grown. AI models are often trained on historical data, which may reflect societal inequities, implicit biases, and systemic discrimination. When these biases are not adequately addressed, AI-driven decisions can reinforce or even amplify existing disparities, leading to unintended and potentially harmful consequences for individuals and communities.

Algorithmic bias occurs when AI models produce systematically prejudiced outcomes due to biases present in the training data or the model's design. These biases can stem from historical data that reflect past inequities, sampling bias where the dataset is not representative of an entire population, or measurement bias due to inconsistent data collection methods. For instance, zoning laws and urban development policies that historically marginalized specific communities may introduce bias into AI models trained on such data. Inaccurate or incomplete datasets will produce fundamentally flawed rules, so training data must accurately reflect the population by representing every demographic category. According to several studies, dark-skinned females are mistakenly identified by facial recognition 40 percent more frequently than white males (U.S. GAO, 2020). Nonrepresentative training data sets are mostly to blame for this.

Biased AI models can have far-reaching consequences in urban planning, potentially exacerbating existing inequalities and leading to unfair or harmful decisions. Examples include inequitable resource allocation, where biased models prioritize infrastructure improvements in wealthier neighborhoods while neglecting underserved communities, or discriminatory zoning practices that reinforce exclusionary policies, limiting access to housing and services for marginalized groups. Moreover, biased traffic data can result in AI systems that unfairly distribute traffic congestion relief measures, disproportionately benefiting certain areas over others.

Planners can employ several strategies to address these issues. Bias detection techniques, such as statistical analysis and fairness metrics, are crucial for identifying biases in training data and model outputs. Ensuring diverse and representative datasets by actively collecting data from underrepresented groups and regions can help mitigate bias. Incorporating fairness constraints and regularization techniques into the model training process can further minimize bias, while continuous monitoring of AI models throughout their lifecycle ensures ongoing bias detection and mitigation. It is also important to immediately resolve any instances we witness of bias in AI.

There may be no easy fixes in these cases, however. Defining and assessing "fairness" can be challenging. Researchers have devised technical definitions of fairness, such as mandating that models have similar outcome values across socioeconomic groups (Corbett-Davies & Goel, 2018). Different fairness criteria typically cannot be satisfied at the same time, which is a considerable challenge. However, researchers have made strides in strategies that can improve how AI systems match fairness requirements and metrics, whether by pre-processing data, reviewing results, or embedding appropriate and transparent rules as part of the data training process (Corbett-Davies & Goel, 2018). "Counterfactual fairness" is a method that ensures a model's conclusions would be valid even if sensitive characteristics like race, gender, or sexual orientation were modified (Kusner et al., 2017). This approach can be used in complex situations in which some impacts from sensitive qualities that affect outcomes are viewed as fair while others are viewed as unfair. The model could be used, for instance, to validate that an applicant's race had no bearing on whether or not they were approved for a mortgage while still allowing the lender to include race as demographic information for later reporting. AI can assist people in overcoming bias, but only if collaboration among stakeholders seeks to address bias in AI.

Error and Misapplication

For example, false positives might involve incorrectly identifying a neighborhood as highly vulnerable to gentrification, leading to unnecessary policy interventions that restrict development and limit housing supply. In contrast, false negatives might fail to detect actual displacement risks, allowing unchecked development to push out long-term residents. Similarly, in transportation planning, a false positive could incorrectly classify an intersection as highly congested, prompting costly infrastructure upgrades that may not be needed. In contrast, a false negative might fail to identify a truly congested area, leading to persistent traffic delays and reduced mobility. In flood risk management, a false positive might designate an area as high risk for flooding, leading to unnecessary investments in flood control infrastructure, while a false negative could overlook a genuinely vulnerable area, leaving it unprepared for extreme weather events. In infrastructure maintenance, a false positive might incorrectly identify a structurally sound bridge as unsafe, leading to unnecessary closures and costly repairs, while a false negative could fail to detect actual structural weaknesses, increasing the risk of collapse. Finally, in land-use planning, a false positive might misidentify an area as suitable for high-density development despite infrastructure constraints, leading to overburdened utilities and transportation networks, while a false negative could exclude viable areas from development, exacerbating housing shortages.

These errors can lead to the misallocation of resources, public safety risks, and loss of trust in AI systems. Misallocated resources might mean deploying emergency services to areas that do not need them while neglecting areas that do. At the same time, inaccurate predictions can undermine public safety by failing to identify areas prone to natural disasters or structural failures. Persistent errors can also erode trust among planners, policymakers, and the public, hindering the adoption of AI technologies.

To mitigate these issues, planners should use effective validation techniques, such as cross-validation, which systematically evaluates model performance by repeatedly training and testing on different subsets of data, and bootstrapping, which assesses model stability and uncertainty by repeatedly sampling the dataset with replacement, to evaluate model reliability and generalizability comprehensively.

Thorough error analysis helps understand the types and sources of errors, allowing for targeted improvements. Ensemble methods, which combine predictions from multiple individual models into a single aggregated prediction, can significantly enhance accuracy and reduce errors by using diverse modeling approaches and reducing reliance on any single model's performance.

Regularly updating models with new data and retraining them to adapt to changing conditions is essential for maintaining accuracy and reducing the likelihood of errors. As urban environments evolve due to factors such as population growth, economic shifts, climate change, and technological advancements, AI models that rely on outdated data can become unreliable or even misleading. For example, transportation demand models must be updated to reflect new commuting patterns influenced by remote work or expanded transit networks. Similarly, land-use and zoning models should incorporate recent development trends, regulatory changes, and demographic shifts to confirm that planning decisions remain relevant and effective. If AI systems are not regularly refreshed with current data, their predictions may lead to suboptimal policy choices, misallocated resources, or missed opportunities for proactive planning.

Beyond simply updating data inputs, model retraining also provides an opportunity to reassess and refine algorithms, improve fairness and transparency, and correct biases that may emerge over time. AI models are susceptible to concept drift, where patterns in data change over time, making past predictions less reliable. For instance, an AI system used to predict flood risks must be updated with new climate projections, rainfall data, and infrastructure modifications to avoid false alarms or overlooked vulnerabilities. Retraining also allows for incorporating expert feedback, adjusting model parameters, and using new machine learning (ML) techniques that enhance predictive performance. By prioritizing regular updates and retraining, urban planners and policymakers can affirm that AI-driven tools remain responsive to current realities and continue to support equitable, data-informed decision-making.

Data Quality and Availability

High-quality data is the foundation of effective AI models. Accurate, comprehensive, and up-to-date data ensures that models can learn effectively and make reliable predictions. In urban planning, high-quality data is crucial for tasks such as traffic management, environmental monitoring, and infrastructure planning (Boeing et al., 2021). One of the biggest obstacles to AI implementation, however, is the lack of sufficient high-quality data (Roh et al., 2019).

Obtaining reliable and comprehensive data for urban planning presents several challenges. Urban data is often fragmented across different sources and agencies, making it difficult to compile a comprehensive dataset. Variations in data collection methods and standards can result in inconsistent and unreliable data. Privacy concerns and regulatory restrictions can limit access to certain types of data, such as individual mobility patterns or detailed demographic information. In some cases, the data will need to be anonymized, which is standard practice for data collected by the U.S. Census. This includes approaches such as "data swapping," which transfers data points from one observation to another, increasing security but potentially decreasing the value of the data for analysis to conclude real-world situations (U.S. Census Bureau, 2021).

To improve data quality and handle missing or incomplete data, planners can develop systems and standards for integrating data from diverse sources, ensuring consistency and completeness. Implementing rigorous data cleaning processes and techniques such as imputation, outlier detection, and normalization can help address inaccuracies, inconsistencies, and missing values. Encouraging collaboration and data sharing among different agencies, organizations, and stakeholders can help build more comprehensive and reliable datasets. Using external data sources, such as satellite imagery, open data platforms, and crowdsourced data, can supplement and enhance existing datasets.

Integration with Existing Systems

Integration with existing systems presents another significant challenge for adopting AI in urban planning. Cities rely extensively on legacy systems, such as geographic information systems (GIS), transportation modeling software, permitting and zoning databases, and other long-established planning platforms. Many of these tools were designed before the widespread emergence of AI and ML methods, leading to compatibility issues, such as incompatible data formats, outdated architectures, or closed software ecosystems. These obstacles often mean that modern AI tools cannot efficiently or effectively interface with legacy systems, creating substantial barriers to seamless adoption, slowing innovation, and potentially increasing implementation costs.

To effectively address this challenge, cities must prioritize scalable and modular AI solutions, meaning these tools can be incrementally integrated into current infrastructures rather than require complete replacement. Modular solutions enable cities to gradually incorporate AI capabilities, adapting and expanding functionalities over time with less disruption. Furthermore, planners should actively invest in interoperability technologies, such as standardized Application Programming Interfaces (APIs), open data formats, and flexible data pipelines. By focusing on these strategies, planners can foster smoother integration between existing platforms and innovative AI methods, ultimately enabling more efficient, effective, and sustainable technological advancements across urban planning processes.

Organizational and Practitioner Challenges

The successful adoption of AI in urban planning involves far more than investments in new technology, datasets, and employee training. Organizations frequently encounter challenges related to unclear or ambiguous goals, resistance to change among practitioners, gaps in necessary skill sets, and significant financial costs. Even substantial investments in upgraded hardware, specialized training programs, or comprehensive data collection efforts do not guarantee successful implementation if these underlying organizational and practitioner barriers are not addressed. Effective performance management, clear strategic objectives, proactive change management, targeted skill development, and careful cost planning are essential for investments in AI to yield meaningful, sustainable improvements in planning practice.

Unclear Goals

Without clear and well-defined goals, even the most sophisticated AI systems and well-intentioned efforts can falter, leading to inefficiencies, unmet expectations, and wasted opportunities. A lack of clear goals can result in a misalignment of time, money, and talent. For example, a company may purchase advanced AI tools or spend considerable time training staff without a precise understanding of how these actions will contribute to specific outcomes. This lack of alignment can result in underused tools and missed opportunities, undermining the very purpose of adopting AI.

Vague goals make it difficult to measure success and improve iteratively. Effective performance management relies on the ability to track progress against defined benchmarks. For instance, an organization might aim to "improve productivity" by using AI. However, without specifying what this means—whether it is reducing processing times, increasing output, or streamlining decision-making—it becomes impossible to assess whether the initiative is delivering value and identify what is working, what is not, and where adjustments are needed. Clearly defined goals provide a framework for assessing progress and making data-driven changes. For instance, if an organization aims to reduce energy usage by

25% using AI, periodic reviews can reveal whether the initiative is on track or if modifications are required.

Unclear goals can also lead to inconsistent decision-making within the organization. Different teams or departments may pursue conflicting priorities if they do not share a unified understanding of what the AI initiative aims to achieve. One team might focus on cutting costs, while another prioritizes innovation. This lack of cohesion can slow progress and dilute the overall impact of AI adoption, leaving the organization without a clear path forward.

Employees can also become confused or disengaged when goals are unclear. Without a clear understanding of why the organization is adopting AI and what is expected, employees may feel disconnected from the process. This uncertainty can lead to resistance, as they perceive the new technology as a vague solution, looking for a problem rather than as a tool designed to address specific challenges. Communicating clear goals helps employees understand how their roles contribute to the broader initiative, fostering engagement and reducing skepticism.

Unclear goals also make it difficult to assign responsibility or to identify where failures occur. For instance, if an organization sets a goal to "enhance data capabilities," it is unclear who is responsible for various components, such as collecting the data, building AI models, or implementing insights. Clear goals help delineate roles and responsibilities, ensuring that everyone involved knows their part in achieving success.

To avoid these pitfalls, organizations should start with a distinct vision for the use of AI and prioritize goal-setting as a primary step in AI adoption. Goals should be specific, measurable, actionable, relevant, and time-bound (SMART). For example, instead of a broad goal like "enhance customer service," an organization might aim to "reduce customer query resolution times by 20% within six months using an AI-powered chatbot." Engaging stakeholders across departments ensures goals are aligned with broader organizational priorities, while regular reviews allow for adjustments as needs evolve. The vision and goals, together with long- and short-term objectives, should be communicated to staff clearly and frequently. Coordinated oversight and evaluation of AI use within the organization is also important for goals to be met, aims to be achieved, and budget resources to be appropriate.

Resistance to Change

Cultural and institutional resistance to change can hinder the integration of AI into urban planning. Planners and decision-makers may be skeptical about AI's reliability or fear its impact on employment and decision-making autonomy.

Fear and uncertainty are inevitable during the transition to new technologies along the road to digital transformation. Though fear can be an effective decision-making motivator, it can also deter us from making significant changes or from taking actions that might be advantageous in the long run. Anxiety can be a warning indication of a potentially poor choice, signaling that the suggested course of action has a sizable risk. Suppose a planning department is considering adopting AI technologies; in that case, it is therefore important to make sure that staff are fully informed about AI and involved in assessing perceived risks to adoption.

Three related types of fear generally shape adoption anxiety: fear of making the decision, fear of the unknown, and fear of failure (Hindle, 2021; Rogers et al., 2014).

- **Fear of making the decision**. When faced with important decisions, our fear of the consequences of making the wrong choice can cause us to take no action or minimize the advantages of innovation. Understanding the organizational context, the dangers of doing nothing, and the risks of various potential solutions is crucial. Clearly outline the project's goals, the benefits of applying AI, and the risk of not achieving those goals. Identifying and addressing any dangers that the technology may introduce can help to take advantage of the opportunity. The decision-making process should be analytical, fact-driven, and focused on the opportunity balanced with the risk.
- **Fear of the unknown**. When something is unfamiliar to us, we often focus on the potential dangers of change rather than the hazards of inaction. Solving this requires understanding the innovation or technology under consideration—both the big picture and the technical details. Even when we understand how the solution is supposed to function, embracing new technology can be scary. Support from technology providers, including communication, collaboration, and training, can help overcome this fear.

- **Fear of failure**. Fears of failure may include concerns that the technology is untested, that it will not work for a particular use case, or that the transition to or adoption of the technology will not proceed smoothly. Demonstrations of the technology can help, as can testimonials from others using the technology to learn what has and has not worked for them. Understanding the technology and assessing its advantages and risks towards achieving project goals is key.

Effective communication is essential for overcoming resistance to change. Managers should put themselves in the position of their staff and determine how the adoption of new technology will affect their day-to-day activities, both positively and negatively. Leaders should also identify the supporters and detractors of the new technology. Internal champions are essential for promoting new technologies, and they are frequently those who are closest to the day-to-day activities of individual planners or staff. The change will go more smoothly if the main advantages and justification for new technology are communicated, especially to the doubters. Buy-in does not happen when technology is pursued simply for technology's sake.

The Need for New Skills

The increasing digitalization of urban planning will require planners to learn new skills. However, AI is not the only driver of this change. Today's workplace is in a constant state of change with new technologies, changes in workplace culture, and evolving business practices. For many professions, the COVID-19 pandemic required the rapid adoption of video conferencing technologies and protocols to accommodate remote work, and electronic alternatives quickly replaced in-person contact. By necessity, we managed to learn new technologies quickly, some of which replaced long-standing previous practices. Updating skill sets to keep up with such changes is becoming a given.

Though most planners will not be directly involved with developing new AI applications, they may be engaging with technologists, such as computer scientists and application developers, to help them do so. Planners must know enough about AI to use these tools in effective and responsible ways. They must represent the interests of community stakeholders and ensure AI is being implemented in ways that will meet community goals. Generally, to stay relevant in a changing world, planners will need to know about these technologies and be prepared to engage with other disciplines involved in shaping the urban landscape, such as civil engineers, architects, landscape architects, and public administrators.

The successful implementation of these new methodologies will also require new expertise in data analytic techniques and information systems. Compounding this challenge, especially for public agencies, is that many planners are not effectively trained in essential elements of data management (Batty, 2021; Sarker et al., 2018). Without effective IT management practices, planning organizations can find it difficult to answer basic questions, such as how many databases an organization has, which database contains a particular piece of information, or how data was initially collected. Within organizations, siloed functional groups and poor communication create challenges for sharing data resources with coworkers, particularly for policymakers and administrators. Given that AI techniques rely heavily on data, these are serious issues.

The skills needed to adopt AI will differ among planners depending on their roles and responsibilities. As discussed in this report, they may include learning a new vocabulary of AI-related terminology, new software packages, programming languages, advanced statistical methods, and other AI-related concepts. Upskilling to learn and maintain these skills will be an important element of adopting these new methods (Andrews et al., 2022). Planning organizations may need to prioritize the recruitment of planners with AI expertise.

Cost

The cost of adopting AI technologies represents a significant barrier, particularly for smaller municipalities with constrained financial resources. Procuring advanced AI tools, upgrading hardware, acquiring extensive datasets, and training staff in specialized skills can place considerable pressure on limited municipal budgets. For instance, investing in high-performance computing infrastructure required for sophisticated traffic simulations, predictive modeling for land-use planning, or smart sensors for real-time environmental monitoring can often surpass the financial capacities of smaller or rural communities.

This challenge can amplify existing inequities, exacerbating the digital divide by enabling only wealthier or larger cities, such as New York City or San Francisco, to afford advanced AI-driven planning systems, leaving smaller municipalities further behind. As wealthier cities continue to advance technologically—integrating real-time traffic analytics, AI-powered predictive crime modeling, or sophisticated digital twins—less affluent communities risk becoming increasingly disconnected from innovations that could significantly improve service delivery and decision-making.

Creative and diversified funding solutions are essential to mitigate these disparities. Public–private partnerships (PPPs) provide one avenue for addressing budget constraints, enabling municipalities to share costs and risks associated with technology investments. For example, a city might collaborate with private transportation companies to deploy AI-driven mobility solutions or partner with technology firms to develop innovative streetlight systems that collect valuable urban data. Additionally, federal, state, or regional grants dedicated explicitly to technology modernization and digital equity initiatives can provide municipalities with essential funding to support AI adoption.

Open-source AI tools and platforms represent another practical alternative to costly proprietary solutions, making advanced technologies more accessible to resource-constrained communities. Open-source software, such as QGIS for geospatial analytics, TensorFlow and PyTorch for ML applications, or OpenStreetMap for collaborative mapping, allows smaller cities to leverage powerful AI capabilities without heavy licensing fees. By combining open-source resources with strategic partnerships and targeted grant opportunities, smaller municipalities can more effectively participate in the benefits of AI innovations, reducing the risk of widening the technological gap between communities.

Legal and Ethical Challenges

As urban planners increasingly integrate AI technologies into decision-making processes, the collection, use, and storage of vast amounts of data raise significant privacy and confidentiality concerns. AI-driven urban planning often relies on extensive datasets, including geospatial information, transportation patterns, socioeconomic demographics, and even real-time surveillance or sensor data. While these data sources enhance predictive capabilities and enable more informed planning decisions, they also introduce risks related to data security, unauthorized access, and the potential misuse of personal or sensitive information. Public trust in AI-powered urban planning depends on ensuring that data is collected responsibly, stored securely, and used in ways that respect individuals' privacy rights.

Addressing these concerns is critical to ensuring ethical practices and compliance with legal and regulatory standards. Many jurisdictions have implemented data protection laws, such as the General Data Protection Regulation (GDPR) in Europe and various privacy acts in the United States, which place strict requirements on how personal data is collected, processed, and stored. Urban planners and AI practitioners must navigate these legal frameworks while also implementing effective data governance policies, including anonymization techniques, data minimization strategies, and secure storage solutions. Transparency in data usage, clear communication about privacy safeguards, and public engagement in data-driven planning initiatives are essential to maintaining public trust.

This section explores key issues related to data collection, privacy risks, and the importance of maintaining confidentiality in AI-driven urban planning. It examines challenges such as balancing the need for detailed urban data with the imperative to protect personal information, ensuring data security in an era of increasing cyber threats, and adopting best practices for ethical data handling. By addressing these concerns proactively, urban planners can leverage AI to improve cities while safeguarding the rights and privacy of the communities they serve.

Data Privacy and Confidentiality

The integration of AI in urban planning involves the collection and analysis of vast amounts of data, including personal and sensitive information. This raises several privacy concerns that must be addressed to protect individuals' rights and maintain ethical standards.

Privacy concerns stem from the potential misuse of personal data, unauthorized access, and the risk of data breaches. For instance, data collected from smart city sensors, traffic cameras, and social media platforms can include detailed information about individuals' movements, behaviors, and preferences. Without proper safeguards, this data could be exploited for malicious purposes or result in unintended consequences.

The legal and ethical implications of data collection in urban planning are significant. Laws and regulations, such as the GDPR in the European Union, set stringent requirements for data protection and privacy. These regulations mandate that data collection practices must be transparent, data subjects must provide informed consent, and organizations must implement effective security measures to protect data. In the United States, the GDPR, Payment Card Industry Data Security Standard (PCI DSS), Health Insurance Portability and Accountability Act (HIPAA), Federal Information Security Management Act of 2002 (FISMA), Family Educational Rights and Privacy Act (FERPA), and Gramm-Leach-Bliley Act are just a few of the laws that forbid the use of confidential or sensitive information (i.e., personally identifiable information, or personally identifiable information (PII)) as input for ML models (Moallem, 2018). While urban planners have not often used credit cards, health care, or educational data in the past, the increasing ubiquity of data collection and its commercialization will require ethical decisions about the appropriateness of specific data that may reveal personal identities.

Several techniques can help secure data privacy and protection:

- **Anonymization**: Transforming personal data into a form that cannot be traced back to individuals. Techniques include removing or masking identifiers and aggregating data to ensure anonymity.
- **Secure data storage**: Implementing effective security measures to protect data from unauthorized access and breaches. This includes encryption, access controls, and regular security audits.
- **Data minimization**: Collecting only the data necessary for specific purposes and retaining it only for as long as needed. This reduces the risk of data misuse and exposure.

Maintaining confidentiality in urban planning data is crucial for several reasons. It protects sensitive information, such as the locations of critical infrastructure and personal details of residents, from unauthorized access and misuse. Ensuring confidentiality also fosters public trust, as individuals are more likely to support AI initiatives if they believe their data is being handled responsibly and securely. The box on p. xx provides several case study examples of how cities around the world have addressed data privacy and confidentiality concerns.

PROTECTING DATA PRIVACY AND CONFIDENTIALITY

The following case studies illustrate the diversity in approaches to privacy across global cities. While local governments may employ different strategies—decentralization, transparency, ethics frameworks, or data minimization—they all strive to build public trust so that AI enhances urban planning without compromising privacy.

Barcelona's Decentralized Data and Citizen Control

In Barcelona, Spain, the city launched the Decentralized Citizen Owned Data Ecosystem (DECODE) initiative to ensure residents control their data while enabling urban planners to use AI for better public services. The DECODE project empowers residents by providing them with tools to decide what data to share and under what conditions, addressing privacy concerns in AI applications. This data-sharing framework supports the city's efforts to improve air quality monitoring, mobility systems, and energy efficiency. AI models in the initiative operate exclusively on anonymized or aggregated datasets, reducing the risks of reidentification. Encryption and blockchain technologies add further protection by ensuring that shared data remains secure and tamper-proof. Barcelona's success in balancing innovative AI solutions with privacy through resident control has become a model for other cities seeking to adopt decentralized approaches to data governance.

Helsinki's Transparency in AI-Driven Mobility Solutions

Helsinki, Finland, has implemented AI-powered tools to improve public transportation planning by optimizing routes, monitoring congestion, and analyzing mobility patterns. To maintain public trust and protect personal privacy, the AI models rely on pseudonymization techniques, masking personal identifiers such as GPS data before analysis, ensuring that individuals cannot be tracked. Helsinki also promotes transparency by publishing anonymized mobility datasets on open-data platforms, encouraging public participation and independent analysis. In addition, the city provides a digital platform where residents can view, manage, and control what data is collected about their movements through public transit systems. This participatory approach allows citizens to decide whether and how their data can be used, strengthening trust between the public and the city government. Helsinki's initiative showcases how AI can deliver data-driven improvements in urban planning while safeguarding individual privacy and encouraging civic engagement.

Singapore's Data Trust Framework for Smart Nation Projects

Singapore's "Smart Nation" initiative leverages AI across multiple urban planning domains, including traffic management, energy distribution, and predictive policing. To address privacy concerns, AI models used in Smart Nation projects are trained on anonymized datasets and operate within strict access controls. Sensitive information is encrypted, and only authorized individuals have access to raw data. Additionally, Singapore has developed AI ethics guidelines that ensure algorithms are used responsibly and transparently, with regular impact assessments to detect potential privacy risks. For example, in predictive policing efforts, the AI models are trained on historical data while avoiding sensitive attributes that could lead to biased outcomes. Data governance policies are overseen by regulatory bodies to maintain continuous accountability and compliance with privacy standards. This approach allows Singapore to apply AI for urban innovation while safeguarding personal data and promoting trust among citizens and stakeholders.

San Francisco's Data Privacy in Predictive Policing and Housing Policy

In the U.S., the city of San Francisco has integrated AI tools to support housing policy development and crime reduction while addressing privacy and equity concerns. Predictive policing models analyze historical crime data to forecast high-risk areas, helping police departments to allocate resources more efficiently. However, to avoid potential privacy violations and profiling, the city adopted a data minimization strategy, ensuring that the AI models only process the minimum data necessary. Sensitive information is stripped from datasets, and the algorithms are trained using aggregated data to prevent individual identification. In housing policy, AI tools help identify trends in rental prices and housing availability, supporting planners in developing affordable housing strategies. Privacy audits and impact assessments are conducted regularly to ensure that AI systems align with ethical standards and do not inadvertently contribute to discrimination. San Francisco's initiatives illustrate how local governments can use AI to address complex urban challenges while mitigating risks of bias and ensuring transparent, privacy-conscious data practices.

Data Security

Data security presents another critical challenge in adopting AI for urban planning. As planners increasingly leverage data from diverse sources—including Internet of Things (IoT) sensors, surveillance cameras, smart transit systems, and mobile applications—the volume and variety of data collected grow significantly. While this expanded data ecosystem enables planners to gain rich, detailed insights into mobility patterns, land use, environmental quality, and public safety, it simultaneously raises serious privacy and security concerns. Much of the collected data, such as real-time location data from smartphones, license plate recognition from surveillance systems, or demographic details from citizen feedback apps, often contains sensitive PII.

Without effective governance frameworks and clearly defined responsibilities, these valuable but sensitive datasets become highly vulnerable to misuse, unauthorized access, and security breaches, potentially resulting in compromised privacy, legal liability, and significant damage to public trust.

Urban planners and their IT departments share distinct but complementary responsibilities for addressing data security:

- **Urban planners** typically have primary responsibility for defining what data is collected, ensuring its appropriateness for planning objectives, and clearly communicating these purposes to stakeholders. They must advocate for privacy-conscious data practices, including minimizing the collection of sensitive information and ensuring that data is used ethically and transparently. Planners are also responsible for understanding and adhering to privacy regulations, such as the GDPR, the California Consumer Privacy Act (CCPA), or other local privacy laws, and ensuring compliance when developing plans, making policy decisions, and sharing data externally.
- **IT department staff**, on the other hand, are primarily responsible for implementing technical safeguards and ensuring infrastructure security. They handle measures such as encryption of data at rest and in transit, anonymization or pseudonymization processes, regular security audits, and strict data access controls. IT professionals manage secure storage solutions, configure secure access protocols, maintain firewalls and intrusion detection systems, and respond promptly to potential breaches or cyber threats. Additionally, IT departments provide guidance and technical support to planners about secure data management practices and regulatory compliance requirements.

Urban planners and IT staff should collaborate closely, establishing comprehensive data governance policies, including clearly defined roles and responsibilities, secure data management protocols, periodic security reviews, and privacy impact assessments. By jointly ensuring effective data security practices, urban planning agencies can confidently use data-driven and AI-based solutions, safeguarding individuals' privacy, maintaining compliance with regulatory standards, and ultimately protecting the public's trust in how cities use emerging technologies.

Legal and Regulatory Barriers

Legal and regulatory barriers add another significant layer of complexity to the adoption of AI in urban planning. Existing legal frameworks around AI use, data privacy, liability, and ethical considerations often lag behind the rapid pace of technological advancement, leaving planners uncertain about acceptable practices and potential legal risks. For example, regulations surrounding data collection through public sensors, surveillance cameras, or mobile apps may be ambiguous or nonexistent in many municipalities. This creates uncertainty about planners' responsibilities and permissible uses of this data.

Rather than expecting individual planners to shape or establish new AI regulations directly—tasks typically beyond the scope and influence of everyday planning practice—planners can take practical steps within their capacity. A realistic approach includes first checking whether their city or municipality already has policies or guidelines related to AI or data usage. If no clear policies exist, planners should proactively seek guidance by consulting with their local government's legal department or senior leadership. Requesting clarity from local authorities on data privacy standards, data-sharing protocols, and acceptable uses of AI technologies is an achievable and practical starting point.

Additionally, planners can advocate internally within their organizations for the creation of clear and concise guidelines or operational frameworks around AI use, data governance, and privacy protections. For instance, working closely with municipal IT and legal teams to clarify appropriate data-handling practices, establishing documented data-sharing agreements with other municipal agencies, and developing internal ethical standards for AI implementation are steps planners can realistically take.

By engaging in these practical actions—such as clarifying existing guidelines, advocating internally for clear policies, and working directly with their city's legal or IT departments—planners can effectively navigate legal uncertainties without needing to assume responsibility for influencing higher-level regulatory processes beyond their roles. These actions support responsible and compliant AI use while helping planners mitigate legal and ethical risks within their immediate professional environments.

Ethical Considerations

The ethical implications of AI demand careful consideration. Planners should ask how AI decisions align with societal values and whether they contribute to the public good. AI and big data are increasingly associated with many aspects of our day-to-day lives. In the realm of urban planning and development, the data collection sensors of smart city initiatives capture human activities at different scales, collecting large amounts of data about us, both with and without our knowledge (Chang, 2021). Further, data is used to make decisions, such as medical diagnoses, credit reporting, and consumer recommendations, that we seem to have little control over. Other significant concerns include bias embedded in search engine results and algorithms (Noble, 2018), which can harm people with low incomes and reinforce racism and inequality (O'Neil, 2017; Eubanks, 2018).

Misapplications of AI have occurred in law enforcement, surveillance, mistaken identity, and hacking, and they have had negative impacts on individuals based on data or other information at the individual level. It is understandable that the public, as well as planners, might assume that similar adverse outcomes may arise while planning communities and neighborhoods. However, very few, if any, of the analyses that urban planners perform use individual-level data for individual persons, so it is unlikely that the use of AI in planning will have the same potential to target individuals for adverse outcomes. More generally, though, planners will need to be cautious that we do not build AI systems that replicate detrimental decisions made in the past related to segregation and racial discrimination.

It is also necessary to determine when a system is deemed fair for use by deciding under what circumstances automated decision-making can be permitted (Araujo et al., 2020). In some cases, "human-in-the-loop" algorithms or AI system responses, which include human intervention or review, will be needed to maintain control or oversight, especially in unusual circumstances that may not have significant machine intelligence to draw upon. These issues call for interdisciplinary approaches from planners, engineers, designers, ethicists, and social scientists. This can be especially tricky in the case of planning, where political forces play a role in decision-making.

Another significant ethical problem is the use of AI to spread false information. Bad actors may use ML models to produce and spread factually incorrect text regarding contentious urban development issues on social media channels (Hollander et al., 2020). The extent to which social media played a role in propagating false information during the 2016 presidential election serves as an example of this on a much larger scale (Shu et al., 2017). The spread of misinformation will likely continue on social media platforms, with or without the intervention of AI technologies. Slowing the spread of misinformation on social media platforms is a complex and multifaceted challenge that requires a multipronged approach. Overall, it will require a combination of fact-checking, algorithm adjustments, education, community engagement, and legal measures (Anderson & Rainie, 2017).

Ensuring accountability in AI-driven urban planning requires establishing comprehensive mechanisms to track, evaluate, and document how decisions are made. One key mechanism is detailed documentation of AI models, including information on the development process, data sources, algorithms used, and decision-making protocols. This documentation focuses on transparency by making critical information accessible to stakeholders, policymakers, and regulatory bodies. Thorough records allow for continuous evaluation, replication of processes, and the identification of issues such as biases or errors in decision-making. Public access to this documentation reinforces trust, giving residents and stakeholders visibility into how AI influences urban planning decisions.

Audits play a crucial role in maintaining ethical standards for AI-driven urban planning. Audits of AI systems are used to systematically review algorithms for biases, inaccuracies, or unintended discriminatory outcomes. These audits help urban planners detect issues such as data bias that could perpetuate existing social inequalities, such as racial disparities in predictive policing or resource allocation. To focus on objectivity and credibility, these audits should be conducted by independent entities with expertise in AI ethics and regulatory compliance. Independent audits promote transparency and public accountability, reassuring residents that AI applications are designed and operated relatively.

Impact assessments are another essential mechanism to evaluate the social, economic, and environmental outcomes of AI-driven decisions.

These assessments aim to identify both positive impacts and unintended consequences, such as inequities or adverse environmental effects, helping urban planners refine AI models and adjust practices as needed. For example, AI models used in public transportation planning may need adjustments if impact assessments reveal unequal service access across different neighborhoods. Ongoing impact evaluations confirm that AI applications remain aligned with urban planning goals, such as sustainability, equity, and public safety, while minimizing unforeseen harm.

Stakeholder engagement is equally critical to ensuring accountability. Involving community members, policymakers, and experts in the evaluation process ensures that AI applications reflect public values, priorities, and ethical standards. Public forums, focus groups, and advisory panels provide opportunities for residents to express concerns and contribute to decision-making processes. Incorporating stakeholder input promotes AI-driven urban planning solutions that are responsive to the needs of diverse communities and aligned with public interests, fostering trust and legitimacy.

Transparency

Transparency in the public realm can be a challenge, and it has several facets. Building public trust through transparent practices and communication is essential.

Transparency in data use involves clearly communicating how data is collected, used, and protected. This can be achieved through public information campaigns, detailed privacy policies, and open data portals where individuals can access and understand how their data is being used. For AI, the main priority for planners should be being open about the use of AI for making predictions, recommendations, or decisions (Gaur & Sahoo, 2022). Engaging with communities and involving them in decision-making processes related to data collection and AI applications can further enhance trust and acceptance.

Transparency also involves enabling users to understand the elements of an AI system. The ability to deliver clear, relevant information regarding the outputs of an AI system and the justification for its use is another example of transparency, as is the facilitation of open, multistakeholder conversations and the creation of specialized organizations, where required, to promote public understanding and acceptance of AI systems. Because AI and ML models may be too technically challenging to be practical or helpful for understanding an output, transparency generally does not include disclosing source code or sharing proprietary datasets. Source code and datasets could also be considered intellectual property, which has its types of legal protections.

Enabling those who will be affected by the output from an AI-based decision to understand how it was reached is referred to as *explainability*. This requires giving stakeholders simple-to-understand information that will allow those who are negatively impacted to contest outcomes and, when possible, the causes and logic that led to those outcomes. For some AI systems, requiring explainability may have a negative impact on accuracy, performance, privacy, and security, as it may necessitate condensing the solution variables to a set small enough for humans to understand, which may not be optimal in complex, high-dimensional problems. However, this will not likely be the case for many planning-related analyses.

When AI actors explain an outcome in clear and simple terms, as appropriate to the context, they may include the main factors in a decision, the data, logic, or algorithm behind the specific outcome, or an explanation of why similar-looking circumstances generated different outcomes. If applicable, personal data protection standards should be respected while allowing people to understand and contest the conclusion.

Identifying and Addressing Stakeholder Concerns

The adoption of AI in urban planning involves various stakeholders, each with different concerns and perspectives. Understanding and addressing these concerns is crucial for the successful integration of AI technologies. The general public's perception of AI technologies can significantly influence the acceptance and implementation of AI in urban planning. Many people view AI with suspicion and fear, often due to a lack of understanding of how AI is portrayed in the media. Concerns about surveillance, data privacy, and the potential misuse of AI are common. For example, the use of AI to monitor public spaces may be seen as intrusive or a violation of privacy.

To address these fears, urban planners must prioritize transparency and actively engage with communities. Clear communication about the benefits and limitations of AI, along with assurances about privacy protections, can help build public trust. Transparent data collection practices and informed consent from individuals are essential steps to alleviate concerns. Demonstrating ethical AI applications through case studies and positive outcomes can further reassure the public. Engaging with communities through forums, workshops, and consultations allows residents to learn about AI and express their concerns. Involving community members in decision-making processes and integrating their feedback into AI initiatives fosters trust and acceptance. Educational campaigns that explain how AI can enhance urban living and address specific community needs can also build support.

Government officials and policymakers play a critical role in the adoption and regulation of AI technologies in urban planning. Their concerns often revolve around regulatory compliance, alignment with public policy objectives, and the ethical implications of AI use. Policymakers are mainly focused on ensuring that AI applications adhere to existing regulations and standards while supporting sustainability, equity, and public safety goals. There is also concern about the potential for AI to exacerbate existing inequalities or create new ethical challenges.

Urban planners should work closely with policymakers to affirm that AI initiatives align with public policy objectives, conducting thorough impact assessments and implementing ethical guidelines. Open communication between planners and government officials through regular meetings, joint task forces, and collaborative planning sessions is essential for fostering cooperation. Presenting evidence-based arguments supported by data and case studies can demonstrate the value of AI technologies. Building strong relationships with government stakeholders and showing a commitment to responsible AI use, effective collaboration, and alignment with public policy goals.

Urban planners themselves have concerns about the impact of AI on their roles and responsibilities. Many worry that AI could render their skills obsolete, displacing their expertise and diminishing their professional identity. There is also apprehension about the complexity of AI technologies and the potential for job loss. To address these concerns, it is essential to provide urban planners with training and professional development opportunities, including workshops, courses, and certifications focused on AI tools relevant to their field. This training empowers planners to integrate AI effectively and confidently into their work. AI should be seen as a tool to complement human expertise rather than replace it. While AI excels at data analysis and prediction, urban planners bring valuable context, judgment, and experience that AI cannot replicate. Balancing AI capabilities with human insight allows planners to interpret results, make nuanced decisions, and apply their expertise. Establishing a collaborative approach where AI and human expertise work together leads to more effective urban planning outcomes.

Looking Ahead

As we look to the future, urban planners should engage proactively with the challenges and concerns associated with AI. Addressing these issues head-on will not only mitigate risks but also unlock the full potential of AI technologies to enhance urban planning practices. A vision for the future of urban planning involves the responsible and equitable integration of AI. This means developing AI systems that are transparent, accountable, and aligned with the values and needs of all community members. It also involves fostering a culture of continuous learning and adaptation, where urban planners stay informed about the latest advancements in AI and are equipped to navigate its evolving landscape.

By prioritizing ethical considerations and addressing the technical and practical challenges of AI integration, urban planners can harness the transformative power of AI to create more innovative, sustainable, and inclusive cities. This vision for the future is not only achievable but also essential for the advancement of urban planning in the 21st century. Through proactive engagement and collaborative efforts, urban planners can ensure that AI technologies are used to enhance the quality of life for all urban residents, driving positive change and fostering resilient, equitable urban environments.

Chapter Summary

With the adoption of AI technologies to enhance the planning, development, and management of urban environments, several challenges and concerns should be addressed to the ethical and practical use of these powerful tools. This chapter provided a brief introduction to the various challenges associated with adopting AI in urban planning and underscores the importance of being proactive in addressing them. AI technologies, as discussed in the previous chapters, provide significant potential for urban planning. They enable the analysis of vast amounts of data, the simulation of complex urban dynamics, and the generation of innovative planning solutions. However, alongside these benefits come challenges that must be navigated carefully.

Addressing the technical challenges of bias and fairness, error and misapplication, and data quality and availability is essential for the successful adoption of AI in urban planning. Implementing strategies to detect and mitigate bias, ensuring effective model validation, and improving data quality will enable urban planners to harness the power of AI to make more accurate, fair, and effective planning decisions. Overcoming these challenges will support the development of AI systems that promote sustainable, inclusive, and resilient urban environments.

One of the most pressing concerns is the issue of bias in AI systems. These systems are inherently shaped by the data they are trained on, and in the context of urban planning, such data often reflects historical inequities. For example, zoning and housing policies shaped by discriminatory practices like redlining can inadvertently influence AI models, perpetuating and even amplifying inequality. Addressing this requires a rigorous approach to ensuring datasets are representative and free from harmful biases. Transparency in how AI models make decisions is also critical for building trust and mitigating the risk of reinforcing systemic discrimination.

Privacy and data security present another critical challenge. Urban planning increasingly relies on data from diverse sources, including IoT devices, surveillance systems, and mobile applications. While this data provides invaluable insights, it often includes sensitive personal information. Without effective governance frameworks, this data can be

⌐isuse or breaches. Planners must implement measures
⌐ption, anonymization, and strict data access controls,
⌐npliance with privacy regulations like GDPR. These efforts
⌐al to safeguarding public trust and protecting individuals'
Addressing privacy and confidentiality concerns is paramount
ethical and practical use of AI in urban planning. Ensuring
privacy through anonymization, secure data storage, and data
⌐imization techniques helps protect individuals' rights and comply
⌐ith legal standards. Maintaining confidentiality and building public
⌐rust through transparent data practices and community engagement are
essential for the successful adoption of AI technologies. By prioritizing
privacy and confidentiality, urban planners can leverage AI to enhance
urban environments while respecting individuals' rights and fostering
public confidence.

A lack of technical expertise among urban planners also poses a
barrier to the effective use of AI. Many planners lack the specialized skills
needed to deploy and interpret AI tools, often resulting in a reliance on
external vendors or consultants. This dependence can lead to a loss of
control over the tools and an inability to assess their outputs critically. To
overcome this, urban planning education must evolve to include training
in AI and data science. Collaborative efforts between planners and AI
experts can also bridge the knowledge gap, fostering more effective and
informed use of these technologies.

The cost of adopting AI technologies is another hurdle, especially for
smaller municipalities with limited budgets. Procuring AI tools, training
staff, and maintaining the necessary infrastructure can strain financial
resources. Moreover, the digital divide can widen if only wealthier
cities and regions can afford to implement these technologies. Creative
funding solutions, such as public–private partnerships and grants, can
help address this disparity, while open-source tools may provide more
accessible alternatives for resource-constrained communities.

Public trust and ethical concerns are also central to the discussion of
AI adoption in urban planning. The opaque nature of many AI systems
can lead to skepticism and resistance, mainly if decisions appear unfair or
unaccountable. Ethical dilemmas, such as balancing surveillance needs
with privacy or ensuring equitable access to AI-driven services, must

be navigated with care. Transparent communication and participatory planning processes that involve the community can help build trust and ensure AI solutions align with public values.

Integration with existing systems presents another significant challenge. Urban planning relies heavily on legacy systems, such as GIS and transportation modeling software, which may not easily interface with modern AI tools. This lack of compatibility can slow down or complicate the adoption of AI. Cities must prioritize scalable, modular AI solutions that can complement existing systems while investing in technologies that support interoperability.

Legal and regulatory barriers add yet another layer of complexity. The legal frameworks surrounding AI use in urban planning are often unclear or lag behind technological advancements. This creates uncertainty for planners regarding data sharing, liability, and ethical considerations. Proactively engaging with policymakers and legal experts is critical for establishing regulations that support ethical and practical AI adoption.

Finally, cultural and institutional resistance to change can hinder the integration of AI into urban planning. Planners and stakeholders may be skeptical about the reliability of AI or fear its impact on employment and decision-making autonomy. To address these concerns, planners must foster a culture of innovation through education, pilot projects, and success stories that demonstrate AI's value in solving urban challenges.

Understanding these challenges provides a foundation for strategic action. By identifying barriers early, planners can develop targeted strategies to mitigate them. Acknowledging public concerns fosters trust and shows that AI initiatives align with community values. Furthermore, these challenges highlight areas for future research and innovation, driving the development of tools and frameworks tailored to the unique needs of urban planning.

In navigating these complexities, urban planners have an opportunity to harness the transformative potential of AI. By addressing these challenges thoughtfully and proactively, the profession can use AI technologies as not only powerful tools for innovation but also catalysts for more equitable, transparent, and sustainable urban futures.

The importance of ethical considerations cannot be overstated in AI-driven urban planning. Urban planners must understand the historical context of discriminatory practices, such as redlining, to avoid replicating or amplifying these biases through AI. Effective ethical frameworks, including guidelines for fairness, transparency, and accountability, should guide the development and deployment of AI systems. This involves selecting appropriate datasets, ensuring equitable outcomes, and applying inclusive design principles that consider the diverse needs of all urban residents.

Urban planners can further strengthen the ethical foundation of AI applications by prioritizing transparency and accountability through clear documentation, regular audits, comprehensive impact assessments, and meaningful stakeholder engagement. A commitment to ethical AI shows that urban planning decisions are transparent, equitable, and aligned with public values. Ultimately, by fostering accountability and building trust through these mechanisms, urban planners can leverage AI responsibly to create more inclusive, sustainable, and just urban environments.

References and Further Reading

Anderson, J. & Rainie, L. (2017). *The Future of Truth and Misinformation Online.* Pew Research Center, Washington, DC.

Andrews, C., Cooke, K., Gomez, A., Hurtado, P., Sanchez, T. W., Shah, S., & Wright, N. (2022). AI in Planning Opportunities and Challenges and How to Prepare Conclusions and Recommendations from APA's "AI in Planning" Foresight Community, American Planning Association, Chicago, IL.

Araujo, T., Helberger, N., Kruikemeier, S., & De Vreese, C. H. (2020). In AI we trust? Perceptions about automated decision-making by artificial intelligence. *AI & Society,* 35(3), 611–623.

Batty, M. (2021). Science and design in the age of COVID-19. *Environment and Planning B: Urban Analytics and City Science,* 48(1), 3–8.

Boeing, G., Batty, M., Jiang, S., & Schweitzer, L. (2022). Urban analytics: History, trajectory and critique. In *Handbook of Spatial Analysis in the Social Sciences* (pp. 503–516). Edward Elgar Publishing.

Chang, V. (2021). An ethical framework for big data and smart cities. *Technological Forecasting and Social Change,* 165, 120559.

Corbett-Davies, S., & Goel, S. (2018). The measure and mismeasure of fairness: A critical review of fair machine learning. arXiv preprint arXiv:1808.00023.

Eubanks, V. (2018). *Automating inequality: How high-tech tools profile, police, and punish the poor.* St. Martin's Press.

Gaur, L., & Sahoo, B. M. (2022). *Explainable Artificial Intelligence for Intelligent Transportation Systems: Ethics and Applications.* Springer Nature.

Hindle, K. (2021, July 14). The Time is Now! The Adoption of New Technology is the Way of Tomorrow, Fear of Adoption, https://carego.com/blog-fear-of-adoption/.

Hollander, J. B., Potts, R., Hartt, M., & Situ, M. (2020). The role of artificial intelligence in community planning. *International Journal of Community Well-Being*, 3(4), 507–521.

Kusner, M. J., Loftus, J., Russell, C., & Silva, R. (2017). Counterfactual fairness. *Advances in Neural Information Processing Systems*, 30.

Moallem, A. (2018). Smart home network and devices. *Human-Computer Interaction and Cybersecurity Handbook*, 177–190.

Noble, S. U. (2018). *Algorithms of oppression*. New York University Press.

O'Neil, C. (2017). *Weapons of math destruction: How big data increases inequality and threatens democracy*. Broadway Books.

Rogers, E. M., Singhal, A., & Quinlan, M. M. (2014). *Diffusion of innovations. In An integrated approach to communication theory and research* (pp. 432–448). Routledge.

Roh, Y., Heo, G., & Whang, S. E. (2019). A survey on data collection for machine learning: a big data-ai integration perspective. *IEEE Transactions on Knowledge and Data Engineering*, 33(4), 1328–1347.

Roselli, D., Matthews, J., & Talagala, N. (2019, May). Managing bias in AI. In *Companion Proceedings of The 2019 World Wide Web Conference* (pp. 539–544).

Sarker, M. N. I., Wu, M., & Hossin, M. A. (2018, May). Smart governance through bigdata: Digital transformation of public agencies. In *2018 international conference on artificial intelligence and big data (ICAIBD)* (pp. 62–70). IEEE.

Shu, K., Sliva, A., Wang, S., Tang, J., & Liu, H. (2017). Fake news detection on social media: A data mining perspective. *ACM SIGKDD Explorations Newsletter*, 19(1), 22–36.

U.S. Census Bureau. (2021). *Disclosure Avoidance for the 2020 Census: An Introduction*. U.S. Government Publishing Office, Washington, DC.

U.S. Government Accountability Office. (2020). Facial Recognition Technology: Privacy and Accuracy Issues Related to Commercial Uses. GAO-20–522.

8

MOVING TOWARDS THE INTEGRATION OF AI IN URBAN PLANNING

Artificial intelligence (AI) has and will continue to have a significant impact on urban planning, providing planners with powerful tools to analyze complex urban systems and make informed decisions. This book has explored AI's fundamental concepts, methodologies, practical applications, and the challenges planners may face in integrating these technologies into their professional practice.

At its core, AI enhances planners' abilities to handle vast datasets and complex problems through automation, predictive analysis, and innovative simulations. Machine learning (ML), as a pivotal component of AI, enables planners to uncover patterns within extensive data sets, predict future urban conditions, and optimize resource allocation in ways previously unattainable with traditional computational approaches. By learning directly from data, ML models become increasingly accurate and adaptive, helping planners respond proactively to urban challenges such as traffic congestion, land-use changes, and environmental sustainability.

DOI: 10.4324/9781003476818-8

Neural networks (NNs) represent a significant advancement within ML. These networks are effective at interpreting complex and high-dimensional data, making them particularly valuable for urban applications like infrastructure forecasting and demographic trend analysis. With their layered architecture, NNs process information at multiple levels of abstraction, enabling planners to gain nuanced insights into urban dynamics. Yet, their inherent complexity also presents interpretability challenges, underscoring the importance of transparency and clear communication with stakeholders.

Natural language processing (NLP) and computer vision (CV) are additional AI technologies integral to urban planning, bridging gaps between human communication, visual analysis, and automated processes. NLP allows planners to efficiently parse vast amounts of textual data, such as community feedback, regulatory documents, and policy proposals, turning qualitative information into actionable insights. Meanwhile, CV automates the interpretation of visual data, facilitating real-time urban monitoring, accurate spatial analysis, and detailed infrastructure assessments. These technologies significantly enhance planners' ability to understand and manage urban environments, although their use demands careful attention to ethical concerns such as privacy and data security.

Generative AI (GenAI) expands planners' creative and analytical horizons by enabling the generation of new, realistic content based on learned data patterns. Unlike traditional AI models designed primarily for classification or prediction, GenAI produces novel scenarios, visualizations, and simulations, empowering planners to explore diverse urban design possibilities and policy impacts proactively. Applications include generating potential urban growth scenarios, visualizing infrastructure projects, and simulating future land-use developments. While generative models provide exciting new tools for urban innovation, planners must remain vigilant about ethical implications, including misinformation risks and data biases.

Despite AI's transformative potential, its integration into urban planning practice faces significant challenges. Technical hurdles, such as data bias, model errors, and difficulties integrating with legacy planning systems, can limit AI's effectiveness. Organizational barriers, including unclear objectives, resistance to change, and skill gaps among planners, further complicate adoption efforts. Moreover, legal and regulatory uncertainties related to data privacy and AI ethics necessitate proactive engagement with city legal departments and careful consideration of existing policies.

Addressing these challenges requires planners to collaborate closely with IT specialists, policymakers, and community stakeholders. Prioritizing scalable, interoperable solutions and investing in transparent AI governance frameworks are practical steps planners can take. Ensuring data quality, fairness, and robust validation methods, such as cross-validation and bootstrapping, is critical to maintaining public trust and achieving equitable outcomes. Ultimately, the successful adoption of AI in urban planning hinges not only on technological advancements but also on thoughtful, ethically grounded implementation strategies.

Overall, AI presents unprecedented opportunities to enhance urban planning practice, providing powerful analytical tools, innovative methodologies, and creative potential. As planners navigate the complexities of integrating AI, maintaining a clear focus on transparency, ethics, and inclusive participation will be essential to leveraging AI's full potential planning actions.

Assessing the Current Integration of AI in Urban Planning

AI integration in urban planning is still in its nascent stages, with varying levels of adoption across different regions and planning departments. While some cities and planning organizations have successfully implemented AI for tasks such as traffic management, land-use classification, and environmental monitoring, others are just beginning to explore its potential. The current state is characterized by pilot projects, experimentation, and a growing recognition of AI's benefits and challenges.

To gain a clear and actionable understanding of AI's current integration into urban planning, conducting comprehensive assessments is not just beneficial—it is essential. These assessments should systematically evaluate the extent to which AI tools are being utilized in the field, identify successful case studies that illustrate best practices, and highlight areas where AI adoption remains underdeveloped or untapped. By taking a critical and structured look at the current landscape, urban planners and policymakers can identify gaps in knowledge, resources, and application, as well as uncover significant opportunities for enhancing AI integration to meet future challenges.

Understanding how and where AI is currently applied enables urban planners to learn from proven successes. Successful case studies, for instance, can demonstrate how predictive analytics have optimized resource allocation in rapidly growing cities or how GenAI has been used to create more realistic urban simulations for public engagement. These examples serve as practical benchmarks, providing insights into how AI can be applied effectively and what factors contribute to success, such as data quality, interdisciplinary collaboration, or robust stakeholder engagement. They also provide evidence to advocate for increased investment in AI tools and training, as they illustrate tangible benefits in real-world contexts.

Equally important is identifying areas where AI adoption is lagging. This might include smaller municipalities lacking the resources to invest in AI or specific urban planning domains, such as public engagement or equity analysis, where AI applications are underexplored. By recognizing these gaps, urban planners can prioritize initiatives to address them, whether through funding, partnerships, or targeted innovation. For example, a lag in AI adoption for analyzing public feedback might prompt investments in NLP tools, enabling planners to better incorporate community voices into decision-making processes.

Moreover, these assessments provide a roadmap for capacity building within the urban planning profession. As AI tools become integral to the planning process, there is an urgent need to upskill existing professionals, equipping them with the knowledge and technical expertise to leverage AI effectively. This might involve integrating AI training into professional development programs or offering workshops on specific applications, such as ML for land-use forecasting or computer vision for infrastructure monitoring. In parallel, the profession must also focus on attracting and hiring a new generation of planners who are already well-versed in these technologies. These individuals can serve as leaders in advancing AI adoption and fostering a culture of innovation within planning organizations.

Ultimately, a thorough understanding of AI's current integration is crucial for bridging the gap between potential and practice. It ensures that urban planning professionals are not only aware of the tools at their disposal but also equipped to use them to their full advantage.

By addressing gaps, learning from successes, and investing in human capital, urban planners and policymakers can create a more adaptive, data-driven, and equitable approach to shaping the cities of the future. This proactive strategy not only enhances the profession's ability to tackle complex urban challenges but also positions it to lead in the ethical and practical use of AI technologies.

Promoting AI Implementation in Urban Planning

AI holds great promise for enhancing urban planning by providing tools to analyze complex data, simulate scenarios, and optimize decisions for improved urban outcomes. However, realizing these benefits requires proactive efforts to overcome the technical, organizational, and ethical barriers that often hinder AI adoption. Promoting effective AI implementation involves more than simply introducing new technologies; it necessitates creating an enabling environment in which planners are knowledgeable, skilled, and supported in integrating AI into their practice. Cities and planning organizations must foster a culture that values continuous learning, interdisciplinary collaboration, and responsible experimentation. By taking targeted steps to build planners' AI literacy, encourage cross-sector collaboration, and pilot innovative solutions, urban planning agencies can confidently embrace AI's transformative potential, ensuring that technological advancements translate into meaningful outcomes.

Immediate Steps to Enhance AI Adoption

To accelerate the adoption of AI in urban planning, several strategies can help create a robust foundation for effective and responsible implementation. Successfully integrating AI into planning practice requires coordinated efforts among multiple stakeholders, including professional planners, planning organizations, researchers, planning students, and planning educators. Each of these groups plays an essential role: planners need practical skills and clear guidance to apply AI tools confidently; planning organizations must create supportive environments and infrastructure; researchers contribute by advancing knowledge and developing innovative methods; students represent the future of planning, necessitating AI integration into their education; and educators shape curricula to ensure new planners are adequately prepared.

The following actions are critical for engaging these diverse stakeholders, enabling planners and planning organizations to adopt AI technologies confidently, and ensuring their implementation aligns with urban development goals, public interest, and ethical standards.

AI education. Building AI literacy among urban planners is essential to bridge the gap between technology and practical urban planning applications. Planners need not only an understanding of the technical capabilities of AI but also insight into how these tools can align with planning processes and policies. Educational initiatives can include targeted workshops, professional training programs, certification courses, and academic modules focusing on AI for urban systems. These programs should balance technical content, such as data analytics and algorithmic design, with discussions on the ethical implications of AI, including bias, transparency, and accountability. Providing planners with access to real-world case studies, hands-on projects, and interactive tools will further enhance their ability to make informed decisions about how and when to use AI. Long-term partnerships with universities and industry experts to provide continuing education will ensure planners stay updated with emerging technologies.

Interdisciplinary collaboration. Effective AI integration requires collaboration between urban planners, data scientists, technologists, and community stakeholders. Each group brings distinct and vital perspectives—planners understand local contexts and policy frameworks, data scientists contribute technical expertise, and community stakeholders provide insights into public needs and priorities. Interdisciplinary teams ensure that AI applications are not only technically sound but also contextually relevant and aligned with community values. Creating formal and informal opportunities for collaboration, such as joint research projects, interdisciplinary task forces, and regular cross-sector meetings, can enhance knowledge sharing. These collaborations can also help identify gaps in AI tools and co-design solutions that respond to local challenges. Importantly, engaging community members in the planning process ensures that AI is deployed in ways that address real needs and promote trust.

Pilot projects. Pilot projects provide urban planners with a controlled environment to explore the potential of AI technologies and experiment with new approaches on a smaller scale. These projects allow for real-time learning, helping planners identify challenges, refine methodologies, and address any unintended consequences before expanding AI use city-wide. Pilot initiatives can focus on specific aspects of urban planning, such as traffic management, public transportation, or environmental monitoring, demonstrating the tangible benefits of AI in solving real-world problems. By showcasing successful applications, pilot projects can serve as proof of concept, building confidence among stakeholders and generating support for broader adoption. To maximize the impact of pilot projects, planners should document outcomes, share insights with peers, and use lessons learned to develop best practices for future AI initiatives.

Accelerating AI adoption in urban planning requires coordinated action across planners, planning organizations, researchers, students, and educators. Planners need targeted education to build practical AI skills, combining technical training with ethical considerations. Planning organizations must establish environments that facilitate interdisciplinary collaboration, connecting planners with data scientists, technologists, and community stakeholders to ensure AI applications align with community needs. Researchers play a crucial role by advancing methods and supporting evidence-based practices while planning educators and students help ensure the profession remains updated and prepared for future challenges. Pilot projects also provide a practical means to test AI tools, identify potential issues, and demonstrate the value of AI in addressing real-world urban planning challenges.

Strategic Planning for Long-Term AI Integration

Long-term integration of AI in urban planning will involve strategic planning that considers not only the immediate benefits but also the future scalability, adaptability, and evolving landscape of technology. To effectively harness AI's potential over the coming decades, planners must develop comprehensive strategies that articulate a clear vision, specific goals, and actionable roadmaps for AI adoption. This approach ensures that AI becomes an integral part of urban planning practices, enabling more innovative and sustainable cities. Several essential elements must be considered to achieve this long-term integration.

Building large datasets with future applications in mind. AI's effectiveness in urban planning depends heavily on the quality and comprehensiveness of the data it analyzes. Planners should focus on collecting and organizing large datasets that are not only relevant to current needs but also structured to support future AI applications. This includes gathering diverse data across domains—such as transportation, housing, public health, and environmental factors—while ensuring interoperability across systems. Planners must also prioritize data governance practices, such as metadata standards and data sharing protocols, to enable smooth integration and reuse of datasets over time. Equally important is maintaining data privacy and security to safeguard public trust as more personal and sensitive data are collected.

Investing in scalable infrastructure. Long-term AI adoption requires robust and scalable infrastructure capable of handling increasing volumes of data and more sophisticated algorithms. Investments in cloud computing services, high-performance computing systems, and data storage solutions will allow planners to manage complex AI models efficiently. The infrastructure must also accommodate growth, ensuring that it can evolve alongside new technological developments and expanding datasets. Planners should explore hybrid infrastructure models that combine on-premises resources with cloud-based solutions, providing flexibility and resilience. Additionally, integrating open-source tools and platforms can help urban planning agencies stay agile, minimize costs, and foster innovation by leveraging global advancements in AI technologies.

Continuous learning and professional development. Given the rapid pace of AI advancement, ongoing education and professional development are essential for urban planners to remain effective and knowledgeable. Continuous learning opportunities can include workshops, seminars, online courses, and certifications covering both the technical and ethical aspects of AI. Partnerships with universities, professional organizations, and online learning platforms will ensure that planners have access to up-to-date knowledge and best practices.

Establishing mentorship programs and knowledge-sharing networks within planning departments can also facilitate the dissemination of AI expertise. By fostering a culture of lifelong learning, urban planning organizations will empower their workforce to adapt to technological changes and leverage AI tools confidently.

Promoting adaptability in planning processes. For AI to have a lasting impact, urban planning frameworks must be flexible and adaptable. This involves creating planning processes that are capable of integrating new data sources, algorithms, and AI-generated insights in real time. Planners should embrace iterative and data-driven planning approaches where AI outputs continuously inform decisions, enabling responsive adjustments to policies and strategies. This shift requires a mindset change, encouraging planners to view planning as an ongoing process rather than a fixed outcome. Incorporating AI-generated forecasts, scenario modeling, and predictive analytics into routine planning will improve the ability to anticipate future challenges and opportunities. In addition, fostering collaboration between AI specialists and urban planners will enhance the integration of new tools and innovations as they emerge.

By strategically focusing on infrastructure, data, continuous education, and adaptability, urban planners can build a resilient framework for long-term AI integration. These efforts will ensure that AI becomes a powerful tool in shaping sustainable, inclusive, and forward-looking urban environments. As cities continue to evolve, planners who embrace a proactive approach to AI adoption will be better equipped to address emerging challenges and unlock new opportunities for improving the quality of life for all residents.

Policies for Guiding Ethical AI Use

Policies play a crucial role in guiding the ethical and responsible use of AI in urban planning, ensuring that these technologies align with societal values, legal frameworks, and public interests. Clear, comprehensive policies provide the foundation for responsible AI deployment, establishing principles that govern how AI is designed, implemented, and monitored. By embedding ethical considerations into policies and fostering trust through transparency and accountability, urban planners can harness the benefits of AI while mitigating risks. Several key elements are essential to building effective policy frameworks for AI in urban planning:

Ethical guidelines. Ethical guidelines must be at the core of AI policies so as to address critical issues such as bias mitigation, data privacy, transparency, and accountability. These guidelines ensure that AI systems promote fairness, protect individual rights, and reflect the values of the communities they serve. For instance, policies should mandate strategies to identify and mitigate biases in AI models, preventing discriminatory outcomes that could exacerbate social inequalities. Data privacy protections are equally essential, requiring responsible handling of sensitive data in compliance with relevant privacy laws. Ethical guidelines should also emphasize the importance of transparency in the development and deployment of AI systems, ensuring that citizens understand how AI influences decisions that affect their lives. Promoting public trust through fairness, openness, and accountability is essential for the successful adoption of AI in urban planning.

Transparency and accountability. Policies must prioritize openness in AI development and decision-making processes, ensuring that AI tools are understandable and explainable to both planners and the public. Transparency can be achieved by documenting data sources, algorithms, and methodologies used in AI models. Planners should also be required to provide clear, accessible explanations for AI-driven decisions, especially those affecting resource allocation, zoning, or public services. In addition, accountability mechanisms such as regular audits, ethical reviews, and impact assessments are essential to monitor AI systems' performance and ethical implications over time. These measures ensure that AI applications remain aligned with evolving societal standards and values. Establishing mechanisms for corrective action in case of unintended outcomes also reinforces accountability, demonstrating a commitment to responsible AI use.

Data protection regulations. Robust data protection regulations are necessary to secure personal and sensitive information used in AI applications. Such laws should establish requirements for data anonymization, secure storage, and informed consent, ensuring that individuals understand how their data will be used and retain control over their information. Compliance with data privacy laws, such as the General Data Protection Regulation (GDPR) or similar frameworks, is essential for building public trust. Planners and developers must also implement protocols for data minimization, ensuring that only the necessary data is collected and used.

AI regulations and deployment standards. For AI to be used responsibly in urban planning, it is essential to develop clear rules and standards that guide every stage of AI integration. Policymakers, urban planners, technologists, and community stakeholders must collaborate to design regulations that are relevant, inclusive, and forward-looking. Standards are essential to ensure consistency, reliability, and ethical compliance in AI applications. These standards should cover aspects such as data quality, model transparency, bias detection, and performance evaluation. Developing benchmarks for validating AI models ensures that they are both accurate and fair. Standardizing the processes for deploying AI tools in urban planning promotes trust among stakeholders, as it guarantees that the tools meet minimum quality and ethical standards. Additionally, adherence to standards facilitates interoperability, enabling different AI systems to work together seamlessly across various urban planning functions.

Public engagement and consultation. Public engagement and consultation are essential components of AI policy development, ensuring that AI applications reflect community values and address societal concerns. Regulations should mandate opportunities for public input throughout the policymaking and implementation processes. Involving residents in decisions about AI technologies fosters trust and promotes inclusivity, particularly for marginalized communities that could be disproportionately affected by AI-driven policies. Transparent communication with the public about the benefits and risks of AI, as well as the safeguards in place, strengthens community buy-in and promotes responsible use.

Balancing immediate needs and long-term considerations. The successful implementation of AI in urban planning requires a balanced approach that addresses both current challenges and future opportunities. While policies and regulations provide a framework for responsible use, planners must also invest in the fundamental elements necessary for long-term AI integration. This includes promoting AI education and training, fostering interdisciplinary collaboration, developing scalable infrastructure, and adopting flexible planning frameworks. Together, these strategies enhance planners' ability to adapt to new technologies and evolving urban challenges.

Through proactive engagement, strategic planning, and transparent policies, urban planners can harness AI's potential to create more innovative, more sustainable, and inclusive cities. Policies that emphasize transparency, accountability, and public trust will be essential to guiding AI adoption in ways that promote the common good and ensure that technological advances benefit all residents. By embedding ethical considerations into AI systems and aligning them with public values, urban planners can leverage AI to enhance decision-making processes and create urban environments that are equitable, resilient, and responsive to future needs.

WORKING WITH AI EXPERTS IN IMPLEMENTING AI

Addressing the many challenges of AI in urban planning previously discussed necessitates collaboration among diverse stakeholders, including technologists. Data scientists and AI experts have expertise in AI algorithms, data processing, and model optimization. Knowing when to bring these experts into your project and how to work with them effectively can make all the difference.

Consider collaborating with AI experts at several key stages of your project. At the very beginning, their input can be invaluable in defining your project goals and determining how AI can best be used. They can help you understand the feasibility of your ideas and suggest the best approaches and technologies to achieve your objectives.

As you move into data preparation, AI experts can assist in gathering, cleaning, and organizing data. This step is crucial because high-quality data is the foundation of any successful AI project. Their expertise ensures that the data is properly formatted and ready for training AI models.

When it comes to selecting and training models, AI experts should be consulted. They can help choose the most suitable models for your specific needs, fine-tune them for optimal performance, and ensure that they are effectively trained. Their experience can save you time and help avoid common pitfalls.

During the implementation phase, these experts can assist in integrating the AI-generated outputs into your planning processes and systems. This integration ensures that the AI solutions are practical and usable within existing workflows.

Finally, after deployment, AI projects often require ongoing evaluation and iteration. AI experts can help continuously assess the performance of the models and refine them based on feedback and new data, ensuring that they remain accurate and effective over time.

Effective collaboration involves clear communication and defined roles. Start by clearly articulating your project goals and how you envision AI enhancing your planning efforts. This clarity helps align everyone's expectations and focuses efforts on shared objectives. Establishing roles and responsibilities early on ensures that everyone knows their contributions and can work together efficiently. Regular communication, such as scheduled meetings, helps keep the project on track and allows for the timely resolution of any issues.

Guidance for Urban Planners

As AI continues to revolutionize urban planning, it is essential for planners to actively engage with these technologies and build the necessary competencies to leverage AI effectively. Planners can take action to build AI competency, embrace change, and foster collaboration and community engagement.

Build AI competency through continuous education and professional development. To harness the full potential of AI in urban planning, planners must develop a strong foundation in AI technologies. Continuous education and professional development are crucial for building AI competency. Planners should seek out training programs, workshops, and courses that provide a comprehensive understanding of AI principles, tools, and applications. Look for opportunities to learn technical skills such as data analysis, ML, and programming, as well as ethical considerations and best practices for AI deployment.

Stay informed about AI advancements and best practices. The field of AI is rapidly evolving, with new advancements and best practices emerging regularly. Urban planners must stay informed about these developments to ensure they are using the most effective and up-to-date tools and methodologies. This can be achieved through ongoing professional development, attending industry conferences, participating in online forums, and subscribing to relevant publications. Staying current with AI advancements allows planners to continually refine their skills and adopt innovative approaches to urban planning challenges.

Embrace AI-driven changes in urban planning. AI technologies are transforming urban planning, and planners must adopt a proactive approach to embrace these changes. Rather than resisting or merely reacting to AI advancements, planners should actively seek opportunities to integrate AI into their workflows. This involves being open to experimentation, learning from pilot projects, and iteratively improving AI applications based on feedback and outcomes.

Collaborate with technologists, policymakers, and the community. Successful AI implementation in urban planning requires collaboration across various stakeholders. Planners must work closely with technologists to understand the technical aspects of AI and develop solutions that are technically feasible and effective. Collaboration with policymakers ensures that AI applications align with regulatory requirements and public policy goals. Engaging with the community is essential to ensure that AI implementations reflect the needs and values of residents.

Ensure that community goals and needs drive AI implementation. Inclusive AI implementation considers the diverse perspectives and needs of all stakeholders. Planners should engage with community members through public consultations, workshops, and participatory planning processes. These interactions provide valuable insights into local priorities, concerns, and aspirations, ensuring that AI-driven solutions address real-world challenges and promote equity.

Planning organizations must also take steps to support the successful adoption of AI. Strategies to guide responsible and effective implementation of AI and foster a culture of innovation and adaptability include the following.

Establish a vision and goals to guide implementation. A clear vision and measurable goals are essential for successfully integrating AI into urban planning. Planning organizations should collaboratively define objectives detailing how AI will improve planning processes and support community priorities like equity and sustainability. Establishing and communicating these goals transparently helps secure stakeholder buy-in, guides planners and technologists, and provides clear benchmarks to evaluate progress and refine AI-driven initiatives over time.

Encourage experimentation. Allowing planners to experiment with AI tools and techniques in a low-risk environment fosters creativity and innovation. Pilot projects and sandbox environments can provide opportunities to test new ideas and approaches without the pressure of immediate large-scale implementation.

Provide support and resources. Ensuring that planners have access to the necessary resources, including training, technical support, and funding, enables them to explore AI applications effectively. Investing in infrastructure and tools that support AI integration is also crucial.

Recognize and reward innovation. Celebrating successes and recognizing innovative contributions can motivate planners to embrace AI-driven changes. Incentives such as awards, public recognition, and professional development opportunities can reinforce a culture of innovation.

By actively pursuing these strategies, planners and planning organizations can thoughtfully integrate AI into their daily practices, addressing challenges as they arise and making the most of new technologies. Committing to ongoing education will equip planners with the skills necessary to apply AI tools effectively. At the same time, a willingness to experiment with innovative approaches can uncover new opportunities for addressing complex urban issues. Strong collaboration among planners, technology experts, policymakers, and community stakeholders ensures that AI solutions are both technically sound and aligned with the specific needs and priorities of local communities.

Looking Ahead

The future of urban planning in the AI era is both promising and challenging. AI provides unprecedented opportunities to transform urban environments, making them more innovative, more sustainable, and more livable. However, realizing this potential requires a thoughtful and responsible approach. Urban planners must navigate the complexities of AI technologies, address ethical considerations, and ensure that AI implementations promote equity and justice.

As AI continues to evolve, urban planners are encouraged to lead the way in integrating these technologies responsibly and innovatively. By embracing a proactive mindset and fostering a culture of continuous learning and adaptation, planners can stay ahead of technological advancements and leverage AI to drive positive change.

This book seeks to provide urban planners with fundamental knowledge about AI and encourages them to apply it in their work. The insights and recommendations provided throughout this book give a clear vision and actionable guidance for integrating AI into urban planning practice. By synthesizing the background information on AI techniques and their applications to urban planning practice provided in each chapter with the recommendations for practice provided in this chapter, urban planners will be empowered to harness AI's potential while navigating its challenges responsibly. The ultimate goal is to create more innovative, more sustainable, and more inclusive urban environments. Through dedication, innovation, and collaboration, urban planners can lead the way in shaping the cities of the future, ensuring that AI technologies contribute to a better quality of life for all urban residents.

GLOSSARY

Abstractive Summarization: An NLP summarization method generating original, condensed text summaries, going beyond merely extracting sentences from the source document.

Accountability: Mechanisms ensuring that planners and technologists are responsible for AI decisions and outcomes, enhancing public confidence.

Accuracy (Model Evaluation): The percentage of correctly predicted cases compared to the total number of cases, reflecting overall model effectiveness.

Activation Function: A mathematical function within a NN determining whether neurons activate, enabling modeling of complex, non-linear relationships.

Agent (in Reinforcement Learning): An entity in reinforcement learning that makes decisions and learns from the outcomes based on interactions with its environment.

AI Literacy: The understanding of AI's principles, capabilities, and limitations, enabling planners to apply AI tools effectively and responsibly.

AI Winter: A period of reduced interest, funding, and progress in AI research, typically following periods of overly ambitious expectations not met by practical results.

Algorithm: Instructions or computational rules used by ML systems to process data, learn from it, and identify patterns.

Algorithmic Bias: Systematic inaccuracies in ML outcomes due to biased training data or flawed algorithms, potentially perpetuating existing inequalities.

Algorithmic Fairness: The concept of ensuring AI models make decisions that are unbiased and equitable across different demographic groups.

Anonymization: Techniques to transform personal data to prevent identification of individuals, preserving privacy and confidentiality.

Application Programming Interface (API):   Software tools allowing access and integration of external data sources (such as social media content) into NLP models.

Artificial General Intelligence (AGI):   AI capable of performing a broad range of tasks, demonstrating near-human cognitive and adaptive capabilities.

Artificial Intelligence (AI):   A field of computer science focused on creating systems that can perform tasks typically requiring human intelligence, such as learning, reasoning, and problem-solving.

Artificial Narrow Intelligence (ANI):   AI designed to perform specific, limited tasks without general understanding or broader adaptability.

Artificial Neural Network (ANN):   Computational systems inspired by the human brain's structure, consisting of interconnected nodes or neurons used to model complex data relationships.

Artificial Super Intelligence (ASI):   Hypothetical AI with intelligence vastly surpassing human cognitive capabilities, potentially excelling in creativity, decision-making, and problem-solving across all domains.

Autoencoders: NNs using unsupervised learning to compress data into simpler forms (latent spaces), then reconstructing it, useful in data representation and feature extraction.

Automated Annotation: Techniques that automatically label data (images or video frames), reducing the manual effort required for creating training datasets.

Automation: Technology-driven processes that perform tasks automatically with minimal human intervention.

Autonomous Vehicle (AV):   Vehicles equipped with AI technologies enabling them to sense their environment and navigate without human intervention, commonly known as self-driving vehicles.

Backpropagation: A method for training NNs where prediction errors are propagated backward through the network to update weights and biases, minimizing future errors.

Bag of Words (BoW): A simplified text analysis model that counts word occurrences without considering context, grammar, or syntax.

BERT (Bidirectional Encoder Representations from Transformers): A transformer-based NLP model that understands context by analyzing words in both directions within a sentence.

Bias Detection: Techniques and methods used to identify biases in data and AI models, crucial for promoting fairness and accuracy.

Bias in AI: Systematic errors in AI models that can lead to unfair outcomes, often due to biased training data or model design.

Bias in Decision-Making: The presence of unfair preferences or prejudices that can influence AI models, urban planning policies, or resource allocation.

Biases: Parameters in NNs allowing adjustments to the activation function threshold, improving model fitting and prediction accuracy.

Bootstrapping: A statistical method used in ML for estimating model performance by resampling data.

Chatbot: An automated system using NLP to interact with humans conversationally, commonly employed for customer service and information dissemination.

Cloud Computing: Providing remote access to powerful computing resources, enabling scalable and cost-effective deployment of AI models.

Clustering: An unsupervised ML technique grouping similar data points based on shared characteristics or features, revealing hidden structures.

Color Spaces (RGB, Grayscale): Systems used to represent color in images. RGB combines red, green, and blue channels, while grayscale represents images using varying shades of gray.

Community Engagement: Inclusive involvement of community members in AI planning processes, ensuring AI solutions align with public needs, values, and priorities.

Comprehensive Plan: A long-term plan that outlines a community's goals for land use, transportation, and development.

Computational Infrastructure: Hardware and software (cloud computing, high-performance servers) needed to support AI processes effectively, and crucial for scalability and reliability.

Computational Resources: Hardware (e.g., GPUs, servers) required for AI implementation, impacting cost, scalability, and accessibility, especially for smaller or resource-constrained communities.

Computer Vision (CV): A branch of AI enabling machines to analyze and interpret visual information from images or videos.

Concept Drift: A phenomenon where the patterns learned by an AI model become outdated as data evolves, requiring regular updates and retraining.

Conditional GANs (cGANs): GAN variants that generate outputs conditioned on specific input data or characteristics, useful for targeted designs like urban landscape renderings.

Continuous Learning: Ongoing professional development and education to keep planners updated with AI advancements and best practices.

Convolutional Neural Network (CNN): A NN architecture optimized for image and spatial data processing, employing filters to recognize visual patterns and features.

Cross-validation: A statistical method to systematically evaluate the reliability and accuracy of AI models by testing them on different subsets of data.

Cybersecurity: Protective measures against unauthorized access, misuse, and breaches of digital systems containing sensitive urban planning data.

Data Augmentation: Techniques creating additional, synthetic data to expand and diversify limited or incomplete datasets.

Data Bias: Systematic errors in AI outcomes caused by skewed or prejudiced data, potentially resulting in unfair or inaccurate decisions.

Data Fragmentation: The dispersion of data across different systems or organizations, complicating comprehensive data integration and analysis.

Data Governance: Policies and processes for managing data availability, usability, integrity, and security, critical for responsible AI use.

Data Minimization: Collecting and using only the necessary data, limiting risks related to privacy and security.

Data Preprocessing: Preparing data for ML by cleaning, handling missing values, normalizing, and encoding categorical variables for improved model accuracy.

Data Privacy: Measures to protect personal information and individual privacy, critical when using visual data captured from surveillance or other imaging technologies.

Data Quality: Accuracy, completeness, reliability, and timeliness of datasets used in AI systems, essential for reliable model outcomes.

Decision Trees: Supervised ML algorithms used for classification or regression by recursively splitting data based on feature values.

Deep Learning: A subset of ML involving multi-layered NNs for complex data analysis.

Deepfakes: Realistic synthetic media (images, videos, audio) generated using GANs or similar AI, often raising ethical and social concerns.

Digital Divide: The gap between communities with and without access to advanced digital technologies, potentially exacerbated by the uneven adoption of AI.

Digital Transformation: The integration of digital technologies into urban life, fundamentally changing city operations and interactions.

Digital Twin: A digital replica of physical assets or urban systems, enabling simulation, monitoring, and predictive analysis.

Dimensionality Reduction: Techniques to simplify data by reducing the number of variables while retaining essential patterns, making analysis more manageable.

Drone Imagery: Aerial imagery collected via drones, providing detailed visual information for focused areas, essential for infrastructure inspection or detailed urban assessment.

Edge Computing: Processing data near the source (such as sensors or cameras) instead of in centralized servers, significantly reducing latency and improving real-time analysis capabilities.

Edge Detection: A CV technique used to identify the boundaries of objects in an image.

Environmental Impact Assessments (EIAs):   Evaluations predicting the environmental consequences of proposed developments, ensuring sustainability and compliance with environmental standards.

Epoch: One complete cycle through the training dataset during NN training, used to iteratively refine model accuracy.

Equity in Urban Planning: Ensuring that all communities, particularly marginalized groups, have equal access to opportunities, resources, and decision-making processes.

Ethical AI: AI deployment that emphasizes fairness, transparency, privacy, accountability, and social equity to ensure responsible use.

Explainable AI (XAI):   Techniques enabling AI models to provide understandable explanations of their predictions or decisions, promoting transparency and accountability.

Extractive Summarization: An NLP technique selecting key sentences directly from the original text to form concise summaries, without generating new phrasing.

F1 Score: A balanced metric combining precision and recall, ideal for situations where false positives and negatives have equal significance.

Faster R-CNN: A highly accurate but computationally intensive object detection algorithm focusing on regions of interest within images for detailed analysis.

Feature Extraction (Transfer Learning):   Using pre-trained model layers to extract visual patterns for new tasks, minimizing training time by retraining only a small portion of the model.

Federated Learning: A decentralized AI training approach allowing models to learn from distributed data sources without compromising individual privacy.

Feedforward Neural Network (FNN):   A basic NN structure where information moves only forward, from inputs to outputs, with no cycles or loops.

Fifth-generation Computing: A computing era characterized by AI integration, parallel processing, advanced human-computer interactions, and sophisticated problem-solving capabilities that has emerged since the 1980s.

Filtering (Image Processing):   The application of mathematical operations to images (using kernels) to enhance features or reduce noise, such as smoothing (Gaussian filters) or sharpening (Laplacian filters).

Fine-tuning: The process of adjusting an AI model trained on one dataset to perform better on a new dataset.

Forward Propagation: The NN process of moving inputs forward through the network layers to produce outputs or predictions.

Gaussian Mixture Models (GMMs): Probabilistic models using multiple Gaussian distributions (bell-shaped curves) to capture complexity and variability in datasets.

General Data Protection Regulation (GDPR): The European regulation governing personal data privacy and security, influencing global data handling standards.

General Problem Solver: An early AI program developed by Allen Newell and Herbert Simon, designed to simulate human problem-solving processes to solve a wide range of complex tasks.

Generative Adversarial Networks (GANs): A type of generative AI model that consists of two competing networks (a generator and a discriminator) used for creating realistic synthetic data.

Generative AI (GenAI): A category of AI focused on creating new content, such as text, images, and videos, by learning patterns from existing data.

Generative Design: The use of algorithms to automatically generate multiple design solutions based on specified criteria, constraints, or objectives.

Gentrification: The process of urban renewal that often results in displacement of lower-income residents due to rising property values.

Geocoding: The assigning of geographical coordinates to textual references, linking textual data to spatial locations, useful in analyzing spatial aspects of textual information.

Geographic Information Systems (GIS): Software systems for analyzing and visualizing spatial and geographic data, commonly integrated with ML for urban planning tasks.

GloVe (Global Vectors for Word Representation): An NLP model generating numerical word embeddings by combining global word co-occurrence statistics with local context to better capture semantic relationships.

Governance: The systems, policies, and regulations that guide urban planning decisions and AI adoption.

GPT (Generative Pre-trained Transformer): A large language model designed to generate human-like text based on context and prompts.

GPU (Graphics Processing Unit): Specialized hardware enabling parallel processing, significantly speeding up the training of large AI models.

Green Computing: Environmentally sustainable computing practices minimizing energy consumption and carbon footprint associated with data-intensive ML processes.

Hidden Layer: Intermediate layers of a NN where data processing and feature extraction occur, situated between input and output layers.

Hidden Markov Models (HMMs): Models predicting sequential data patterns by assuming data points are influenced by hidden, inferred states, useful in speech and handwriting synthesis.

Human-Centered AI: AI development and deployment that prioritizes human well-being, fairness, and usability.

Human-in-the-Loop: AI systems involving human oversight or intervention, particularly valuable in decision-making contexts requiring ethical judgment or nuanced interpretation.

Hybrid Infrastructure: A combination of local (on-premises) and cloud-based computing resources, providing flexibility and resilience for evolving AI needs.

Hybrid Neural Networks: Models combining different NN architectures (e.g., CNN and RNN) to leverage complementary strengths for complex urban analyses.

Hyperparameters: Settings in a ML model that determine how the model learns and optimizes itself.

Image Processing: Techniques for enhancing, transforming, and analyzing digital images to extract useful information.

Image Segmentation: The dividing of an image into distinct regions to identify different objects or features at the pixel level, essential for detailed spatial analysis.

Impact Assessment: Evaluations of AI's potential social, economic, environmental, and ethical impacts to guide responsible implementation.

Impact Assessments: Evaluations assessing the social, economic, environmental, and ethical implications of AI-driven decisions, ensuring positive outcomes and minimizing harm.

Infrastructure: The physical and organizational structures, such as roads, bridges, water systems, and telecommunications, that support urban life.

Input Layer: The first NN layer that receives raw data for processing.

Instance Segmentation: The segmenting of an image into distinct objects, identifying individual instances separately, even within the same category.

Interactive Visualization: Tools and techniques allowing users to dynamically explore, manipulate, and engage with visual representations of proposed urban developments.

Interdisciplinary Collaboration: Cooperative efforts between planners, technologists, policymakers, and community stakeholders, essential for successful AI implementation.

Internet of Things (IoT):   A network of interconnected physical devices and sensors collecting and exchanging real-time data used in ML-driven analysis.

Interoperability: The ability of AI systems and legacy platforms (e.g., GIS) to effectively exchange and utilize data, essential for seamless integration.

Keras: A high-level, user-friendly NN library written in Python that runs on top of TensorFlow, designed to enable fast experimentation and simplified development of deep learning models.

Land Use: The designation of specific areas for different types of development, such as residential, commercial, industrial, or recreational purposes.

Large Language Models (LLMs):   AI models using deep learning to analyze large text datasets, enabling sophisticated language understanding, generation, and interaction capabilities.

Latent Dirichlet Allocation (LDA):   A probabilistic topic modeling technique used to identify underlying themes within large collections of text documents without pre-labeled categories.

Latent Space: A compressed representation of input data learned by AI models, used to generate variations of data.

Legacy Systems: Established technology platforms (e.g., GIS, transportation software) often incompatible with modern AI tools, presenting integration challenges.

Lemmatization: An NLP technique that reduces words to their base or root form (lemma), ensuring consistent analysis across different variations of words.

Logic Theorist: The first AI computer program developed by Allen Newell, Herbert Simon, and Cliff Shaw in 1956, capable of proving logical theorems and performing symbolic reasoning.

Long Short-Term Memory (LSTM):   A specialized type of RNN capable of learning long-term dependencies in sequential data, ideal for predicting traffic flows or temporal patterns.

Loss Function: A measure of prediction error in NNs, guiding the learning process by quantifying discrepancies between predicted and actual outcomes.

Machine Learning (ML):   A subset of AI that enables computers to learn from data and improve their performance on tasks without being explicitly programmed.

Mobility: The ease with which people can move around a city using different modes of transportation, including walking, biking, public transit, and personal vehicles.

Mode Collapse: A GAN-specific training issue where generated outputs lack diversity, repeatedly producing similar outcomes.

Model: A representation of learned relationships from data, enabling predictions or decisions for new or unseen data.

Model Evaluation: The assessment of ML model performance using metrics such as accuracy, precision, and recall, ensuring reliability and generalizability to new data.

Modular Solutions: Scalable AI implementations allowing incremental integration into existing urban planning systems, reducing disruption and improving adoption.

Morphology: The analysis of the structure and formation of words, focusing on roots, prefixes, and suffixes, essential for understanding grammatical meaning.

Multimodal Models: AI models capable of processing and integrating multiple data types (text, images, spatial data), enhancing complexity and context-awareness in analysis.

Named Entity Recognition (NER):   A task in NLP that involves identifying and classifying entities, such as names of people, organizations, and locations, within text.

Natural Language Processing (NLP):   A field of AI that enables computers to understand, interpret, and generate human language.

Neural Networks: A computing system inspired by the human brain that consists of layers of interconnected nodes (neurons) used for recognizing patterns and making predictions.

Neuron: The fundamental unit in a NN, receiving inputs, performing calculations, and producing outputs to subsequent layers.

Object Detection: A computer vision task that identifies and classifies objects within an image or video.

Open-Source Software: Freely available software platforms (e.g., TensorFlow, QGIS, OpenStreetMap) allowing cost-effective AI implementation, particularly valuable for smaller municipalities.

Optimization Algorithms: Mathematical techniques used to minimize errors in AI models during training.

Output Layer: The final NN layer that produces predictions or decisions based on processed data.

Overfitting: A condition where an ML model performs well on training data but poorly on new, unseen data due to overly capturing noise rather than general patterns.

Part-of-Speech (POS) Tagging: The assigning of grammatical categories (noun, verb, adjective, etc.) to individual words in text to identify syntactic roles.

Pilot Projects: Smaller-scale, controlled AI implementations used to evaluate effectiveness, refine methodologies, and demonstrate benefits before broader deployment.

Pixel: The smallest unit of a digital image, containing information about brightness and color intensity.

Policy Implementation: The process of enacting laws, regulations, and initiatives that shape urban development and AI usage.

Pragmatics: A subfield of linguistics and NLP concerned with how context influences meaning in communication.

Precision: A measure indicating how many of the positive predictions were actually correct, emphasizing reliability in avoiding false positives.

Predictive Analysis: Techniques using historical data to forecast future events or trends, essential for proactive urban planning.

Predictive Modeling: The use of historical data to predict future scenarios, commonly applied to forecasting urban trends and impacts.

Principal Component Analysis (PCA): A dimensionality reduction technique that transforms complex datasets into simpler representations by identifying key features.

Probabilistic Modeling: Statistical methods modeling uncertainty and variability in data to predict and generate realistic new data points.

Public Engagement: The process of involving residents and stakeholders in decision-making about urban planning and development.

Public-Private Partnerships (PPP):   Collaborative agreements between public agencies and private entities to share resources and risks for AI technology adoption.

Python: A versatile programming language widely used in ML, data analysis, and geospatial applications, favored for its extensive ML libraries and integration with other tools.

PyTorch: An open-source ML framework developed primarily by Facebook's AI Research lab, known for its flexibility, dynamic computation graphs, and ease of use, popular among researchers for deep learning applications.

R Programming: A programming language specializing in statistical analysis and visualization, commonly applied to detailed data analysis and spatial modeling in urban planning.

Random Forests: ML algorithms combining multiple decision trees to enhance prediction accuracy and robustness by averaging outcomes.

Reactive AI: AI systems that respond directly to inputs without memory or context-based reasoning.

Recall (Sensitivity):   The proportion of actual positives correctly identified by the model, emphasizing the detection of all relevant instances.

Recurrent Neural Network (RNN):   NNs specifically designed for sequential data, maintaining memory of past inputs to inform current decisions, commonly used in time-series analysis.

Regression Models: ML models predicting continuous outcomes (e.g., housing prices) by analyzing relationships between variables.

Regulatory Compliance: The adhering to laws and standards governing AI use, particularly regarding data privacy and ethical concerns.

Reinforcement Learning: An ML technique where an agent learns by interacting with an environment and receiving rewards or penalties for actions taken.

Resilience: The ability of cities and communities to recover from environmental, social, or economic disruptions.

Sandbox Environments: Safe testing platforms allowing planners to experiment with AI applications without immediate large-scale risks, facilitating innovation.

Satellite Imagery: Images captured by satellites, critical for large-scale urban analysis such as land-use classification, urban expansion, and environmental monitoring.

Scalable Solutions: AI solutions designed to grow and adapt efficiently to future demands, ensuring long-term viability and effectiveness.

Scenario Generation: Creating realistic predictive simulations or visualizations of future developments or impacts, particularly useful for urban planning and environmental assessments.

Scenario Modeling: The use of AI-generated scenarios to simulate and explore potential urban developments and impacts, enabling informed planning decisions.

Semantic Analysis: The process of understanding the meaning and relationships between words in NLP.

Semantic Segmentation: Assigning class labels to every pixel within an image without differentiating individual instances, grouping similar objects as one entity.

Semantics: The meaning behind words, phrases, and sentences, focusing on context and word relationships to derive accurate interpretations.

Sentiment Analysis: An NLP technique used to determine the sentiment (positive, negative, or neutral) expressed in a piece of text.

Smart Cities: Urban areas that integrate technology, data, and AI to improve infrastructure, governance, and quality of life.

Stakeholder: Any individual, group, or organization with an interest in an urban planning or AI-related decision or project.

Stakeholder Engagement: Active involvement of community members, policymakers, and planners in AI decision-making, promoting transparency and responsiveness to community needs.

Supervised Learning: An ML technique where models are trained on labeled datasets, meaning that each training example includes both input data and the correct output.

Sustainability: The principle of developing cities and communities in ways that meet present needs without compromising future generations' ability to meet their needs.

Syntax: The rules governing the structure and arrangement of words within sentences, essential for understanding grammatical relationships and sentence structure.

Synthetic Data: Artificially generated data closely resembling real-world datasets, used for data augmentation, model training, and scenario analysis.

TensorFlow: An open-source software library developed by Google for ML and deep learning applications, widely used for building, training, and deploying NNs and AI models.

Term Frequency-Inverse Document Frequency (TF-IDF):   A statistical method assessing word importance by weighting frequency within documents against how common the word is across a corpus, improving relevance detection.

Text Summarization: The automatic condensing of long text documents into concise summaries, preserving essential information for quick comprehension.

Tokenization: The breaking of text into individual tokens or units (words, phrases, or characters) to facilitate further NLP analysis.

TPU (Tensor Processing Unit):   Google's AI-specific processor optimized for training NNs, particularly suited to AI model development.

Traffic Flow Prediction: The use of AI models to analyze and predict traffic patterns to optimize urban mobility.

Training Data: Datasets used to train ML algorithms, providing examples from which models learn patterns and relationships.

Transfer Learning: Leveraging pre-trained models on extensive datasets to efficiently train models on new, smaller, or specific datasets.

Transformers: A type of deep learning model architecture used in NLP tasks, known for its ability to process sequential data efficiently.

Transparency: Clear documentation and explanation of AI methodologies, algorithms, and decisions to build trust and accountability.

Underfitting: When a NN is too simple, failing to capture essential patterns, resulting in poor performance on training and new data.

Unsupervised Learning: An ML technique where models find patterns and structures in data without labeled outputs.

Urban Planning: The process of designing and managing land use, infrastructure, transportation, and public spaces to create sustainable, functional, and livable communities.

Variational Autoencoders (VAEs):   Autoencoder models adding probabilistic methods to latent spaces, enabling the generation of realistic, diverse, and novel data samples.

Vision Transformers (ViTs):   A deep learning model used in CV that applies transformer architectures to image processing.

Wasserstein GANs (WGANs):   An improved GAN variant designed to stabilize training and prevent common problems like mode collapse or instability in generating realistic data.

Weights: Parameters in NNs that adjust input significance, determining how much each input influences the neuron's output.

Word Embeddings: An NLP technique capturing semantic relationships between words through numerical representations, enabling deeper linguistic understanding.

Word2Vec: An NLP method that converts words into numerical vectors capturing semantic meaning, allowing models to understand relationships and similarities between words based on their usage context.

YOLO (You Only Look Once):   A popular real-time object detection algorithm known for speed, analyzing the entire image simultaneously to detect multiple objects efficiently.

Zoning: Regulations that determine how land can be used and developed, typically enforced by municipalities.

Zoning Compliance: The process of ensuring that buildings and land use conform to municipal zoning laws, sometimes analyzed using AI.

INDEX

For Product Safety Concerns and Information please contact our EU
representative GPSR@taylorandfrancis.com
Taylor & Francis Verlag GmbH, Kaufingerstraße 24, 80331 München, Germany